Lecture Notes in Computer S

Edited by G. Goos, J. Hartmanis, and J.

T0250848

Springer
Berlin
Heidelberg
New York
Barcelona
Hong Kong
London
Milan
Paris
Tokyo

Thomas Arts   Markus Mohnen (Eds.)

Implementation of Functional Languages

13th International Workshop, IFL 2001
Stockholm, Sweden, September 24-26, 2001
Selected Papers

 Springer

Series Editors

Gerhard Goos, Karlsruhe University, Germany
Juris Hartmanis, Cornell University, NY, USA
Jan van Leeuwen, Utrecht University, The Netherlands

Volume Editors

Thomas Arts
Ericsson, Computer Science Laboratory
P.O. Box 1505, 125 25 Älvsjö, Sweden
E-mail: thomas@cslab.ericsson.se

Markus Mohnen
RWTH Aachen, Lehrstuhl für Informatik II
Ahornstr. 55, 52056 Aachen, Germany
E-mail: mohnen@informatik.rwth-aachen.de

Cataloging-in-Publication Data applied for

Die Deutsche Bibliothek - CIP-Einheitsaufnahme

Implementation of functional languages : 13th international workshop ;
selected papers / IFL 2001, Stockholm, Sweden, September 24 - 26, 2001.
Thomas Arts ; Markus Mohnen (ed.). - Berlin ; Heidelberg ; New York ;
Barcelona ; Hong Kong ; London ; Milan ; Paris ; Tokyo : Springer, 2002
    (Lecture notes in computer science ; Vol. 2312)
    ISBN 3-540-43537-9

CR Subject Classification (1998): D.3, D.1.1, F.3

ISSN 0302-9743
ISBN 3-540-43537-9 Springer-Verlag Berlin Heidelberg New York

Springer-Verlag Berlin Heidelberg New York
a member of BertelsmannSpringer Science+Business Media GmbH

http://www.springer.de

© Springer-Verlag Berlin Heidelberg 2002
Printed in Germany

Typesetting: Camera-ready by author, data conversion by Steingräber Satztechnik GmbH, Heidelberg
Printed on acid-free paper   SPIN: 10846589   06/3142   5 4 3 2 1 0

Preface

The 13th International Workshop on the Implementation of Functional Languages (IFL 2001) was hosted this year by Ericsson in Stockholm. The growing importance of functional languages in Ericsson products makes strong cooperation with universities attractive, and hosting IFL was one nice way to interact. Consecutive to IFL 2001, Ericsson had organized the annual *Erlang User Conference*, which over 100 (mostly industrial) users of the functional language Erlang attended. All participants of IFL 2001 were invited to stay for that conference as well. In this way, academia got a better insight into the potential of functional languages in industry, and industry got a feeling for upcoming ideas in this area.

IFL 2001 was held in September 2001 and attracted 43 researchers from the international functional language community. During the 3 days of the workshop, they presented no fewer than 28 contributions. The contributions covered topics on the implementation, and also the use of functional languages.

This volume follows the lead of the last five IFL workshops in publishing a high-quality subset of the contributions in Springer's Lecture Notes in Computer Science series. All speakers at the workshop were invited to submit a paper afterwards. These submissions were reviewed by three or four referees and thoroughly discussed by the program committee. From all submissions, 11 papers were selected for publication in this volume.

The overall balance of the papers is representative, both in scope and technical substance, of the contributions made to the workshop in Stockholm as well as to those that preceded it. Publication in the LNCS series is not only intended to make these contributions more widely known in the computer science community but also to encourage researchers in the field to participate in future workshops. The next IFL will be held in Madrid, Spain in September 2002.

We would like to thank the program committee, the referees, and the authors of the papers for the work and time they have put into the workshop.

January 2002   Thomas Arts and Markus Mohnen

The international workshops on Implementation of Functional Languages (IFL) are a tradition that has lasted for over a decade. The aim of these workshops is to bring together researchers to discuss new results and new directions of research related primarily but not exclusively to the implementation of functional or function–based languages. A not necessarily exhaustive list of topics includes: language concepts, type checking, compilation techniques, (abstract) interpretation, automatic program generation, (abstract) machine architectures, array processing, concurrent/parallel programming and program execution, heap management, runtime profiling and performance measurements, debugging and tracing, tools and programming techniques.

Program Committee

Peter Achten	(University of Nijmegen, The Netherlands)
Thomas Arts	(Ericsson, Sweden)
Olaf Chitil	(University of York, UK)
Chris Clack	(University College London, UK)
Kevin Hammond	(University of St. Andrews, UK)
John Hughes	(Chalmers University of Technology, Sweden)
Pieter Koopman	(University of Nijmegen, The Netherlands)
Rita Loogen	(Philipps University of Marburg, Germany)
Markus Mohnen	(RWTH Aachen, Germany)
John O'Donnell	(University of Glasgow, UK)
Ricardo Peña	(Universidad Complutense de Madrid, Spain)
Sven-Bodo Scholz	(University of Kiel, Germany)
Phil Trinder	(Heriot-Watt University Edinburgh, UK)

Referees

Mustafa Aswad	Frank Huch	Konstantinos Sagonas
Adam Bakewell	Werner Kluge	Clara Segura
Andre R. Du Bois	Hans-Wolfgang Loidl	Volker Stolz
Marko van Eekelen	Yolanda Ortega-Mallén	S. Doaitse Swierstra
Karl-Filip Faxén	Maarten de Mol	Malcolm Wallace
Lars-Åke Fredlund	Thomas Noll	Michael Weber
Clemens Grelck	Mikael Pettersson	
Dilian Gurov	Robert Pointon	

Table of Contents

Sized Types for Typing Eden Skeletons*

Ricardo Peña and Clara Segura

Departamento de Sistemas Informáticos y Programación
Universidad Complutense de Madrid
{ricardo,csegura}@sip.ucm.es

Abstract. The parallel-functional language Eden extends Haskell with constructs to explicitly define and communicate processes. These extensions allow the easy definition of skeletons as higher-order functions. However, the programmer can inadvertently introduce busy loops or deadlocks in them. In this paper a sized type system is extended in order to use it for Eden programs, so that those well-typed skeletons are guaranteed either to terminate or to be productive. The problems raised by Eden features and their possible solutions are described in detail, and several skeletons are manually type checked in this modified system such as the parallel map, farm, pipeline, and replicated workers.

1 Introduction

The parallel-functional language Eden [BLOP98] extends the lazy functional language Haskell with constructs to explicitly define and communicate processes. It is implemented by modifying the *Glasgow Haskell Compiler* (GHC) [PHH+93]. The three main additional concepts are *process abstractions*, *process instantiations* and the non-deterministic process abstraction merge. Process abstractions of type Process a b can be compared to functions of type a -> b, and process instantiations can be compared to function applications, the main difference being that the former, when instantiated, are executed in parallel. An instantiation is achieved by using the predefined infix operator (#) :: Process a b -> a -> b. Each time an expression e1 # e2 is evaluated, a new parallel process is created to evaluate (e1 e2). Non-determinism is introduced in Eden by means of a predefined process abstraction merge :: Process [[a]] [a] which *fairly* interleaves a set of input lists, to produce a single non-deterministic list.

These extensions allow the easy definition of *skeletons* as higher-order functions [PR01]. A skeleton [Col89] is a generic scheme for solving in parallel a particular family of problems. They are very useful because they are defined once and reused many times. However the programmer can inadvertently introduce busy loops, deadlocks or any other runtime error in them. So, it is very important to formally verify that they are free from these undesirable problems. The theory of sized types has been developed in recent years by John Hughes

---

* Work partially supported by the Spanish-British Acción Integrada HB 1999-0102 and Spanish project TIC 2000-0738.

T. Arts and M. Mohnen (Eds.): IFL 2001, LNCS 2312, pp. 1–17, 2002.

and Lars Pareto [HPS96,Par97,Par00] to provide a framework in which type checking based analysis of both program termination and program productivity can be done. A simplified version of Haskell, *Synchronous Haskell*, is given a sized type system so that well-typed programs are guaranteed to be free from runtime errors.

The objective of this paper is to prove Eden skeletons correct. As they are not many, for the moment we will be glad with type checking them manually. In the way of conjecturing and proving their types correct, we have found some weaknesses in Hughes and Pareto's system. Thus, another objective is to propose extensions to the sized type system so that it could more be useful for typing Eden programs. The problems due to Eden's features and their possible solutions are described in detail, and several skeletons are type ckecked in this modified system.

The plan of the paper is as follows: Section 2 describes the theory of sized types developed by Hughes and Pareto and the type system for Synchronous Haskell. In Section 3 some problems introduced by Eden features are described and the type rules are extended consequently. Two simple examples, a naïve version of a parallel map skeleton and a pipeline are type checked using the new rules. In Section 4 more complex skeletons, such as the farm skeleton and the replicated workers topology are type checked. The problems posed by these skeletons and their possible solutions are discussed. In Section 5 we draw some conclusions and future work.

2   Huges and Pareto's Sized Types

From a semantic point of view, the denotation of a sized type is an upwards closed subset of a lattice which may not include $\perp$, where $\perp$ means at the same time non-termination (for finite types) and deadlock (for infinite types). So, if a function can be successfully typed in this system, it is sure that either it terminates (if the function produces a finite value), or it is productive (if it produces an infinite value). To this purpose, finite types must be carefully distinguished from infinite ones. Additionally, types may have one or more *size parameters* which carry size information. These can be constants, universally quantified variables or, in general (restricted) expressions. Intuitively, the size of a value of a certain type is the number of constructor applications needed to construct the value. For instance, for a finite list, it is the number of *cons* constructors plus one (the latter takes into account the *nil* constructor). For a binary tree, it is the number of levels plus one, and so on.

2.1   The Syntax of Sized Types and Datatype Terms

Syntactically, finite non-recursive types are introduced by a **data** declaration, finite recursive types by an **idata** declaration, and infinite ones by a **codata** declaration. Figure 1 shows the syntax of signatures and type declarations. There, τ, σ, s, k and t respectively denote types, type schemes, size expressions, size

$$\begin{array}{ll}
\tau ::= t \mid \tau \to \tau \mid T\,\bar{s}\,\bar{\tau} & D ::= \mathbf{data}\ E \mid \mathbf{idata}\ E \mid \mathbf{codata}\ E \\
\sigma ::= \forall t.\tau \mid \forall k.\tau \mid \tau & E ::= L = R \mid \forall t.E \mid \forall k.E \\
s ::= w \mid i & L ::= T\,\bar{s}\,\bar{\tau} \\
i ::= k \mid n \mid p * i \mid i + i & R ::= c_1\,\overline{\tau_1} \mid \dots \mid c_n\,\overline{\tau_n}
\end{array}$$

Fig. 1. Syntax of syzed types and datatype definitions

variables and type variables. A size expression can be either finite, denoted i, or infinite, denoted ω. In the former case, notice that they are restricted to be linear natural number expressions in a set of size variables. Size and type variables can be universally quantified in a type scheme and in a type declaration. There are some additional restrictions of well-formedness (e.g. that constructors must be unique, or that mutually recursive definitions are not allowed), all of which can be statically checked, in order that types have a well defined semantics. See [Par00] for details. Examples of valid type declarations are:

> **data** Bool = true | false,   **idata** $\forall a$. List ω a = nil | cons a (List ω a),
> **idata** Nat ω = zero | succ (Nat ω),   **codata** $\forall a$. Strm ω a = make a (Strm ω a)

representing respectively, the boolean type, finite lists of any size, natural numbers of any size, and streams of any size. Examples of valid type schemes are: List 3 (Nat ω), $(a \to b) \to$ Strm k $a \to$ Strm k b, $\forall a.\forall k$. List k $a \to$ Nat k.

2.2 Semantics of Sized Types

The first parameter of an **idata** or a **codata** type is a size expression bounding the size of the values of that type. For **idata** it is an *upper bound*, and for **codata** it is a *lower bound*. So, the type **List** 2 **a** denotes lists of zero or one value (i.e. having at most two constructors), while **Stream** 2 **a** denotes streams of two or more values (i.e. having at least two make constructors). Partial streams such as $1; 2; \bot$ and infinite streams such as $1; 2; \dots$ (where ; is the infix version of make) belong to this type. This size parameter can be instantiated with the infinite size ω. For **idata** types such as **List** ω **a** this means finite lists of *any* size, while for **codata** types such as **Stream** ω **a** this means strictly *infinite* streams.

A program consists of a set of well-formed type declarations followed by a term written in an enriched λ-calculus having constructor applications, **case** expressions, and **letrec** expressions, each one with a set of mutually recursive simple bindings. In order to preserve type soundness, there is also the restriction that all constructors of the corresponding type must appear exactly once in the branches of every **case** expression.

The universe of values **U** is defined as the solution to the following isomorphism: $\mathbf{U} \sim [\mathbf{U} \to \mathbf{U}]_\bot \oplus (\mathbf{U} \times \mathbf{U})_\bot \oplus 1_\bot \oplus CON_\bot$, where CON is the set of constructors. In this universe, the enriched λ-calculus is given a standard non-strict semantics. The set of types $\mathbf{T} = \{\mathcal{T} \mid \mathcal{T}$ is an upwards closed subset of $\mathbf{U}\}$ form a complete lattice under the subset ordering $\subseteq$ where $\top_{\mathbf{T}} = \mathbf{U}$ is the top element, $\bot_{\mathbf{T}} = \emptyset$ is the bottom element, and $\cup, \cap$ are respectively the least upper bound and greatest lower bound operators. It is a cpo but not a domain.

As types are upwards closed subsets of $\mathbf{U}$, the only type containing $\perp_{\mathbf{U}}$ is just $\mathbf{U}$. In this cpo, recursive types are interpreted by using functionals $\mathcal{F} : \mathbf{T} \to \mathbf{T}$. To define these functionals from type declarations, in [Par00] several type operators, $\boxed{\times}$ for non-strict cartesian products of types, $\boxed{+}$ for sums of types, and $\boxed{\to}$ for functions between types, are defined. It is proved that these operators preserve the upwards closedness property.

From now on, we will use an overline to represent several elements. For example, $\overline{s}$ represents that there exists some number $l \geq 0$ such that $s = s_1 \ldots s_l$. The denotation of a recursive type constructor instantiation $T \, \overline{s} \, \overline{\tau}$ is the application of a function that takes as parameters $l - 1$ naturals corresponding to the sizes $s_2, \ldots, s_l$, j types corresponding to the types $\tau_1, \ldots, \tau_j$, and returns a *type iterator* $\mathcal{F} : \mathbf{T} \to \mathbf{T}$. If all declarations respect the forementioned static semantics restrictions, the resulting type iterators are continuous for **idata** declarations and co-continuous for **codata** ones. This type iterator takes as parameter a type corresponding to the recursive ocurrences of the type being defined, and returns a new type corresponding to its right hand side definition. The first size parameter s_1 determines the number of times the iterator is applied (respectively to $\perp_{\mathbf{T}}$ for **idata** or to $\top_{\mathbf{T}}$ for **codata**). If it is applied k times, then values of at most (at least, for **codata**) size k are obtained. In the limit (size ω), values of any size (infinite size, for **codata**) are obtained. For inductive types (those defined by an **idata** declaration) the interpretation is the least fixpoint of the iterator, while for co-inductive types (those defined by a **codata** declaration) it is the greatest fixpoint of the iterator. These fixpoints can respectively be reached by the limits of the ascending chain $\mathcal{F}^i(\perp_{\mathbf{T}})$ and of the descending chain $\mathcal{F}^i(\top_{\mathbf{T}})$.

A subtype relation can be defined between sized types with the same underlying type but different size. It is a subset based relation, that is, $\tau \rhd \tau'$ when the interpretation of τ is a subset of the interpretation of τ'. It is a monotone relation with the sizes in **idata** types, while antimonotone in the **codata** types. For example **List** 2 $a \rhd$ **List** 3 a, while **Strm** 3 $a \rhd$ **Strm** 2 a. In [Par00] the rules for checking this subtyping relation are shown. They provide a way of weakening size information. This weakening will be applied in $[APP]$, $[LET]$, $[LETREC]$ and $[CASE]$ rules, see Figure 4.

The interpretation of type polymorphism is, as usual, the intersection of the interpretations of every single type. In formal terms, if $\mathcal{I}$ denotes the interpretation function, γ is a type environment mapping type variables to types in $\mathbf{T}$, and δ is a size environment mapping size variables to sizes in $\mathbb{N}^\omega$, then $\mathcal{I}[\![\forall t.\sigma]\!] \, \gamma \, \delta = \bigcap_{\mathcal{T} \in \mathbf{T}} \mathcal{I}[\![\sigma]\!] \, \gamma[\mathcal{T}/t] \, \delta$. Similarly, size polymorphism is interpreted as the intersection of the interpretation for all sizes: $\mathcal{I}[\![\forall k.\sigma]\!] \, \gamma \, \delta = \bigcap_{n \in \mathbb{N}} \mathcal{I}[\![\sigma]\!] \, \gamma \, \delta[n/k]$; but in this case the intersection is restricted to finite sizes. The reason for that is to be able to use induction on natural numbers to assign types to recursive definitions. This restriction makes size instantiation of polymorphic types safe only for finite sizes. *Omega instantiation* is not always safe. Indeed, there are some types for which omega instantiation delivers a type *smaller* than the polymorphic one instead of bigger. An example is $\forall k.(\mathbf{Stream} \; \omega \; (Nat \; k) \to Bool)$ substituting ω for k. In [Par00], a sufficient decidable condition (namely that a type scheme is *undershooting* with respect to a size variable, denoted as $\sigma \overset{\cup}{\sim} k$) is given for a scheme to be able to be safely instantiated with ω.

2.3   Synchronous Haskell Type System

In [Par00] the programming language Synchronous Haskell is defined. This is a simplified version of the functional language Haskell. Thanks to its demand driven evaluation it can be seen as a concurrent language where programs are visualized as networks of processes executing in parallel and communicating through message channels.

A program consists of a set of type declarations followed by a term written in an enriched λ-calculus. Each **let** and **letrec** binding is annotated by the programmer with a type scheme to be (type) checked by the system. The whole type system is not shown here as our extended type rules in Figures 4 are just an extension of these. To recover the original type system, first eliminate $[PABS]$, $[PINST]$ and $[MERGE]$. Then, eliminate the classes F and T in the type schemes and the environments Γ_T^T and Γ_T^F in the type assertions. Finally, eliminate all those conditions where $\overline{t}^F$, $\overline{t}^T$, Γ_T^T, Γ_T^F or any of their variants are involved. So the type assertions are of the form $\Gamma \vdash e :: \tau$. In this section we only explain $[VAR]$ and $[LETREC]$. Different indexes will be used when different sequences of elements appear in the same rule. We will not use i because it is reserved for finite size expressions. So for example in $[VAR]$, $\tau \overset{\cup}{\sim} k_j'$ means that being $\overline{k'} = k_1' \dots k_n'$, then $\forall j \in \{1..n\}.\tau \overset{\cup}{\sim} k_j'$. There, instantiation of both type and size variables takes place. We can only instantiate with ω the size variables k_j' such that τ is undershooting w.r.t. them. In [Par00] sufficient conditions are given to prove this property, which imply the definition of other relations between types and size variables, such as monotonicity $\tau \overset{+}{\sim} k$ and antimonotonicity $\tau \overset{-}{\sim} k$.

In $[LETREC]$, induction on natural numbers is applied. To illustrate how this rule works we will explain the typing of function $map :: \forall a, b, k.(a \to b) \to$ **List** $k\ a \to$ **List** $k\ b$, where $map = \lambda f.\lambda xs.$**case** xs **of** $nil \to nil; cons\ x\ xs' \to cons\ (f\ x)\ (map\ f\ xs')$. First of all we have to choose the size variable on which the induction is made. In the rule it is always the first one k_j in each binding. Then the base case is studied $\sigma_j[0] = \mathbf{U}$. This is called the *bottom check*. The rules for checking it need the definition of other relations on types as emptiness ($= \mathbf{E}$) and non-emptiness ($\neq \mathbf{E}$); and some other on sizes, like $= 0$ and $\neq 0$. All the rules are in [Par00], but we show the most useful ones in Figure 2. In general, a **codata** type (T_C) of size 0 denotes the universe, while a **idata** type (T_I) of size 0 denotes the empty type. Some examples where the bottom check holds are: $\forall k.$**Strm** $k\ a$, $\forall a, b, k.(a \to b) \to$ **List** $k\ a \to$ **List** $k\ b$ and $\forall a, k.$**Strm** $k\ a \to$ **Strm** $k\ a$. Then, assuming the induction hypothesis for each $j \in \{1..n\}$: $x_j :: \forall \overline{k_j}.\tau_j[k]$ we must prove that the types of the right hand sides of the bindings e_j are subtypes of $\tau_j[k + 1]$. In the example, assuming that $map :: (a \to b) \to$ **List** $k\ a \to$ **List** $k\ b$ we must prove that its body definition has type $(a \to b) \to$ **List** $(k + 1)\ a \to$ **List** $(k + 1)\ b$. This implies $f :: a \to b$ and $xs :: $ **List** $(k + 1)\ a$. In the **case** expression, if xs is an empty list, $nil :: $ **List** $1\ a$

$\tau_2 = \mathbf{U}$	$\tau_1 = \mathbf{E}$	$s_1 = 0$	$\sigma = \mathbf{U}$	$\sigma = \mathbf{U}$	$s_1 = 0$
$\tau_1 \rightarrow \tau_2 = \mathbf{U}$	$\tau_1 \rightarrow \tau_2 = \mathbf{U}$	$T_C\ \overline{s}\ \overline{\tau} = \mathbf{U}$	$\forall t.\sigma = \mathbf{U}$	$\forall k.\sigma = \mathbf{U}$	$T_I\ \overline{s}\ \overline{\tau} = \mathbf{E}$

Fig. 2. Rules for bottom check and one rule for emptiness check

is returned, which is a subtype of **List** $(k+1)$ a as $1 \leq k+1$. If it is non-empty, the value is destroyed, so xs' has one constructor less $xs' :: $ **List** k a. By induction hypothesis then $map\ f\ xs' :: $ **List** k b, so adding a new element gives us $cons\ (f\ x)\ (map\ f\ xs') :: $ **List** $(k+1)$ b, the desired type. Polymorphic recursion in all the size variables but the inductive one is allowed, and it is quite useful, for example to type the *reverse* function, as shown in [Par00].

3   New Problems Introduced by Eden

Eden is a parallel functional language where processes communicate through channels, so it is very close to the view Synchronous Haskell provides to programs. However, some problems arise when trying to apply Synchronous Haskell type system to Eden programs. If we take into account Eden features, some extensions to the type system are needed. The most important features are the way in which values are transmitted through the channels, the eager evaluation of some expressions, and the use of lists to represent both Haskell lists and stream-like transmission of values.

The instantiation protocol of e1 # e2 deserves some attention in order to understand Eden's semantics: (1) closure e1 together with all its dependent closures are *copied* unevaluated to a new processor and the child process is created there to evaluate it; (2) once created, the child process starts producing eagerly its output expression; (3) expression e2 is eagerly evaluated in the parent process. If it is a tuple, an independent concurrent thread is created to evaluate each component (we will refer to each tuple element as a *channel*). Once a process is running, only fully evaluated data objects are communicated. The only exception are lists: they are transmitted in a *stream*-like fashion, i.e. element by element. Each list element is first evaluated to normal form and then transmitted.

3.1   Transmission of Values

The communication of data through channels leads us to two different problems. Firstly, as values are evaluated to normal form before sending them, it is necessary that the types of the communicated values are finite: tuple, **data** or **idata** types with finite components and function types. Secondly, this implies that instantiation of type variables must be restricted in some places to finite types. We propose a mechanism similar to the class system of Haskell. We define a *finiteness relation* $\Gamma_T \vdash_F \tau$, see Figure 3, where Γ_T is a set of type variables that may appear in τ. This assertion means that assuming the type variables in Γ_T can only be instantiated with finite types, τ is also a finite type. In Figure 3

$$\dfrac{a \in \Gamma_T}{\Gamma_T \vdash_F a} \qquad \dfrac{\Gamma_T \vdash_F \tau_1 \quad \Gamma_T \vdash_F \tau_2}{\Gamma_T \vdash_F (\tau_1, \tau_2)} \qquad \dfrac{}{\Gamma_T \vdash_F \tau \to \tau'} \qquad \dfrac{}{\Gamma_T \vdash_F F}$$

$$\dfrac{\Gamma_T \vdash_F R[\overline{\tau}/\overline{t}][\overline{s}/\overline{k}]}{\Gamma_T \vdash_F T_d \ \overline{s} \ \overline{\tau}} \qquad \dfrac{\Gamma_T \vdash_F S[F][\overline{\tau}/\overline{t}][\overline{s}/\overline{k}]}{\Gamma_T \vdash_F T_i \ s_1 \ \overline{s} \ \overline{\tau}} \qquad \dfrac{\forall j \in \{1..n\}, l \in \{1..m_j\} \quad \Gamma_T \vdash_F \tau_{jl}}{\Gamma_T \vdash_F c_1 \ \overline{\tau_1} \mid \ldots \mid c_n \ \overline{\tau_n}}$$

where **data** $\forall \overline{k} \ \overline{t}.T_d \ \overline{k} \ \overline{t} = R$ $\qquad R = c_1 \ \overline{\tau_1} \mid \ldots \mid c_n \ \overline{\tau_n}$

$\qquad$ **idata** $\forall \overline{k} \ \overline{t}.T_i \ w \ \overline{k} \ \overline{t} = S[T_i \ w \ \overline{k} \ \overline{t}]$ $\qquad S = c_1 \ \overline{\tau_1} \mid \ldots \mid c_n \ \overline{\tau_n}$

Fig. 3. Finiteness relation

we use a pseudo-variable F to substitute a finite type for the recursive positions of an **idata** type, that is, to prove by structural induction that it is finite.

We use this relation to control the instantiation of variables. As there are different ways of sending values, depending on the channel type, we can use different types to represent a channel: if it is a single value channel, its type is represented by the type of the value; if it is a stream-like channel, we can use a **List** or a **Strm** type (see discussion below). This separation imposes different restrictions: if it is a single value channel, its type must be finite, but if it is a stream-like channel, only the type of the elements must be finite. This leads us to introduce two different classes of values, F (from finite) and T (from transmission interface). The first one indicates that the type variable can only be instantiated with finite types, and the second one that it can only be instantiated with *'interface'* types. An interface type is either a finite type (this includes the **List** type with finite components) or a **Strm** with finite components. A process usually has several input and output channels, represented by a tuple of channels, so interface types must also include tuples of the two previous types. The types are extended with these classes: $\tau' ::= \tau \mid [T \ \overline{a}], [F \ \overline{b}] \Rightarrow \tau$; and a new rule for bottom check is needed, expressing that it is not affected by the contexts:

$$\dfrac{\tau = \mathbf{U}}{[T \ \overline{a}], [F \ \overline{b}] \Rightarrow \tau = \mathbf{U}}$$

Additionally, two new environments, Γ_T^F and Γ_T^T are introduced in the rules, carrying the type variables that appear respectively in a F or a T context. So our assertions are of the form $\Gamma_T^F, \Gamma_T^T, \Gamma \vdash e :: \tau$. The predicate $P(\Gamma_T^F, \Gamma_T^T, \tau)$, defined in Figure 4 tells us whether τ is a interface type.

In Figure 4 the modified type rules are shown. We describe here only the newly introduced elements. In $[VAR]$ the instantiation of type variables is controlled: those that appear in an F context are instantiated with finite types, and those that appear in a T context are instantiated with a interface type. In a **Process** $\tau \ \tau'$ type, τ and τ' represent the communication interfaces, so in $[PABS]$ and $[PINST]$ it must be checked that they are in fact interface types. In $[MERGE]$, the values transmitted through the channels must be of finite type. We use angle brackets there to represent strict tuples, explained in Section 4.2.

In $[LET]$ ($[LETREC]$ is similar), the bindings are annotated with their types. If a universally quantified type variable is qualified by a class F or T, we force the programmer to indicate the same quantification in all the annotations where

$$\frac{\begin{array}{ccc} & \sigma = \forall \overline{a}\ \overline{k}\ \overline{k'}.T\ \overline{b}, F\ \overline{c} \Rightarrow \tau & \\ \overline{t^T} = \overline{a} \cap \overline{b} & \overline{t^F} = \overline{a} \cap \overline{c} & \overline{t} = \overline{a} \backslash (\overline{t^T} \cup \overline{t^F}) \\ \tau \overset{\cup}{\sim} k'_j & \Gamma_T^F \vdash_F \tau_m^F & P(\Gamma_T^F, \Gamma_T^T, \tau_l^T) \end{array}}{\Gamma_T^F,\ \Gamma_T^T,\ \Gamma \cup \{x :: \sigma\} \vdash x :: \tau[\overline{i/k}][\overline{s/k'}][\overline{\tau/t}][\overline{\tau^T/t^T}][\overline{\tau^F/t^F}]}\ VAR$$

$$\frac{\Gamma_T^F, \Gamma_T^T, \Gamma \cup \{x :: \tau\} \vdash e :: \tau' \quad P(\Gamma_T^F, \Gamma_T^T, \tau) \quad P(\Gamma_T^F, \Gamma_T^T, \tau')}{\Gamma_T^T, \Gamma_T^T, \Gamma \vdash \textbf{process}\ x \to e :: \textbf{Process}\ \tau\ \tau'}\ PABS$$

$$\frac{\begin{array}{cccc} \Gamma_T^F, \Gamma_T^T, \Gamma \vdash e_1 :: \textbf{Process}\ \tau\ \tau' & \Gamma_T^F, \Gamma_T^T, \Gamma \vdash e_2 :: \tau'' & \tau'' \rhd \tau \\ P(\Gamma_T^F, \Gamma_T^T, \tau) & P(\Gamma_T^F, \Gamma_T^T, \tau') & \end{array}}{\Gamma_T^F, \Gamma_T^T, \Gamma \vdash e_1 \# e_2 :: \tau'}\ PINST$$

$$\frac{\Gamma_T^F, \Gamma_T^T, \Gamma \vdash e :: \langle \textbf{Strm}\ k_1\ \tau, \ldots, \textbf{Strm}\ k_n\ \tau \rangle \quad \Gamma_T^F \vdash_F \tau}{\Gamma_T^F, \Gamma_T^T, \Gamma \vdash merge \# e :: \textbf{Strm}\ (\sum_{j=1}^n k_j)\ \tau}\ MERGE$$

$$\frac{\begin{array}{ccc} & \sigma = \forall \overline{a}\ \overline{k}.T\ \overline{b}, F\ \overline{c} \Rightarrow \tau \quad \overline{a}, \overline{k} \notin FV(\Gamma) & \\ \overline{t^T} = \overline{b} \backslash \overline{a} & \overline{t^F} = \overline{c} \backslash \overline{a} \quad \Gamma_T^{T'} = \overline{b} \quad \Gamma_T^{F'} = \overline{c} \\ \Gamma_T^F, \Gamma_T^T, \Gamma \cup \{x :: \sigma\} \vdash e' :: \tau' & \Gamma_T^{F'}, \Gamma_T^{T'}, \Gamma \vdash e :: \tau'' \quad \tau'' \rhd \tau \\ \overline{t^T} \subseteq \Gamma_T^T & \overline{t^F} \subseteq \Gamma_T^F \end{array}}{\Gamma_T^F, \Gamma_T^T, \Gamma \vdash \textbf{let}\ x :: \sigma = e\ \textbf{in}\ e' :: \tau'}\ LET$$

$$\frac{\begin{array}{c} j \in \{1..n\}, \sigma_j[k_j] = \forall \overline{a_j}\ \overline{k_j}.T\ \overline{b_j}, F\ \overline{c_j} \Rightarrow \tau_j[k_j] \quad \overline{a_j}, \overline{k_j}, k_j \notin FV(\Gamma) \\ \Gamma' = \Gamma, x_1 :: \forall k_1.\tau_1[k] \ldots x_n :: \forall k_n.\tau_n[k] \\ \Gamma'' = \Gamma, x_1 :: \forall k_1.\sigma_1[k_1] \ldots x_n :: \forall k_n.\sigma_n[k_n] \\ \Gamma_T^{T'} = \overline{b_1} \cup \ldots \cup \overline{b_n} \quad \Gamma_T^{F'} = \overline{c_1} \cup \ldots \cup \overline{c_n} \quad \overline{t} = \overline{a_1} \cup \ldots \cup \overline{a_n} \\ \overline{t^T} = \Gamma_T^{T'} \backslash \overline{t} \quad \overline{t^F} = \Gamma_T^F \backslash \overline{t} \quad \overline{t^T} \subseteq \Gamma_T^T \quad \overline{t^F} \subseteq \Gamma_T^F \\ \sigma_j[0] = \textbf{U} \quad \Gamma_T^{F'}, \Gamma_T^{T'}, \Gamma' \vdash e_j :: \tau'_j \quad \tau'_j \rhd \tau_j[k+1] \quad \Gamma_T^F, \Gamma_T^T, \Gamma'' \vdash e :: \tau \end{array}}{\Gamma_T^F, \Gamma_T^T, \Gamma \vdash \textbf{letrec}\ x_1 :: \forall k_1.\sigma_1[k_1] = e_1 \ldots x_n :: \forall k_n.\sigma_n[k_n] = e_n\ \textbf{in}\ e :: \tau}\ LETREC$$

$$\frac{\Gamma_T^F, \Gamma_T^T, \Gamma \cup \{x :: \tau_1\} \vdash e_. : \tau_2}{\Gamma_T^F, \Gamma_T^T, \Gamma \vdash \lambda x.e :: \tau_1 \to \tau_2}\ ABS$$

$$\frac{\Gamma_T^F, \Gamma_T^T, \Gamma \vdash e_1 :: \tau_1 \to \tau_2 \quad \Gamma_T^F, \Gamma_T^T, \Gamma \vdash e_2 :: \tau_3 \quad \tau_3 \rhd \tau_1}{\Gamma_T^F, \Gamma_T^T, \Gamma \vdash e_1\ e_2 :: \tau_2}\ APP$$

$$\frac{\begin{array}{ccc} & \vdash_= \tau = c_1\ \overline{\tau_1} \mid \ldots \mid c_n\ \overline{\tau_n} & \\ \Gamma_T^F, \Gamma_T^T, \Gamma \vdash e :: \tau & \Gamma_T^F, \Gamma_T^T, \Gamma \cup \{x_{j1} :: \tau_{j1}, \ldots, x_{jn_j} :: \tau_{jn_j}\} \vdash e_j :: \tau'_j(\forall j) & \tau'_j \rhd \tau'(\forall j) \end{array}}{\Gamma_T^F, \Gamma_T^T, \Gamma \vdash \textbf{case}\ e\ \textbf{of}\ c_1\ \overline{x_1} \to e_1 \ldots c_n\ \overline{x_n} \to e_n :: \tau'}\ CASE$$

$$\begin{aligned} P(\Gamma_T^F, \Gamma_T^T, \tau) = \ &if\ (\tau = \textbf{Strm}\ s\ \tau')\ then\ \Gamma_T^F \vdash_F \tau' \\ &else\ if\ (\tau = (\tau_1, \ldots, \tau_n))\ then\ \forall j. \\ &\quad\quad if\ \tau_j = \textbf{Strm}\ s_j\ \tau'_j\ then\ \Gamma_T^F \vdash_F \tau'_j \\ &\quad\quad else\ \quad \Gamma_T^F \cup \Gamma_T^T \vdash_F \tau_j \\ &else\ \quad \Gamma_T^F \cup \Gamma_T^T \vdash_F \tau \end{aligned}$$

Fig. 4. Type rules

such variable appears free ($\overline{t^T} \subseteq \Gamma_T^T$ and $\overline{t^F} \subseteq \Gamma_T^F$). Additionally, the class information needed to type the right hand side of a binding is extracted from its annotation ($\Gamma_T^{T'} = \overline{b}$ and $\Gamma_T^{F'} = \overline{c}$). The rest of rules ($\lambda$-abstraction, application and **case**) are similar to the original ones.

3.2 Eager Evaluation

In Eden, lazy evaluation is changed to eager in two cases: (1) processes are eagerly instantiated when the expression under evaluation demands the creation of a closure of the form $o = e_1 \# e_2$, and (2) instantiated processes produce their output even if it is not demanded. These semantics modifications are aimed at increasing the degree of parallelism and at speeding up the distribution of the computation.

Eager evaluation does not affect the type rules. From the type system point of view, eagerness means that some values of interface types, like o in $o = e_1 \# e_2$, are produced without being demanded. If o is finite, its type gives us an upper bound of its size. With lazy evaluation, this size needs not be reached in all cases, while with eager evaluation, this size is probably reached all times the expression $e_1 \# e_2$ is evaluated. If o is a stream, its type gives a lower bound of the number of elements produced, provided there is demand for them. With eager evaluation the only difference is that this demand is guaranteed.

3.3 Types List and Strm

In Eden, the list type $[\tau]$ is used both for Haskell lists and for stream-like channels, and they are transformed from one to the other in a way transparent to the programmer. However, in this type system it is necessary first to divide Haskell lists into finite ones (**List** type) and partial or infinite ones (**Strm** type). This is a problem inherited from Haskell. A **List** type gives us a proof of termination, while a **Strm** type gives us a proof of productivity. Additionally it is necessary to identify the stream-like channels. We usually want to prove the productivity of our skeletons, so we will use mainly the **Strm** type in such cases. But there are some skeletons that work with finite types and require a version with **List** of another skeleton. In such cases we would like to have both versions of the skeleton, one for lists and another one for streams, so that both termination and productivity are proved. In some cases we obtain the two versions for free, thanks to polymorphism, as in the naïve map and pipe skeletons shown below.

3.4 Two Simple Examples

We study now two simple examples of skeletons that illustrate some of the ideas shown in this section. In the following section we will study more complex skeletons and the problems they produce. In all of them, we first show the Eden skeleton as it is written in [PR01] and then the sized typed version appears. The latter is usually modified somehow for different reasons we will explain in turn. Similarly to Hughes and Pareto's system there is not an automatic way of transforming the programs (so that they are easier to type) or of conjecturing a correct type in a first attempt.

In order to abbreviate type proofs, in those functions and skeletons where, to type them, induction has been used, we will write as a subscript the size of those program variables whose type contains the size variable over which we are doing induction. Sometimes we will write the size of a complete expression. When a compound type is used, as in **List** k (**Strm** l a), we will use brackets to represent the size, in the example $k[l]$. In the original text [PR01] a `Transmissible` class (abbreviated `Tr` here) is used. It subsumes both the T and F classes used in the type system.

A Naïve Implementation of a Parallel Map Skeleton. We first show a naïve implementation of a map skeleton:

```
map_naive :: (Tr a, Tr b) => (a -> b) -> [a] -> [b]
map_naive f xs = [pf # x | x <- xs]    where pf = process x -> f x
```

For each element of the list, a different process instantiation is done, where each process simply applies the function `f` to the corresponding input.

The ZF notation is rewritten into a simple map and the **where** clause into a **let**. The type is obtained by composing functions:

$$map\_naiveL :: \forall a, b, k.T\ a, b \Rightarrow (a \rightarrow b) \rightarrow \textbf{List}\ k\ a \rightarrow \textbf{List}\ k\ b$$
$$map\_naiveL = \lambda f.\lambda xs.\textbf{let}\ g :: T\ a, b \Rightarrow a \rightarrow b$$
$$g = \lambda x.(\textbf{process}\ y \rightarrow f\ y)\#x$$
$$\textbf{in}\ map\ g\ xs$$

A Pipeline Skeleton. Now we show a pipeline skeleton instantiating a different process to evaluate each of the pipeline stages. Each process in the pipe creates its successor process:

```
pipe :: Tr a => [[a] -> [a]] -> [a] -> [a]
pipe fs xs  = (ppipe fs) # xs
ppipe :: Tr a => [[a] -> [a]] -> Process [a] [a]
ppipe [f]    = process xs -> f xs
ppipe (f:fs) = process xs -> (ppipe fs) # (f xs)
```

The following type can be checked by induction on the length k of fs:

$$ppipe :: \forall a, k, l.F\ a \Rightarrow \textbf{List}\ k\ (\textbf{Strm}\ l\ a \rightarrow \textbf{Strm}\ l\ a) \rightarrow \textbf{Process}\ (\textbf{Strm}\ l\ a)\ (\textbf{Strm}\ l\ a)$$
$$ppipe = \lambda fs_{k+1}.\textbf{case}\ fs_{k+1}\ \textbf{of}$$
$$nil \qquad\qquad \rightarrow \textbf{process}\ s \rightarrow s$$
$$cons\ f\ fs'_k \rightarrow \textbf{process}\ s \rightarrow (ppipe\ fs'_k)\#(f\ s)$$

$$pipe :: \forall a, k, l.F\ a \Rightarrow \textbf{List}\ k\ (\textbf{Strm}\ l\ a \rightarrow \textbf{Strm}\ l\ a) \rightarrow \textbf{Strm}\ l\ a \rightarrow \textbf{Strm}\ l\ a$$
$$pipe = \lambda fs.\lambda s.(ppipe\ fs)\#s$$

In this example we have encountered and solved a couple of problems. First, the empty list case is not included in the original `ppipe`, which violates the restrictions for **case**. So it is added as the identity process in order to be able to type the skeleton.

Second, we have chosen to represent the processes as consuming and producing a stream of data in order to study its productivity. This means that the type a cannot be an interface type, but must be a finite type, so the context in this case is F and not T. However we could have given less restrictive types: $ppipe :: \forall a,k,l.T\ a \Rightarrow$ **List** $k\ (a \rightarrow a) \rightarrow$ **Process** $a\ a$ and $pipe :: \forall a,k,l.T\ a \Rightarrow$ **List** $k\ (a \rightarrow a) \rightarrow a \rightarrow a$, using T class. By instantiating a with $F\ a \Rightarrow$ **Strm** $l\ a$ we obtain the previous type.

4   Skeletons in Eden

4.1   The Farm Implementation of the Parallel Map Skeleton

The map_naive version can be improved by reducing the number of worker processes to be created. In a map_farm a process is created for every processor, tasks are evenly distributed between processors, and the results are collected. Here is its implementation in terms of map_naive:

```
map_farm :: (Tr a,Tr b) => (a -> b) -> [a] -> [b]
map_farm = farm noPe unshuffle shuffle
farm :: (Tr a, Tr b) => Int -> (Int->[a]->[[a]]) -> ([[b]]->[b]) ->
        (a -> b) -> [a] -> [b]
farm np unshuffle shuffle f tasks =
                    shuffle (map_naive (map f) (unshuffle np tasks))
```

where noPe is a constant giving the number of available processors. Different strategies to split the work into the different processes can be used provided that, for every list xs, (shuffle . unshuffle) xs == xs. For instance, the following scheme distributes the tasks using a round-robin strategy:

```
unshuffle :: Int -> [a] -> [[a]]
unshuffle n ins
   | length firsts < n = take n (map (:[]) firsts ++ repeat [])
   | otherwise         = zipWith (:) firsts (unshuffle n rest)
  where (firsts, rest) = splitAt n ins
shuffle :: [[a]] -> [a]
shuffle = concat . transpose
```

In Figure 5 the typings of auxiliary functions used in the farm skeleton are shown. Function $zipWiths$ (we only show its type), $takes$, $drops$ and $(+\!\!+)_s$ are proved by induction on k. Notice the use of the subtyping relation $\rhd$. In Figure 6 the modified farm skeleton is shown with its type. There, functions $unshuffles^n$ and $shuffles$ are proved by induction on l.

The first thing to decide is which list types are finite lists and which ones are streams. In order to study the productivity we have chosen stream types for the input [a] and output [b] lists in the skeleton. As the number of processes is finite, the distribution of tasks between processes is considered a list of streams. This decision leads us to slightly change the definitions of shuffle and unshuffle, so they have now a different type. In particular, shuffle needs

sidata sList $w\ a = snil\ |\ scons\ a\ (\textbf{sList}\ w\ a)$
$zipWiths :: \forall a, b, c, k.(a \to b \to c) \to \textbf{sList}\ k\ a \to \textbf{sList}\ k\ b \to \textbf{sList}\ k\ c$
$takes :: \forall a, k, l.Nat\ k \to \textbf{Strm}\ (k + l)\ a \to \textbf{sList}\ k\ a$
$takes = \lambda n_{k+1}.\lambda s.\textbf{case}\ n_{k+1}\ \textbf{of}\ zero \to snil_{1 \triangleright k+1}$
$\qquad\qquad\qquad\qquad\qquad succ\ n'_k \to \textbf{case}\ s_{k+l+1}\ \textbf{of}$
$\qquad\qquad\qquad\qquad\qquad\qquad\qquad x; s'_{k+l} \to (scons\ x\ (takes\ n'_k\ s'_{k+l})_k)_{k+1}$
$drops :: \forall a, k, l.Nat\ k \to \textbf{Strm}\ (k + l)\ a \to \textbf{Strm}\ l\ a$
$drops = \lambda n_{k+1}.\lambda s_{k+l+1}.\textbf{case}\ n_{k+1}\ \textbf{of}\ zero \to s_{k+l+1 \triangleright l}$
$\qquad\qquad\qquad\qquad\qquad\qquad succ\ n'_k \to \textbf{case}\ s_{k+l+1}\ \textbf{of}$
$\qquad\qquad\qquad\qquad\qquad\qquad\qquad\qquad x; s'_{k+l} \to (drops\ n'_k\ s'_{k+l})_l$
$splitAts :: \forall a, k, l.Nat\ k \to \textbf{Strm}\ (k + l)\ a \to (\textbf{sList}\ k\ a, \textbf{Strm}\ l\ a)$
$splitAts = \lambda n.\lambda s.(takes\ n\ s, drops\ n\ s)$
$(+\!\!+_s) :: \forall a, k, l.\textbf{sList}\ k\ a \to \textbf{Strm}\ l\ a \to \textbf{Strm}\ l\ a$
$xs_{k+1} +\!\!+_s\ s = \textbf{case}\ xs_{k+1}\ \textbf{of}\ snil \to s_l;\ scons\ x\ xs'_k \to (x; (xs'_k +\!\!+_s\ s)_l)_{l+1 \triangleright l}$

Fig. 5. Auxiliary functions for the farm skeleton

an auxiliary stream in order to cope with a possibly empty list of channels, even though this situation will never arise in practice, as it would correspond to having zero processors.

Some problems have been found when typing this skeleton: The first one arises when typing `unshuffle`. We are dividing a stream of elements into n lists of streams. This means that the original stream should have at least $n * k$ elements, so that we obtain n lists of at least k elements. This implies a product of size variables, which is not allowed by the type system. There are two possibilities to solve this. One is to define a family $unshuffles^n$ of functions, one for each fixed number of processes n, so that $n*k$ is a product of a constant and a variable. This means that the natural parameter would disappear, and consequently $farm^n$ and map_farm^n would also be a family of functions. The drawback of this alternative is that we need to define many versions of the same skeleton for several values of n. The other possibility is to allow products of two (or more) variables, or size expressions, in order to obtain a parametric skeleton. In this case some new rules (not shown) for checking the relations $= 0$, $\neq 0$, $\overset{+}{\sim}k$ and $\sim k$ should be added. The drawback of this alternative is that products of variables are not included in the type checking algorithm, and they may even make it undecidable.

The second problem is also related to `unshuffle`. Its resulting type is a list of streams. The bottom check fails when $l = 0$, as $\textbf{List}\ n\ \textbf{U} \neq \textbf{U}$. This problem arises when we use a list or a tuple to represent several channels coming out of a process. As a simpler example with tuples we show the following version of $unshuffle$ for two streams:

$unshuffle2 :: \forall a, k.\textbf{Strm}\ (2k)\ a \to (\textbf{Strm}\ k\ a, \textbf{Strm}\ k\ a)$
$unshuffle2 = \lambda s_{2(k+1)}.\textbf{case}\ s_{2(k+1)}\ \textbf{of}$
$\qquad\qquad\qquad\qquad x; s'_{2k+1} \to \textbf{case}\ s'_{2k+1}\ \textbf{of}$
$\qquad\qquad\qquad\qquad\qquad y; s''_{2k} \to \textbf{let}\ \langle s1_k, s2_k\rangle = unshuffle2\ s''_{2k}\ \textbf{in}\ ((x; s1)_{k+1}, (y; s2)_{k+1})$

A similar problem arised in [Par00] when trying to type mutually recursive definitions. This was solved by building a special fixpoint definition for a set of simultaneous equations. A function from tuples to tuples would not work in principle as the bottom check fails because $(\textbf{U}, \textbf{U}) \neq \textbf{U}$. The solution we propose is to untag the tuples, that is, to define strict tuples. We define strict data, **sdata** (T_s), and idata, **sidata** (T_{si}). We add a new rule to represent the strictness, and another one to establish when an **sidata** is empty:

$$farm^n :: \forall a, b, l.F\ a, b \Rightarrow (\mathbf{Strm}\ (n*l)\ a \rightarrow \mathbf{sList}\ n\ (\mathbf{Strm}\ l\ a)) \rightarrow$$
$$(\mathbf{sList}\ n\ (\mathbf{Strm}\ l\ a) \rightarrow \mathbf{Strm}\ l\ b \rightarrow \mathbf{Strm}\ l\ b) \rightarrow$$
$$(a \rightarrow b) \rightarrow \mathbf{Strm}\ l\ b \rightarrow \mathbf{Strm}\ (n*l)\ a \rightarrow \mathbf{Strm}\ l\ b$$
$$farm^n = \lambda unshuffle^n.\lambda shuffle.\lambda f.\lambda aux.\lambda s.\ shuffle\ (map\_naiveLs\ (mapS\ f)\ (unshuffle^n\ s))\ aux$$

$$map\_farm^n :: \forall a, b, k.F\ a, b \Rightarrow (a \rightarrow b) \rightarrow \mathbf{Strm}\ k\ b \rightarrow \mathbf{Strm}\ (n*k)\ a \rightarrow \mathbf{Strm}\ k\ b$$
$$map\_farm^n = farm^n\ unshuffles^n\ shuffles$$

$$unshuffles^n :: \forall a, l.\mathbf{Strm}\ (n*l)\ a \rightarrow \mathbf{sList}\ n\ (\mathbf{Strm}\ l\ a)$$
$$unshuffles^n = \lambda s_{n(l+1)}.\mathbf{let}\ (firsts_n, rest_{nl}) = splitAts\ n\ s_{n(l+1)}$$
$$\mathbf{in}\ (zipWiths\ (;)\ firsts_n\ (unshuffles^n\ rest_{nl})_{n[l]})_{n[l+1]}$$

$$shuffles :: \forall a, l, k.\mathbf{sList}\ (k+1)\ (\mathbf{Strm}\ l\ a) \rightarrow \mathbf{Strm}\ l\ b \rightarrow \mathbf{Strm}\ l\ b$$
$$shuffles = \lambda xs_{k+1[l+1]}.\lambda aux_{l+1}.\mathbf{case}\ xs_{k+1[l+1]}\ \mathbf{of}$$
$$snil \rightarrow aux_{l+1}$$
$$scons\ s_{l+1}\ xs'_{k[l+1]} \rightarrow \mathbf{case}\ s_{l+1}\ \mathbf{of}$$
$$x; s'_l \rightarrow \mathbf{let}\ heads_k = map\ hdS\ xs'_{k[l+1]}$$
$$\mathbf{in\ let}\ tls_{k+1[l]} = map\ tlS\ xs_{k+1[l+1]}$$
$$\mathbf{in}\ (x; (heads_k\ ++_s\ (shuffles\ tls_{k+1[l]}\ aux)_l)_l)_{l+1}$$

Fig. 6. The farm skeleton

$$\frac{\exists i.\tau_i = \mathbf{U}}{T_s / T_{si}\ \overline{s}\ \overline{\tau} = \mathbf{U}} \qquad\qquad \frac{s_1 = 0}{T_{si}\ \overline{s}\ \overline{\tau} = E}$$

From now on angle brackets will represent strict tuples. These were also used in rule [*MERGE*], see Figure 4. Strict lists are defined in Figure 5. In order to make the previous strictness rule semantically correct we define a new type operator $\boxed{\times}'$ used to interpret this kind of types: $T_1\ \boxed{\times}'\ T_2 = \begin{cases} T_1\ \boxed{\times}\ T_2\ \text{if}\ T_1, T_2 \neq \mathbf{U} \\ \mathbf{U}\ \text{otherwise} \end{cases}$

4.2 Replicated Workers Topology

We now show a replicated workers implementation [KPR00] of the parallel map skeleton that distributes work on demand, i.e. a new task is assigned to a process only if it is known that it has already finished its previous work. The programmer cannot predict in advance the order in which processes are going to finish their works, as this depends on runtime issues.

By using the reactive (and non-deterministic) process **merge**, acknowledgments from different processes can be received by the manager as soon as they are produced. Thus, if each acknowledgment contains the identity of the sender process, the list of merged results can be scrutinized to know who has sent the first message, and a new work can be assigned to it:

```
rw :: (Tr a, Tr b) => Int -> Int -> (a->b) -> [a] -> [b]
rw np prefetch fw tasks =    results    where
  results = sortMerge outputsChildren
  outputsChildren =  [(worker fw i) # inputs
                          |(i,inputs) <- zip [0..np-1] inputss]
  inputss         = distribute tasksAndIds
                          (initReqs ++ (map owner unorderedResult))
  tasksAndIds     = zip [1..] tasks
  initReqs        = concat (generate prefetch [0..np-1])
  unorderedResult = merge # outputsChildren    -- Non-deterministic!!

  distribute [] _          = generate np []
```

data $ACK\ k\ b = ACK\ (Nat\ k)\ b$
$generate :: \forall k.Nat\ k \rightarrow \textbf{Strm}\ k\ (Nat\ k)$
$generate = \lambda n_{k+1}.\textbf{case}\ n_{k+1}\ \textbf{of}\ zero \rightarrow zeros_{\omega[1] \rhd k+1[k+1]};$
$$succ\ n'_k \rightarrow (n_{k+1};(generate\ n'_k)_{k[k]})_{k+1[k+1]}$$

$zipS :: \forall a, b, k.\textbf{Strm}\ k\ a \rightarrow \textbf{Strm}\ k\ b \rightarrow \textbf{Strm}\ k\ (a, b)$
$zipS = \lambda s_{k+1}.\lambda t_{k+1}.\textbf{case}\ s_{k+1}\ \textbf{of}\ x; s'_k \rightarrow \textbf{case}\ t_{k+1}\ \textbf{of}\ y; t'_k \rightarrow ((x, y);(zipS\ s'_k\ t'_k)_k)_{k+1}$

$owner :: \forall b, k.ACK\ k\ b \rightarrow Nat\ k$
$owner\ (ACK\ i\ \_) = i$
$result :: \forall b, k.ACK\ k\ b \rightarrow b$
$result\ (ACK\ \_\ b) = b$

$worker :: \forall a, b, k, l.F\ a, b \Rightarrow (a \rightarrow b) \rightarrow Nat\ k \rightarrow \textbf{Process}\ (\textbf{Strm}\ l\ a)\ (\textbf{Strm}\ l\ (ACK\ k\ b))$
$worker = \lambda f.\lambda n.\textbf{process}\ ts \rightarrow \textbf{let}\ f' :: F\ a, b \Rightarrow a \rightarrow ACK\ k\ b$
$$f' = \lambda t.ACK\ n\ (f\ t)$$
$$\textbf{in}\ (mapS\ f'\ ts)$$

$mapt^n :: \forall a, b, k_1, \dots, k_n.F\ a, b \Rightarrow (a \rightarrow b) \rightarrow \langle \textbf{Strm}\ k_1\ a, \dots, \textbf{Strm}\ k_n\ a \rangle \rightarrow$
$$\langle \textbf{Strm}\ k_1\ (ACK\ n\ b), \dots, \textbf{Strm}\ k_n\ (ACK\ n\ b) \rangle$$
$mapt^n = \lambda w.\lambda \langle s_1, \dots, s_n \rangle.\langle (worker\ w\ 0)\#s_1, \dots, (worker\ w\ (n-1))\#s_n \rangle$

Fig. 7. Auxiliary functions for the replicated workers topology

```
distribute (e:es) (i:is) = insert i e (distribute es is)
   where insert 0 e  (x:xs) = (e:x):xs
         insert (n+1) e  (x:xs) = x:(insert n e xs)

worker :: (Tr a, Tr b) => (a->b) -> Int -> Process [(Int,a)]  [ACK b]
worker f i = process ts -> map (\(id_t,t) -> ACK i id_t (f t)) ts

data ACK b =  ACK Int Int b
owner (ACK i _ _ )  = i
```

The skeleton receives as input parameters (1) the number of worker processes to be used; (2) the size of workers' prefetching buffer; (3) the worker function that will perform the actual computation on the tasks; and (4) the list of tasks into which the problem has been split. See [KPR00] for details. In Figure 7 the types of auxiliary functions used in this topology are shown. Functions $generate$ and $zipS$ are proved by induction on k. Notice that we make use of subtyping in $generate$. We are assuming that $mapS :: \forall a, b, k.(a \rightarrow b) \rightarrow \textbf{Strm}\ k\ a \rightarrow \textbf{Strm}\ k\ b$.

In Figure 8 a modified version of the topology is given a type. We have simplified some aspects. The prefetch parameter has been eliminated. The task identity has also been eliminated from the ACK type so we eliminate the sorting function and just return the unordered result. Several problems have been found when typing this skeleton. The first one is the following. As this is a topology where work is distributed on demand, the sizes of the streams communicating the processes are not necessarily the same, so working with lists of streams is not appropriate, as too much information would be lost. So we have decided to use instead strict tuples of streams of different sizes: $\langle \textbf{Strm}\ k_1\ a, \dots, \textbf{Strm}\ k_n\ a \rangle$. This means that the topology is in fact a family of functions, one for a different number of processors. So the natural number parameter is eliminated.

The second problem is that typing the recursive **let** implies proving that all the streams grow at least in one element, and this is not true for `outputChildren` for example. However it can be noticed that once `distribute` is applied, at least one task will be given to a process in `inputss` so that the topology keeps running. Then, we redefine the recursive **let** by defining a single recursive binding for *inputss* in terms of the rest of the bindings. So it is only necessary to prove that *inputss* grows. This is true at the beginning of the execution thanks to the initial list of requests *initReqs*. The rest of requests are appended after these: `initReqs ++ map owner unorderedResult`.

The third problem arises in this append function. We have to append a finite list of length n to a stream of at least, say, k elements. In the type system **List** n a means that the list has a length of at most n, so we cannot safely say that the resulting stream has at least $n + k$ elements. We need to use a stream also for the first parameter. This is *generate* n in Figure 8. It generates the first n requests and then adds an infinite number of 0's at the end. So, given two streams, the new append function, takes n elements from the first one and puts them at the beginning of the second one. But again this is not immediate, because we have to take n elements from the first stream, and again the natural numbers are inductive. So, we need to define a (inductively defined) family of append functions $\{++^j :: \forall a, k.\textbf{Strm } j\ a \rightarrow \textbf{Strm } k\ a \rightarrow \textbf{Strm } (k+j)\ a\}_{j \in \mathbb{N}^+}$, where now each function is defined in terms of the previous one:

$$++^1 :: \forall a, k.\textbf{Strm } 1\ a \rightarrow \textbf{Strm } k\ a \rightarrow \textbf{Strm } (k+1)\ a$$
$$s ++^1 s' = \textbf{case } s \textbf{ of } x; s'' \rightarrow x; s'$$

$$++^{j+1} :: \textbf{Strm } (j+1)\ a \rightarrow \textbf{Strm } k\ a \rightarrow \textbf{Strm } (k+j+1)\ a$$
$$s ++^{j+1} s' = \textbf{case } s \textbf{ of } x; s'' \rightarrow x; (s'' ++^j s')$$

The last problem arises in function `distribute`. This function provides new tasks to idle processes. This means that the streams are not uniformly increased. So it is not possible to type the *distribute*^{n} function of Figure 8 as we do not know which stream will be increased. But we are sure that one of them will be. We need then to make *induction over the sum of the stream sizes* and not separately on one of them. This is not supported by the type system. The process would be the following. First the bottom check: $\sum_{j=1}^n k_j = 0$ implies that for each $j = 1, \ldots, n$, $k_j = 0$. This means that **Strm** k_j a = u and the use of strict tuples leads us to $\langle \textbf{Strm } k_1\ a, \ldots, \textbf{Strm } k_n\ a \rangle = $ u. The induction hypothesis is that *distribute*^{n} :: **Strm** $w\ a \rightarrow \textbf{Strm}(\sum_{j=1}^n k_j)\ (Nat\ n) \rightarrow \langle \textbf{Strm } k_1\ a, \ldots, \textbf{Strm } k_n\ a \rangle$ where $\sum_{j=1}^n k_j = k$. We have to prove that *distribute*^{n} :: **Strm** $w\ a \rightarrow \textbf{Strm}(\sum_{j=1}^n k_j')$ $(Nat\ n) \rightarrow \langle \textbf{Strm } k_1'\ a, \ldots, \textbf{Strm } k_n'\ a \rangle$ where $k + 1 = \sum_{j=1}^n k_j' = \sum_{j=1}^n k_j + 1$. So let $s_1 ::$ **Strm** $w\ a$ and $s_2 ::$ **Strm** $(\sum_{j=1}^n k_j + 1)\ (Nat\ n)$. Then, by applying the **case** rule, $s_1' ::$ **Strm** $w\ a$ and $s_2' ::$ **Strm** $(\sum_{j=1}^n k_j)\ (Nat\ n)$, so applying the induction hypothesis we obtain that *distribute*^{n} s_1' $s_2' :: \langle \textbf{Strm } k_1\ a, \ldots, \textbf{Strm } k_n\ a \rangle$; and then, for each $j = 1, \ldots, n$, $t_j ::$ **Strm** k_j a. In each branch of the **if** expression one of the components is increased by one element, that is, each branch has a type where the sum of sizes is $k + 1$, so the whole expression has a type where the sum of sizes is $k + 1$. This is what we wanted to prove. This kind of induction should be also applied to *inputss*. This is still not included in the extended type system and should be formalised as a new way of induction.

$rw^n :: \forall a, b.F\ a, b \Rightarrow (a \rightarrow b) \rightarrow \mathbf{Strm}\ w\ a \rightarrow \mathbf{Strm}\ w\ b$
$rw^n = \lambda f.\lambda tasks.$
$\quad$ **let** $initReqs :: \mathbf{Strm}\ n\ (Nat\ n)$
$\qquad initReqs = generate\ n$
$\quad$ **in let rec**
$\qquad inputss :: \forall k_1 \ldots k_n.F\ a \Rightarrow \langle \mathbf{Strm}\ k_1\ a, \ldots, \mathbf{Strm}\ k_n\ a \rangle$
$\qquad inputss = \mathbf{let}\ oChildren :: F\ b \Rightarrow \langle \mathbf{Strm}\ k_1\ (ACK\ n\ b), \ldots, \mathbf{Strm}\ k_n\ (ACK\ n\ b) \rangle$
$\qquad\qquad oChildren = mapt^n\ f\ inputss$
$\qquad\quad$ **in let** $unordered :: F\ b \Rightarrow \mathbf{Strm}\ (\sum_{i=1}^{n} k_i)\ (ACK\ n\ b)$
$\qquad\qquad unordered = merge\#oChildren$
$\qquad\quad$ **in let** $restReqs :: \mathbf{Strm}\ (\sum_{i=1}^{n} k_i)\ (Nat\ n)$
$\qquad\qquad restReqs = mapS\ owner\ unordered$
$\qquad\quad$ **in let** $requests :: \mathbf{Strm}\ (\sum_{i=1}^{n} k_i + n)\ (Nat\ n)$
$\qquad\qquad requests = initReqs{+}{+}^n restReqs$
$\qquad\quad$ **in** $distribute^n\ tasks\ requests$
$\quad$ **in let**
$\qquad outputChildren :: \forall k_1 \ldots k_n.F\ b \Rightarrow \langle \mathbf{Strm}\ k_1\ (ACK\ n\ b), \ldots, \mathbf{Strm}\ k_n\ (ACK\ n\ b) \rangle$
$\qquad outputChildren = mapt^n\ f\ inputss$
$\quad$ **in** $mapS\ result\ (merge\#outputChildren)$

$distribute^n :: \forall a, k_1, \ldots k_n.\mathbf{Strm}\ w\ a \rightarrow \mathbf{Strm}(\sum_{k=1}^{n} k_i)\ (Nat\ n) \rightarrow \langle \mathbf{Strm}\ k_1\ a, \ldots, \mathbf{Strm}\ k_n\ a \rangle$
$distribute^n = \lambda s_1.\lambda s_2.\mathbf{case}\ s_1\ \mathbf{of}\ x_1; s_1' \rightarrow \mathbf{case}\ s_2\ \mathbf{of}\ x_2; s_2' \rightarrow$
$\qquad\qquad\qquad\qquad\mathbf{case}\ (distribute^n\ s_1'\ s_2')\ \mathbf{of}\ \langle t_1, \ldots, t_n \rangle \rightarrow$
$\qquad\qquad\qquad\qquad\qquad \mathbf{if}\ (x_2 == 0)\ \mathbf{then}\ \langle x_1; t_1, \ldots, t_n \rangle$
$\qquad\qquad\qquad\qquad\qquad \ldots$
$\qquad\qquad\qquad\qquad\qquad \mathbf{else}\ \{-(x_2 == n-1)-\}\ \langle t_1, \ldots, x_1; t_n \rangle$

Fig. 8. The replicated workers topology

5   Conclusions and Future Work

Eden is a parallel functional language that is sufficiently expressive that the programmer may introduce deadlocks and non-termination in programs. Having a proof that these unwanted effects are not present is highly desirable. Such proofs are even more essential for skeletons because the latter represent parallel topologies reused many times in different applications.

We have extended sized types by Hughes and Pareto in several directions in order to make them more useful for typing our skeletons, and proved that the skeletons are free from abnormal termination and busy loops. Firstly, we have introduced type classes for restricting the instantiation of some type variables. In this way, it can be proved that only finite values are communicated between processes. Secondly, we have added to the system strict types, and their corresponding typing rules, in order to be able to do induction proofs for processes receiving or/and producing tuples or finite lists of channels. Thirdly, we suggest to incorporate products of size variables in size expressions. This would make the type system much more expressive so that many more algorithms could be typed. In the general case the extension would probably make type checking undecidable, but surely many useful subcases could be encountered in which the algorithm is still decidable. Our `map_farm` and `map_rw` skeletons provide real examples showing that this extension is clearly needed. Finally, we propose to extend the induction proof embedded in rule $[LETREC]$ to cope with doing induction on expressions such as the sum of size variables rather than only on single variables.

Even though the proposed extensions can automate the proofs, the programmer is still responsible for conjecturing a type for his/her program and for reformulating it in order to get a proof. We have typed other skeletons not shown here such as different versions of divide and conquer.

There are other techniques to prove termination and productivity of programs. Between the first ones they may be cited the big amount of work done in term rewriting systems and, in the functional field, proposals such as that of David Turner [Tur95], were all programs terminate by construction. On productivity, it may be cited [Sij89]. In Pareto's thesis [Par00] more exhaustive related work can be found.

As future work we plan in the first place to continue trying the typing of other (more complex) skeletons such as the ring and torus. We would also like to work in better formalizing the new features and in extending the current implementation of sized types with them in order to check automatically the proofs presented in this paper.

References

BLOP98. S. Breitinger, R. Loogen, Y. Ortega Mallén, and R. Peña. Eden: Language Definition and Operational Semantics. Technical Report, Bericht 96-10. Revised version 1.998, Philipps-Universität Marburg, Germany, 1998.

Col89. M. Cole. *Algorithmic Skeletons: Structured Management of Parallel Computation.* Research monographs in parallel and distributed computing. Pitman, 1989.

HPS96. J. Hughes, L. Pareto, and A. Sabry. Proving the correctness of reactive systems using sized types. In *Conference Record of POPL '96: The* 23$^{\rm rd}$ *ACM SIGPLAN-SIGACT*, pages 410–423, 1996.

KPR00. U. Klusik, R. Peña, and F. Rubio. Replicated Workers in Eden. 2nd International Workshop on Constructive Methods for Parallel Programming (CMPP 2000). To be published by Nova Science, 2000.

Par97. L. Pareto. Sized types. Licenciate Dissertation, Chalmers University of Technology, G teborg, Sweden, 1997.

Par00. L. Pareto. *Types for Crash Prevention.* PhD thesis, Chalmers University of Technology and G teborg University, Sweden, 2000.

PHH+93. S. L. Peyton Jones, C. V. Hall, K. Hammond, W. D. Partain, and P. L. Wadler. The Glasgow Haskell Compiler: A Technical Overview. In *Joint Framework for Inf. Technology, Keele*, pages 249–257, 1993.

PR01. R. Pe a and F. Rubio. Parallel Functional Programming al Two Levels of Abstraction. In *Principles and Practice of Declarative Programming, PPDP'01*. To appear in ACM Press, 2001.

Sij89. B. A. Sijtsma. On the Productivity of Recursive List Definitions. *ACM Transactions on Programming Languages and Systems*, 11(4):633–649, October 1989.

Tur95. D. A. Turner. Elementary Strong Functional Programming. In *Functional Programming Languages in Education, FPLE'95*, pages 1–13. LNCS 1022, Springer, 1995.

A Compilation Scheme
for a Hierarchy of Array Types

Dietmar Kreye

University of Kiel
Department of Computer Science and Applied Mathematics
D-24098 Kiel, Germany
dkr@informatik.uni-kiel.de

Abstract. In order to achieve a high level of abstraction, array-oriented languages provide language constructs for defining array operations in a shape-invariant way. However, when trying to compile such generic array operations into efficiently executable code, static knowledge of exact shapes is essential. Therefore, modern compilers try to infer the shapes of all arrays used in a program.

Unfortunately, shape inference is generally undecidable. Therefore, most compilers either rule out all programs for which shape inference fails, or they perform no shape inference at all. In the first case the expressive power of the language is restricted, in the latter the generated code has a weak runtime performance.

This paper presents a new compilation scheme for the language SAC which combines these two approaches in order to avoid their individual shortcomings. A preliminary performance evaluation demonstrates the benefits of this compilation scheme.

1 Introduction

One of the key features of array-oriented languages such as APL [11], J [6], NIAL [13], FISH [12], ZPL [15], or SAC [19] is that they support so-called shape-invariant programming, i.e. all operations/functions can be defined in a way that allows arguments to have arbitrary extents in an arbitrary number of dimensions. This high level of abstraction gains the programmer a lot of benefits, among these are simplicity of program development, good readability and re-usability of programs.

However, the large semantical gap between such programming constructs and a given target architecture makes it difficult to develop a compiler that generates code with a high runtime performance. Sophisticated optimization techniques are needed that transform the generic program specifications into more specific ones, which in turn can be compiled into more efficiently executable code. A common method to achieve this is the so-called static shape inference, which tries to infer the shapes of all arrays used in a program as precisely as possible. Several case studies in the context of SAC [18,10] and ZPL [7,16] have shown that reasonably complex array operations can be compiled into code whose runtimes

T. Arts and M. Mohnen (Eds.): IFL 2001, LNCS 2312, pp. 18–35, 2002.

are competitive with those obtained from rather low-level specifications in other languages such as SISAL or FORTRAN.

Unfortunately, inferring shapes statically is impossible in certain situations, e.g. if external module functions are compiled separately or input data have unknown shapes. Even worse, whenever a recursive function is applied to an argument whose shape is changing with each recursive call, shape inference may be undecidable.

There are basically two ways to handle this problem. The first approach, used for instance in the languages FISH, ZPL, and SAC, is to rule out all programs for which static shape inference fails. As a consequence, implementing certain algorithms in these languages requires some awkward code design or is even impossible. The second approach, which gives the language the full expressive power, is to refrain from static shape inference and to generate code for generic programs instead. Past experiences with such languages, for instance APL, J, or NIAL, have shown that this results in a rather weak runtime performance of the generated code.

The aim of this paper is to present a compilation scheme that combines the advantages of both approaches: generation of shape-specific code whenever exact shapes can be statically inferred and generation of more generic code, otherwise. The basic idea is to make use of a hierarchy of array types with different levels of shape information — the most specific array types specify an exact shape, whereas more general types prescribe an exact dimensionality only or contain no shape information at all — and to translate the typed programs into a corresponding hierarchy of array representations.

This compilation scheme has been developed in the context of the language SAC and has been implemented as an extension to the current SAC compiler. Therefore, Section 2 gives a brief introduction to the array concept of SAC and specifies a short SAC program that is used as a running example throughout the paper. Section 3 describes the compilation scheme for a hierarchy of array types, Section 4 presents a preliminary performance figure, and Section 5 sketches some related work. Finally, Section 6 concludes the paper and discusses future work.

2   Arrays in Sac

SAC [17] is a strict functional language based on C-syntax which primarily has been designed for numerical applications. This section gives a brief introduction to the array concept of SAC.

2.1   Representation of Arrays

SAC supports the notion of n-dimensional arrays and of high-level array operations as they are known from array languages such as APL, J, and NIAL. All arrays are represented by two vectors: a **data vector** containing all array elements in canonical order, and a **shape vector** which specifies the number of elements per axis. For instance, a 2×3 matrix $\begin{pmatrix} 1\ 2\ 3 \\ 4\ 5\ 6 \end{pmatrix}$ has the data vector [1,2,3,4,5,6] and the shape vector [2,3]. For reasons of uniformity scalars are considered arrays with empty shape.

2.2   Type System

For each base type (int, float, double, bool, char) SAC provides an entire hierarchy of array types. The most specific array types specify an exact shape, whereas more general types prescribe an exact dimensionality only or contain no shape information at all.

Basically, an array type consists of a base type followed by a shape vector. If the shape is not completely defined, some or all components of the shape vector may be replaced by wildcards (., *, +). The wildcard . means that the extent of a certain dimension is unknown. The wildcards + and * represent arrays with at least dimensionality 1 or completely unknown dimensionality, respectively.

The hierarchy of array types can be classified into three major categories:

- arrays with known dimensionality and known extent, e.g. $\mathcal{T}[3,2], \mathcal{T} \equiv \mathcal{T}[]$, where $\mathcal{T}$ denotes a base type;
- arrays with known dimensionality but unknown extent, e.g. $\mathcal{T}[.], \mathcal{T}[.,.]$;
- arrays with unknown dimensionality and unknown extent, e.g. $\mathcal{T}[+], \mathcal{T}[*]$.

Figure 1 depicts the directed graph of the (reflexive, transitive and antisymmetrical) subtype relation. Vertices of the graph represent types and an edge $(\mathcal{T} \rightarrow \sigma)$ means that σ is a subtype of $\mathcal{T}$. The dashed horizontal lines separate the three categories of array types.

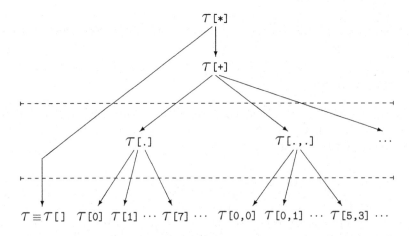

Fig. 1. Hierarchy of array types in SAC.

2.3   User-Defined Array Operations

User-defined functions may have arbitrary numbers of parameters and return values. Moreover, functions can be overloaded with respect to almost[1] arbitrary argument type constellations. The semantics of SAC prescribes that for each function application the most specific instance suitable for the arguments must be used.

Consider as an example computing the determinant of a two-dimensional array. For arrays with shape [2,2] the operation is very simple:

$$\det \begin{pmatrix} a & b \\ c & d \end{pmatrix} = ad - bc \quad . \tag{1}$$

Higher-order determinants may be computed recursively using the Laplace expansion (along the first column):

$$\det(A) = \sum_{i=0}^{n-1} (-1)^i \cdot A_{i0} \cdot \det(\mathcal{A}_{i0}) \quad , \tag{2}$$

where A is an array of shape [n,n] and $\mathcal{A}_{ij}$ denotes the array A without the i-th row and j-th column. This mathematical specification of the algorithm can be translated almost literally into a SAC implementation, defining a separate function for each of the equations (1) and (2), as depicted in Fig. 2.

```
(1):   int Det( int[2,2] A)
(2):   {
(3):     return( A[[0,0]] * A[[1,1]] - A[[0,1]] * A[[1,0]]);
(4):   }

(5):   int Det( int[.,.] A)
(6):   {
(7):     shp = shape( A);
(8):     if (shp[[0]] == shp[[1]]) {
(9):       ret = with ([0] <= [i] < [shp[[0]]]) {
(10):            B = Elim( A, [i,0]);
(11):            det = Det( B);
(12):            val = (-1) i * A[[i,0]] * det;
(13):          } fold( +, val);
(14):     } else {
(15):       ret = ERROR( ''array is not quadratic");
(16):     }
(17):     return( ret);
(18):   }
```

Fig. 2. Computing the determinant of a two-dimensional array.

---

[1] In the next section it will be shown that the signatures of overloaded functions have to meet some side conditions.

This example of a user-defined function is well-suited to explain the basic problems that arise when trying to compile generic SAC code into efficiently executable C code:

It is important to note that the function `Det()` is overloaded. The first instance is suitable for arrays of shape `[2,2]` only, the second one applies for all two-dimensional arrays with bigger shapes. It is the compiler's duty to resolve this overloading correctly.

Note also that the second instance of `Det()` has a non-shape-specific argument. In order to generate code with best possible runtime performance, the compiler has to specialize this instance for all required argument shapes. Moreover, these additional instances must be taken into account during resolution of function overloading.

Whenever the compiler succeeds in inferring all array shapes statically, both tasks — function specialization and resolution of overloading — are quite simple, because functions are specialized for concrete shapes only and overloading can be resolved statically then. But in general things are not that easy.

Consider, for instance, applications of the `Det()` function to arguments of type `int[3,3]`, `int[.,.]`, and `int[+]`. For the first application the compiler builds a specialization of the second instance with argument shape `[3,3]` and resolves the overloading statically. For the second application no specialization is needed, but it is not statically decidable which instance must be used. Each of the three instances available — the two given by the programmer and the one built by the compiler — may be applicable. Thus, the compiler must generate additional code that chooses the matching instance at runtime. For the third application the situation is basically the same, but here an additional dynamic type check is needed to ensure that the argument represents indeed a two-dimensional array.

So, in general it can be a rather complicated and time consuming task to determine which functions have to be specialized for which argument shapes, and to build all the tailor-made code fragments that resolve the overloading.

Another problem arises in the backend of the compiler. The compiler must generate code for three different categories of array types, which include scalars. With respect to runtime efficiency it is obviously a good idea to use different representations for scalars and non-scalars. But in fact even for non-scalar arrays a hierarchy of different representations should be used. However, these different representations have to interact with each other, e.g. formal and actual arguments of a function may have different types. Therefore, they must be designed in a way that allows for cheap conversion from one representation into another.

3   Compilation

The compilation of user-defined array operations into C code is divided into four major phases:

- type inference and function specialization,
- resolution of function overloading,

- high-level code optimization,
- code generation.

In this section, these phases are described in more detail.

Note, that the following subsection about type inference and function specialization is just an excerpt from [20] and is presented here as background information only. The topic of this paper is code generation. It is demonstrated how the partial shape information provided by the type system can be exploited to generate efficiently executable code even in case of failing static shape inference. So, the innovative parts of the compilation scheme are described in the subsections 3.2 and 3.4.

3.1   Type Inference and Function Specialization

The first important task of compilation is to infer the types of all local variables. In order to achieve best possible potential for code optimizations, these types are inferred as shape-specific as possible.

Basically, the inference algorithm works as follows: Starting from the `main()` function, the type inference system traverses all function bodies from outermost to innermost, propagating shapes as far as possible. Whenever a function application is encountered, it has to be determined which function definitions are relevant for it, i.e. which function definitions are possibly needed to compute the result of the application. Then, the type of the application equals the most specific common supertype (short: MSCS) of the return types of all these function definitions. Furthermore, if only a single relevant definition is found which has not yet been specialized for the actual argument shapes, the specialization is enforced.[2]

Take as an example the two definitions of `Det()` in Fig. 2. If `Det()` is applied to an argument of type `int[2,2]`, only the first definition is relevant. However, if the argument is of type `int[3,3]`, only the second definition is relevant. Moreover, the type inference system generates a specialized `int[3,3]` version of this definition, which afterwards is the only relevant one. If the argument is of type `int[.,.]`, both definitions are relevant.

The inference algorithm sketched above has some important implications which will be formalized in the following. Consider a function application

$$f(x_1 : \mathcal{T}_1, \ldots, x_m : \mathcal{T}_m) \quad .$$

(The notation $x : \mathcal{T}$ means that for the variable x the type $\mathcal{T}$ has been inferred.) Let

$$\sigma_1^k, \ldots, \sigma_n^k \; f^{(k)}(\mathcal{T}_1^k \, a_1, \ldots, \mathcal{T}_m^k \, a_m) \; \{ \; \ldots \; \} \quad , \quad k \in \{1, \ldots, M\}$$

---

[2] To avoid non-termination, the number of possible function specializations is limited to a pre-specified number of instances. If this number is exceeded, the generic version of the function is used instead.

denote all the instances of f that occur in the given SAC program where M is the number of these instances. A function definition $f^{(k)}$ is relevant for the above application iff two conditions hold:

$$\forall i \in \{1, ..., m\} : (T_i^k \preceq T_i \vee T_i^k \succeq T_i) \quad ,$$

$$\neg \, \exists l \in \{1, ..., M\} \setminus \{k\} : \forall i \in \{1, ..., m\} : (T_i \preceq T_i^l \preceq T_i^k \vee T_i^l = T_i^k) \quad .$$

(The notation $T \preceq \sigma$ means that T is a subtype of σ.) The first condition ensures that actual and formal parameters of the application have compatible types. The second condition excludes all instances that are under no circumstances needed, because it is guaranteed that always another instance with more specific argument shapes can be found.

Without loss of generality, let

$$\{f^{(k)} \mid k \in \{1, ..., R\}\} \quad , \quad R \leq M$$

denote the set of relevant function definitions. As already mentioned, the type of the j-th return value of the given application is equal to

$$\text{MSCS}(\{\sigma_j^k \mid k \in \{1, ..., R\}\}) \quad .$$

Obviously, such a supertype does not always exist. In order to ensure that the type of the application is well-defined, the type inference system has to check whether the return values of all relevant instances have pairwise a common supertype:

$$\forall k, l \in \{1, ..., R\} : \forall j \in \{1, ..., n\} : \exists \sigma : (\sigma \succeq \sigma_j^k \wedge \sigma \succeq \sigma_j^l) \quad . \tag{3}$$

Note here, that a common supertype of two arbitrary types exists iff the two types have an identical base type. Thus, the constraint (3) can be simplified to:

$$\forall k, l \in \{1, ..., R\} : \forall j \in \{1, ..., n\} : \text{Basetype}(\sigma_j^k) = \text{Basetype}(\sigma_j^l) \quad .$$

3.2 Resolution of Function Overloading

The type inference system of the compiler infers for each function application the set of relevant function definitions. If this set contains more than a single instance, the compiler must generate additional code for the function application, that dynamically chooses the matching instance (i.e. at runtime). Moreover, it may not be statically inferable whether or not a function application is type-correct, i.e. some actual arguments' types are proper supertypes of the formal arguments' types. In this case the compiler has to generate additional code for dynamic type checks as well.

Fortunately, it turns out that it is not necessary to generate individual code that performs the resolution of overloading and the dynamic type checks for

each function application explicitly. Instead, it suffices to generate it for the
most general case only. This code is written in SAC itself and inserted into the
SAC program via a high-level code transformation. Subsequently, individual and
optimized code for each function application is obtained by means of the usual
high-level code optimizations already integrated into the compiler, like function
inlining, constant folding and constant propagation.

```
(1):   int Det__i_2_2( int[2,2] A) { ... }
(2):   int Det__i_X_X( int[.,.] A) { ... Det__i( B) ... }
(3):   int Det__i_3_3( int[3,3] A) { ... Det__i( B) ... }

(4):   inline int Det__i( int[*] A)          /* wrapper */
(5):   {
(6):     if (dim( A) == 2) {
(7):       if (shape( A) == [2,2]) {
(8):         ret = Det__i_2_2( A);
(9):       } else if (shape( A) == [3,3]) {
(10):        ret = Det__i_3_3( A);
(11):      } else {
(12):        ret = Det__i_X_X( A);
(13):      }
(14):    } else {
(15):      ret = ERROR( ``type error");
(16):    }
(17):    return( ret);
(18):  }

(19):  int main()
(20):  {
(21):    int[+] A;
(22):    int[.,.] B;
(23):    int[3,3] C;
(24):    ...
(25):    a = Det__i( A);
(26):    b = Det__i( B);
(27):    c = Det__i( C);
(28):    ...
(29):  }
```

Fig. 3. After resolution of function overloading.

As an example consider a main() function that contains applications of the
familiar Det() function to arguments of type int[+], int[.,.], and int[3,3].
Figure 3 depicts the SAC code with resolved function overloading and explicit
type checks. There exist three instances of the function Det(): Two of them
have been given by the programmer (see lines 1, 2), the third one with argument
shape [3,3] (line 3) is built by the type inference system via specialization of
the [.,.] version. All three instances of Det() have unique names now. This is

done by adding suffixes representing the types of the arguments (e.g. _i_X_X for int[.,.]). The resolution code is implemented as a wrapper function Det__i() with the most general argument type int[*] (lines 4–18). All applications of the function Det() in the SAC source code are replaced by applications of this wrapper (lines 2, 3, 25–27). The wrapper selects the appropriate instance with respect to the actual shape of the argument (lines 8, 10, 12), or causes a runtime error if no appropriate instance has been found (line 15). In order to minimize on average the number of comparisons needed to choose the correct function, the choice is narrowed down by first checking the argument's dimensionality (line 6). The keyword inline in front of the definition of the wrapper function (line 4) directs the compiler to perform function inlining on it.

The interesting part of this code transformation is the generation of the wrapper function(s). Let again

$$\sigma_1^k, \ldots, \sigma_n^k \; f^{(k)} \, (\, \mathcal{T}_1^k \, a_1, \ldots, \mathcal{T}_m^k \, a_m) \; \{ \; \ldots \; \} \quad , \quad k \in \{1, \ldots, M\}$$

denote all the instances of a function f that occur in the given SAC program, and define the set $\mathcal{I}(f)$ of these instances:

$$\mathcal{I}(f) := \{ f^{(k)} \mid k \in \{1, \ldots, M\} \} \quad .$$

Then, the following defines an equivalence relation $\sim$ on $\mathcal{I}(f)$:

$$f^{(k)} \sim f^{(l)} \quad :\Longleftrightarrow \quad \forall i \in \{1, \ldots, m\} : \mathrm{Basetype}(\mathcal{T}_i^k) = \mathrm{Basetype}(\mathcal{T}_i^l) \quad .$$

For each equivalence class of this relation a wrapper function must be generated.

Without loss of generality, let

$$\mathcal{C} := \{ f^{(k)} \mid k \in \{1, \ldots, N\} \} \quad , \quad N \leq M$$

denote an arbitrary equivalence class of $\sim$. Then, the i-th argument of the wrapper function has the type

$$\mathrm{Basetype}(\mathcal{T}_i^k) \, [*] \quad , \quad \text{identical for all } k \in \{1, \ldots, N\} \quad ,$$

and the j-th return value has the type

$$\mathrm{MSCS}(\{ \sigma_j^k \mid k \in \{1, \ldots, N\} \}) \quad .$$

Again, such a supertype exists only if a constraint analogous to (3) is met:

$$\forall k, l \in \{1, \ldots, N\} : \forall j \in \{1, \ldots, n\} : \mathrm{Basetype}(\sigma_j^k) = \mathrm{Basetype}(\sigma_j^l) \quad . \qquad (4)$$

In order to generate the body of the wrapper function, the instances in $\mathcal{C}$ must be sorted according to their argument types. Unfortunately, in case of multiple arguments the subtype relation on its own is not a proper ordering relation. Consider as an example the following two instances of a function fun:

```
int fun( int[.] A, int[2] B) { ... }
int fun( int[2] A, int[.] B) { ... }
```

Regarding the argument A the second instance has a more specific type than the first one, regarding the argument B it is the other way round. Consider an application of fun, where for both arguments the type int[2] has been inferred. Without additional criteria it is undecidable which instance has to be chosen. This problem could be solved by introducing different priorities for different argument positions, but then, the semantics of SAC programs would depend on the order of the function arguments. To avoid confusion about the overloading mechanism, instances with such argument types are ruled out:

$$\forall k, l \in \{1, ..., N\} : ((\exists i : \mathcal{T}_i^k \prec \mathcal{T}_i^l) \Rightarrow (\forall i : \mathcal{T}_i^k \preceq \mathcal{T}_i^l)) \quad . \tag{5}$$

(The notion $\mathcal{T} \prec \sigma$ means $(\mathcal{T} \preceq \sigma \wedge \mathcal{T} \neq \sigma)$.) Besides, all pairwise distinct instances must differ in their argument signatures:

$$\forall k, l \in \{1, ..., N\} : \exists i \in \{1, ..., m\} : \mathcal{T}_i^k \neq \mathcal{T}_i^l \tag{6}$$

Now, an ordering relation $\leq$ on $\mathcal{C}$ can be defined

$$f^{(k)} \leq f^{(l)} \quad :\Longleftrightarrow \quad \forall i \in \{1, ..., m\} : \mathcal{T}_i^k \preceq \mathcal{T}_i^l \quad ,$$

and the following holds:

$$\forall k, l \in \{1, ..., N\} : ((k \neq l) \Rightarrow (f^{(k)} < f^{(l)} \vee f^{(k)} > f^{(l)})) \quad .$$

Thus, it is guaranteed that the function overloading can be resolved uniquely.

3.3   High-Level Code Optimizations

The SAC compiler applies several high-level code optimizations. Among these are standard optimizations [2] like function inlining, constant folding, constant propagation, dead code removal, common subexpression elimination, and loop unrolling. In general, the benefits gained by these optimizations heavily depend on the types inferred for the array objects. The more precisely the shapes have been inferred, the higher is the potential for optimizations. For example, having specialized the function Det() for arguments of shape [3,3], the if-clause in its body (see Fig. 2, line 8) is redundant and can be eliminated, whereas this is not the case for the generic instance. Thus, by allowing arrays whose shapes cannot be inferred statically some overhead is introduced.

Another potential source of overhead are the wrapper functions that resolve function overloading. Since these wrappers are designed for arguments of most general types, they contain a lot of redundancy if applied to arguments of more specific types. Fortunately, this redundancy is eliminated by the optimization techniques mentioned above. Take, for instance, an application of the wrapper function Det__i(), as defined in Fig. 3, to an argument of type int[3,3]. First, the function is inlined, i.e. the function application is replaced by the body of the wrapper function. Subsequently, constant folding detects that the conditions of all `if`-clauses can be evaluated statically, and therefore replaces the whole nesting of `if`-clauses by a call of the function `Det__i_3_3()`. Thus, as intended, the call of the wrapper function has been replaced by a call of the correct specialized function.

3.4   Code Generation

In the final compilation phase the optimized SAC code is translated into ANSI C code. The most important issue in this context is to find an appropriate C representation for the whole hierarchy of array types provided by SAC.

Array Representation. SAC arrays that are statically identified as scalars are represented in C by scalar values.

Other SAC arrays are uniquely defined by means of a data vector and a shape vector. Additionally, a reference counter [8] (short: rc) for the implicit memory management is needed. In order to get a compact representation, the reference counter and the shape vector are combined to a so-called descriptor containing reference counter, dimensionality, and all shape components. Keeping data vector and descriptor separately allows arrays to be handled uniquely irrespective of the length of their data and shape vectors, and it facilitates interfacing to external languages such as C.

The performance evaluation presented in the next section shows that this simple and uniform array representation is not sufficient for obtaining best possible runtime performance. Storing the shape in the descriptor (only) is in many situations inefficient, because the shape information is frequently used. For instance, consider a variable A representing an array of shape [.,.]. In this case it is guaranteed that all descriptors of the arrays, A is pointing to during program execution, contain a dimensionality of 2. So, in order to avoid costly accesses to the main memory, all references to the dimensionality of A should be replaced by the constant value 2. As a consequence, it is superfluous to store the dimensionality of A in the descriptor at all. Moreover, even the shape components of A are constant until a new array object is assigned to A. Therefore, it is recommended to buffer the shape components on the runtime stack or even in registers.

Unfortunately, it is unlikely that the C compiler will be able to apply such optimizations. In an imperative language like C any function call or any reference to a vector may cause a side-effect, hence it is almost impossible to detect that a value behind a pointer is constant or in fact superfluous. Therefore, rather than relying on the C compiler, these optimizations have to be done on the SAC level. For this purpose additional local variables are used, which always mirror the shape information of the descriptor. Whenever the shape has to be inspected, these local variables are accessed rather than the descriptor.

Figure 4 depicts the optimized C representations for the different categories of SAC arrays. For a variable A representing a non-scalar array, a data vector A

Declaration in Sac	Declaration in C
$\mathcal{T}$[] A;	$\mathcal{T}$ A;

$\mathcal{T}$[4,3] A;	$\mathcal{T}$ *A;
	int *A_desc; /* rc */
	const int A_dim = 2;
	const int A_shp0 = 4;
	const int A_shp1 = 3;

$\mathcal{T}$[.,.] A;	$\mathcal{T}$ *A; int *A_desc; /* rc, shp0, shp1 */ const int A_dim = 2; int A_shp0; int A_shp1;
$\mathcal{T}$[+] A; and $\mathcal{T}$[*] A;	$\mathcal{T}$ *A; int *A_desc; /* rc, dim, shp0, ... */ int A_dim;

Fig. 4. C representations for the different categories of SAC arrays.

and a descriptor A_desc is needed. All statically known parts of the shape are not expected in the descriptor, i.e. the corresponding descriptor entries possibly contain undefined values, but are declared as scalar constants instead. Furthermore, all variable parts of the shape are mirrored in scalar variables. Note, that mirroring the shape components is impossible for arrays of shape [+] or [*], because the number of needed scalars is unknown during compilation.

So, the hierarchy of array types in SAC is represented by a hierarchy of C representations. As a result, the compilation scheme for array operations must be parameterized with respect to array categories, and in certain situations arrays must be converted from one representation into another.

Transformation Rules. With an appropriate array representation at hand, the code generation can be specified by means of a transformation scheme $\mathcal{C}$ which transforms SAC code into semantically equivalent C code. The basic set of transformation rules for array operations is depicted in Fig. 5.

Transformation rule (7) applies to variable declarations. The pseudo statement DECL_ARRAY() represents a C declaration as shown in Fig. 4.

A simple example for creating a new array is given in (8). ALLOC_ARRAY() allocates memory for the data vector as well as the descriptor of the array, and initializes the descriptor entries and the mirror variables. ASSIGN_CONST() stores the elements of the constant array [1,2,...] in the data vector.

Assignments of a variable A representing an array of type $\mathcal{T}$ to a variable B representing an array of type σ are compiled into the statement ASSIGN_ARRAY() that also converts the array representation if needed. Take as an example B : int[+] and A : int[.,.]. Then, the following code is created:

```
B = A;
B_desc = A_desc;
B_dim = A_dim;
```

$$\mathcal{C}\left[\!\!\left[\begin{array}{l} T \text{ A;} \\ Rest \end{array}\right]\!\!\right] \longmapsto \left\{\begin{array}{l} \text{DECL\_ARRAY(A:}T\text{)} \\ \mathcal{C}[\![Rest]\!] \end{array}\right. \tag{7}$$

$$\mathcal{C}\left[\!\!\left[\begin{array}{l} \text{A:}T \text{ = [1,2,...];} \\ Rest \end{array}\right]\!\!\right] \longmapsto \left\{\begin{array}{l} \text{ALLOC\_ARRAY(A:}T\text{)} \\ \text{ASSIGN\_CONST(A:}T\text{, [1,2,...])} \\ \mathcal{C}[\![Rest]\!] \end{array}\right. \tag{8}$$

$$\mathcal{C}\left[\!\!\left[\begin{array}{l} \text{B:}\sigma \text{ = A:}T\text{;} \\ Rest \end{array}\right]\!\!\right] \longmapsto \left\{\begin{array}{l} \text{ASSIGN\_ARRAY(B:}\sigma\text{, A:}T\text{)} \\ \mathcal{C}[\![Rest]\!] \end{array}\right. \tag{9}$$

$$\mathcal{C}\left[\!\!\left[\begin{array}{l} \text{B:}\sigma \text{ = fun(A:}T\text{);} \\ Rest \end{array}\right]\!\!\right] \quad \text{where} \quad \sigma' \text{ fun(}T'\text{ A')} \{ ... \}$$

$$\longmapsto \left\{\begin{array}{l} \begin{array}{l} \text{FUN\_AP(B:}\sigma\text{, fun, A:}T\text{)} \\ \text{REFRESH\_MIRROR(B:}\sigma\text{)} \qquad ; \quad \text{iff } (T{=}T' \wedge \sigma{=}\sigma') \\ \mathcal{C}[\![Rest]\!] \end{array} \\ \hline \mathcal{C}\left[\!\!\left[\begin{array}{l} \text{A':}T' \text{ = A:}T\text{;} \\ \text{B':}\sigma' \text{ = fun(A':}T'\text{);} \\ \text{B:}\sigma \text{ = B':}\sigma'\text{;} \\ Rest \end{array}\right]\!\!\right] \qquad ; \quad \text{otherwise} \end{array}\right. \tag{10}$$

$$\mathcal{C}\left[\!\!\left[\begin{array}{l} \sigma \text{ fun(} T \text{ A)} \\ \{ \\ \quad Body \\ \quad \text{return(B:}\sigma\text{);} \\ \} \end{array}\right]\!\!\right] \longmapsto \left\{\begin{array}{l} \text{FUN\_DEF(B:}\sigma\text{, fun, A:}T\text{)} \\ \{ \\ \quad \text{DECL\_ARRAY\_ARG(A:}T\text{)} \\ \quad \mathcal{C}\left[\!\!\left[\begin{array}{l} Body \\ \text{return(B:}\sigma\text{);} \end{array}\right]\!\!\right] \\ \} \end{array}\right. \tag{11}$$

Fig. 5. Rules for transforming SAC code into semantically equivalent C code.

However, if the inferred types are B : int[.,.] and A : int[+], descriptor accesses are needed:

```
B = A;
B_desc = A_desc;
B_shp0 = A_desc[2];
B_shp1 = A_desc[3];
```

Another important situation arises if A is a scalar and B not, e.g. A : int[] and B : int[*]. In this case a new descriptor for B has to be generated.

Assignments with a function application[3] on the right hand side are transformed as shown in (10). If the types of formal and actual parameters / return values are identical, the assignment is directly compiled into the statements FUN_AP() and REFRESH_MIRROR(). Otherwise additional assignments before or after the function application are inserted to convert the array representations

---

[3] Function definitions and applications are, for reasons of clarity, restricted to a single argument and a single return value here.

accordingly. Consider that A and B are both non-scalar arrays. Then, FUN_AP() represents an application of the function fun to the arguments A, A_desc, &B, &B_desc, i.e. return values are implemented as reference parameters, because C functions allow a single return value only. Note, that the mirror variables of the array representation (A_dim, ...) are *not* passed to the function, because the function signature must be suitable for all argument types. Instead, the subsequent statement REFRESH_MIRROR() assures that the mirror variables are initialized with the corresponding values of the descriptor.

The rule for transforming function definitions is depicted in (11). The statement FUN_DEF() defines the function header by analogy with FUN_AP(). Besides, for each function argument a statement DECL_ARRAY_ARG() is inserted into the body which declares and initializes the scalar variables of the array representation. Take as an example an argument A:int[.,.]. In this case A and A_desc are already declared in the argument list of the function header, but the scalar variables for the shape are still missing:

```
const int A_dim = 2;
int A_shp0 = A_desc[2];
int A_shp1 = A_desc[3];
```

4   Preliminary Performance Evaluation

This section evaluates the runtime behaviour of the code generated by the compilation scheme presented in the previous section.

The hardware platform used for the measurements is a SUN ULTRA-10 with 256 MB of main memory running under SOLARIS 7. The GNU C compiler (GCC, version 2.95.3) is used to compile the C code generated by the SAC compiler into native machine code.

The evaluation is based on the function Det() used in the previous sections which is applied to an array of shape [10,10]. This example is compiled with two different compiler versions: The first one uses the simple array representation, i.e. all non-scalar arrays are represented by data vector and descriptor only, and the second one uses the optimized array representation.

Additionally, during compilation four different strategies for function specialization are used. The first strategy builds no specializations at all, i.e. only the original two instances of Det() are available. Whenever Det() is applied to an argument whose shape is not [2,2], the generic instance is used. The second strategy builds a single specialization for argument shape [3,3]. The third one builds specializations for argument shapes [3,3] and [4,4]. The fourth one builds instances for all needed argument shapes [10,10], ..., [3,3]. As a consequence, all array objects have statically known shapes and function overloading can be resolved statically.

The results of the runtime measurements are shown in Fig. 6. The four bars on the left and in the middle relate to the two SAC compilers, whereas the color of each bar indicates the specialization strategy used. The single bar on the

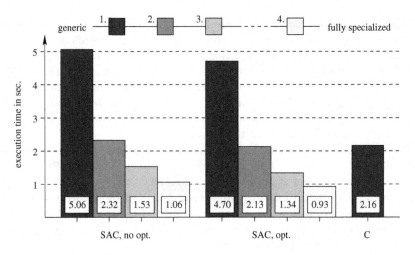

Fig. 6. Time demand for computing the determinant of a 10×10 array.

right depicts the time demand of an equivalent C implementation of the `Det()` function.

The runtime figure shows that the descriptor optimizations have a significant impact on the execution times of the generated code. Enabling the optimizations decreases the execution times by ≈ 8–14%.

Furthermore, the measurements demonstrate that specializing functions is indeed crucial for getting best possible runtime performance. The more specializations are built by the compiler, the lower is the time demand of the generated code. The generic version without any specializations is about a factor of 5 slower than the fully specialized version. Building one or two specialized instances of the `Det()` function reduces the slowdown to a factor of ≈ 2.3 or 1.4 respectively.

However, it is also indicated that by means of the new compilation scheme even generic functions can be compiled into code with an acceptable runtime performance. Note, that it is sufficient to build a single specialization of the `Det()` function to get approximately the same execution time as the C implementation. If the compiler adds additional specializations, the SAC implementation is significantly faster than the C implementation.

5   Related Work

The concept of shape-invariant programming has been invented mainly by the designers of the language APL. Although APL allows for a very concise and elegant way of program specification, it causes difficulties when trying to execute these generic programs efficiently. It usually requires dynamic typing and execution in an interpretating environment. Much effort has been devoted to improve runtime efficiency of such programs by application of sophisticated optimization techniques [4] and by attempts to compile them [21,9,5,3]. But code efficiency in many cases turns out to be less than satisfactory.

In order to overcome this shortcoming, languages like FISH or ZPL are designed in a way that eases static shape inference. As a result, FISH and ZPL programs, although written shape-invariantly, are compiled into very efficiently executable code. However, compilers for these languages lack the ability to generate truly shape-invariant code.

Common techniques to implement overloading, for instance in HASKELL compilers, involve the use of dictionary values [1,14]. A dictionary is a kind of a virtual function table that is passed as additional parameter to overloaded functions to resolve overloading at runtime. This dictionary-passing style must be generated by the backend of the compiler and can incur substantial overhead. In contrast, the compilation scheme presented in this paper uses static branch code written in SAC itself to implement the dynamic dispatches, therefore, no modifications in the backend are needed. A similar approach is used in the SmallEIFFEL compiler, which is described in more detail in [22]. Here, it is also shown that dynamic dispatches that have been implemented via static branch code, rather than function tables, perform better on modern hardware.

6   Conclusion and Future Work

This paper presents a compilation scheme for transforming shape-invariant array operations into efficiently executable code. This scheme has been developed in the context of the language SAC and combines two approaches: On the one hand static shape inference is performed to generate shape-specific code whenever possible, on the other hand more generic code is produced if the shape inference fails. The basic idea is to make use of a hierarchy of array types with different levels of shape information and to translate the typed programs into a corresponding hierarchy of array representations.

In order to support such a hierarchy of array types, basically two problems have to be solved. Firstly, a mechanism must be found that allows the compiler to resolve function overloading dynamically and to generate additional dynamic type checks if needed. The approach suggested in this paper achieves this by means of an elegant high-level code transformation. For each overloaded function a generic wrapper, which is also written in SAC, is generated that dynamically chooses the matching instance and performs all needed type checks. Subsequently, the code of this wrapper function is individually adapted to each function application by means of the code optimizations already integrated into the compiler.

The second problem is to find a hierarchy of array representations that is suitable for the hierarchy of array types. This paper presents two different versions of such representations. The first one is easy to implement but results in a suboptimal runtime performance of the generated code, whereas the second one is much more complex but reduces execution times by approximately 10 %.

However, the code generated for generic SAC functions may show an extremely poor runtime performance in certain situations. That is due to the fact that some high-level code optimizations of the SAC compiler are not implemented for arrays with unknown shape yet, for instance with-loop folding and index vector elimination. Therefore, future work will focus on remedying this shortcoming.

References

1. L. Augustsson: *Implementing Haskell Overloading*. In: Conference on Functional Programming Languages and Computer Architecture (FPCA '93). Copenhagen, Denmark, 1993.
2. D. F. Bacon, S. L. Graham, O. J. Sharp: *Compiler Transformations for High-Performance Computing*. ACM Computing Surveys, 26(4), pp. 345–420, 1994.
3. R. Bernecky: *APEX: The APL Parallel Executor*. Master's Thesis, University of Toronto, Canada, 1997.
4. J. Brown: *Inside the APL2 Workspace*. ACM Quote Quad, 15, pp. 277–282, 1985.
5. T. Budd: *An APL Compiler*. Springer, 1988. ISBN 0-387-96643-9.
6. C. Burke: *J and APL*. Iverson Software Inc., Toronto, Canada, 1996.
7. B. L. Chamberlain, S. J. Deitz, L. Snyder: *A Comparative Study of the NAS MG Benchmark Across Parallel Languages and Architectures*. In: Proceedings of the ACM Conference on Supercomputing. ACM Press, 2000.
8. J. Cohen: *Garbage Collection of Linked Data Structures*. ACM Computing Surveys, 13(3), pp. 341–367, 1981.
9. G. C. Driscoll, D. L. Orth: *Compiling APL: The Yorktown APL Translator*. IBM Journal of Research and Development, 30(6), pp. 583–593, 1986.
10. C. Grelck, S.-B. Scholz: *HPF vs. SAC — A Case Study*. In A. Bode, T. Ludwig, W. Karl, R. Wismüller (Eds.): Euro-Par 2000, Parallel Processing, Proceedings of the 6th International Euro-Par Conference, Munich, Germany. Vol. 1900 of: LNCS. Springer, 2000, pp. 620–624.
11. K. E. Iverson: *A Programming Language*. John Wiley & Sons, 1962.
12. C. B. Jay: *Programming in FISh*. International Journal on Software Tools for Technology Transfer, 2(3), pp. 307–315, 1999.
13. M. A. Jenkins, W. H. Jenkins: *The Q'Nial Language and Reference Manuals*. Nial Systems Ltd., Ottawa, Canada, 1993.
14. M. P. Jones: *Dictionary-Free Overloading by Partial Evaluation*. In: ACM SIGPLAN Workshop on Partial Evaluation and Semantics-Based Program Manipulation. ACM Press, 1994.
15. C. Lin: *ZPL Language Reference Manual*. UW-CSE-TR 94-10-06, Department of Computer Science and Engineering, University of Washington, Seattle, Washington, USA, 1996.
16. C. Lin, L. Snyder, R. Anderson, B. L. Chamberlain, S.-E. Choi, G. Foreman, E. C. Lewis, W. D. Weathersby: *ZPL vs. HPF: A Comparison of Performance and Programming Style*. TR 95-11-05, Department of Computer Science and Engineering, University of Washington, Seattle, Washington, USA, 1995.
17. S.-B. Scholz: *Single Assignment C — Entwurf und Implementierung einer funktionalen C-Variante mit spezieller Unterstützung shape-invarianter Array-Operationen*. PhD Thesis, Institut für Informatik und Praktische Mathematik, Universität Kiel, 1996. ISBN 3-8265-3138-8.

18. S.-B. Scholz: *A Case Study: Effects of WITH-Loop-Folding on the NAS Benchmark MG in SAC.* In C. Clack, T. Davie, K. Hammond (Eds.): Implementation of Functional Languages, 10th International Workshop (IFL '98), London, England, UK, Selected Papers. Vol. 1595 of: LNCS. Springer, 1998, pp. 216–228. ISBN 3-540-66229-4.

19. S.-B. Scholz: *On Defining Application-Specific High-Level Operations by Means of Shape-Invariant Programming Facilities.* In S. Picchi, M. Micocci (Eds.): Proceedings of the Array Processing Language Conference (APL '98), Rome, Italy. ACM Press, 1998, pp. 40–45.

20. S.-B. Scholz: *A Type System for Inferring Array Shapes.* In T. Arts, M. Mohnen (Eds.): Proceedings of the 13th International Workshop on the Implementation of Funtional Languages (IFL '01). Ericsson, Älvsjö, Sweden, 2001, pp. 53–63.

21. J. Weigang: *An Introduction to STSC's APL Compiler.* In: Proceedings of the Array Processing Language Conference (APL '89). Vol. 15 of: ACM Quote Quad. ACM Press, 1989, pp. 231–238.

22. O. Zendra, D. Colnet, S. Collin: *Efficient Dynamic Dispatch without Virtual Function Tables: The SmallEiffel Compiler.* In: Proceeding of the 12th Annual ACM SIGPLAN Conference on Object-Oriented Programming, Systems, Languages and Applications (OOPSLA '97). Atlanta, Georgia, USA, 1997, pp. 125–141.

Optimizations on Array Skeletons
in a Shared Memory Environment

Clemens Grelck

Medical University of Lübeck *
Institute for Software Technology and Programming Languages
D–23569 Lübeck, Germany
grelck@isp.mu-luebeck.de

Abstract. Map- and fold-like skeletons are a suitable abstractions to guide parallel program execution in functional array processing. However, when it comes to achieving high performance, it turns out that confining compilation efforts to individual skeletons is insufficient. This paper proposes compilation schemes which aim at reducing runtime overhead due to communication and synchronization by embedding multiple array skeletons within a so-called `spmd` meta skeleton. Whereas the meta skeleton exclusively takes responsibility for the organization of parallel program execution, the original array skeletons are focussed to their individual numerical operation. While concrete compilation schemes assume multithreading in a shared memory environment as underlying execution model, ideas can be carried over to other settings straightforwardly. Preliminary performance investigations help to quantify potential benefits.

1   Introduction

Algorithmic skeletons [7] are a well-known framework to express parallel computations on a high level of abstraction. In the field of array processing familiar skeletons like `map`, `zip`, and `fold` are complemented by more array-specific ones like `take`, `drop`, or `rotate`. However, serious array processing generally requires many more such basic building blocks. Dedicated languages, both functional and imperative, usually provide a more or less comprehensive collection.

In a shared memory environment, where explicit data decomposition is not necessary, the organization of parallel program execution can completely be confined to specific implementations of these array skeletons. Whereas programs are still executed sequentially by a single thread of control in general, evaluation of array skeletons causes additional *worker threads* to be created. They simultaneously perform the specified computations in a cooperative manner and terminate after synchronization with the initial or *master thread*. Having waited for the termination of the last worker thread, the master thread continues with sequential operations.

---

* Most of the work described in this paper was done while the author was affiliated with the University of Kiel.

T. Arts and M. Mohnen (Eds.): IFL 2001, LNCS 2312, pp. 36–54, 2002.
© Springer-Verlag Berlin Heidelberg 2002

The appealing property of this approach is that it directs all efforts for non-sequential program execution to specific implementations of some high-level language constructs. Unfortunately, it shows some drawbacks as well. Individual compilation and execution of each instance of a skeleton results in a sequence of thread creation, synchronization, and termination operations, all of which are costly with respect to execution time. As a consequence, the runtime overhead associated with non-sequential program execution may severely limit the performance gains actually achieved.

Optimizations which aim at reducing this runtime overhead by combining multiple instances of skeletons into a single one are restricted by the inherent need to represent the combined operation within the given skeletal framework. At this point, it turns out to be an obstacle that array skeletons mix up two different aspects of program execution. On the one hand, they specify some numerical computations to be performed, regardless of whether this is done sequentially or in parallel. On the other hand, they specify a model for organizing parallel program execution. Unfortunately, restrictions with respect to the former aspect usually hinder optimizations concerning the latter one.

As the major contribution we propose transformation schemes which at some intermediate level of compilation explicitly separate the organizational aspects of array skeletons from their computational aspects. Each instance of an array skeleton is embedded within a so-called spmd meta skeleton. The name stands for "single program, multiple data". It refers to the fact that this skeleton represents areas of parallel execution within a program which is executed sequentially otherwise. Multiple threads execute the same code but act on pairwise disjoint parts of the arrays involved. We call it a *meta* skeleton because it has no computational meaning for itself; it solely specifies a program's coordination behaviour.

Embedded within spmd meta skeletons, variants of the original array skeletons define the computations actually to be performed. They differ from their original counterparts in that most organizational aspects of their parallel execution are stripped off. In fact, they expect to be evaluated in a parallel execution environment which is already set up appropriately (by the spmd meta skeleton) rather than doing so themselves.

This two-level representation of parallel array operations forms the basis for optimizations across multiple instances of array skeletons. By merging several spmd meta skeletons into a single one, considerable overhead for the organization of parallel program execution can be shared among multiple array skeletons. As a consequence, the ratio between productive computations and organizational overhead is improved. The application of this optimization is only restricted by data dependencies, whereas embedded numerical operations are not concerned.

The paper is organized as follows. Section 2 sketches out implementations of array skeletons in a shared memory environment. Section 3 introduces the spmd meta skeleton along with the associated optimization and code generation schemes; Section 4 refines the optimization scheme. Preliminary performance investigations are discussed in Section 5 while Section 6 outlines some related work. Section 7 concludes and discusses directions for future work.

2   Implementing Array Skeletons

Various array skeletons have been proposed in different contexts [1,2]. Most of them fall into one of two basic categories: they either create a new array whose elements are individually computed from some arguments based on their index positions or they perform a reduction operation. To abstract from individual properties of concrete skeletons we introduce two generalized skeletons representing the two basic categories:

GenArray(shp, $op_{idx}(arg_1, \ldots, arg_n)$)   ,

FoldArray(shp, $op_{idx}(arg_1, \ldots, arg_n)$, $fold\_op$, $neutral$)   .

The GenArray skeleton creates a new array of shape shp, where shp is considered to denote an integer vector defining both the dimensionality of the new array as well as its extent in each dimension. Explicit specification of the shape vector allows for any relationship between shapes and even values of arguments and the shape of the result array. Its elements are separately computed by some operation op_{idx}. Being parameterized over individual index positions, different operations may actually be realized by op_{idx} on disjoint areas of the result array. With its arity left unspecified any number of scalar and array arguments may occur. So, these skeletons may be considered operational templates rather than concrete higher-order functions.

Similar to GenArray, the FoldArray skeleton evaluates the given function op_{idx} for each legal index position associated with the shape shp. Instead of using the results for initializing a new array, they are pairwise folded using the binary fold operation $fold\_op$ with neutral element $neutral$. Since the concrete sequence of folding operations is left unspecified, legal fold operations must be associative and commutative to ensure deterministic results.

Fig. 1 shows the compilation scheme for the GenArray skeleton into imperative pseudo code both for the master thread (left-hand side) and for worker threads (right-hand side). Whenever the master thread evaluates a GenArray skeleton, it first allocates memory for storing the result array, which is referred to by some previously unused variable tmp. Due to the commitment to shared memory architectures, no explicit data decomposition is required, and implicit dynamic memory management for arrays can be adopted from sequential implementations with little or no alteration. Afterwards, the base address and the shape of the result array as well as the numerical arguments of the skeleton are broadcast, and, last but not least, the desired number of worker threads is created.

At a first glance, it seems to be inconsistent to send data to worker threads before they actually exist. However, in a shared memory environment send and receive operations are nothing but copy operations to and from some specific memory buffer, which may exist independently of the threads themselves. Broadcasting data prior to thread creation allows for a non-blocking implementation of the corresponding receive operations, and, thus, reduces synchronization requirements among threads to their creation.

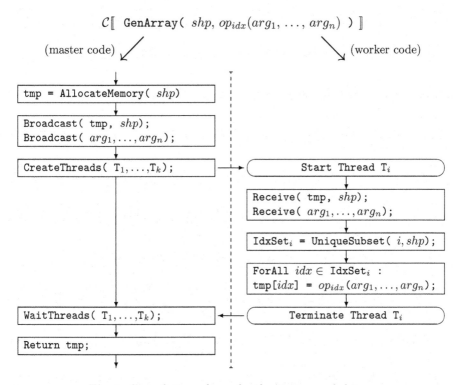

Fig. 1. Compilation scheme for the `GenArray` skeleton.

All worker threads uniformly execute the code shown on the right hand side of Fig. 1, but each thread may identify itself by means of a unique ID. As a first step, a worker thread receives the target array's base address and shape along with the other arguments in order to set up an appropriate execution environment for performing the numerical operation. Then, based on its unique ID, each worker thread identifies a subspace of the entire index space defined by *shp*. Proper implementations of `UniqueSubset` guarantee that each legal index position belongs to exactly one such index subspace. For each element of its individual index subspace a worker thread computes the corresponding numerical operation and initializes the result array accordingly. After having completed their individual computations, the worker threads terminate.

While worker threads are responsible for the parallel execution of the numerical computations represented by the skeleton, the master thread just awaits the termination of all worker threads. As soon as the last worker thread has completed its individual share of work, the master thread returns the result to the surrounding context and continues with sequential program execution until the next skeleton is encountered. Altogether, program execution is organized as a sequence of concurrent stages.

$$\mathcal{C} \llbracket \text{ FoldArray}(\ shp, \ op_{idx}(arg_1, \ \ldots, \ arg_n), \ fold\_op, \ neutral \ ) \rrbracket$$

(master code)   (worker code)

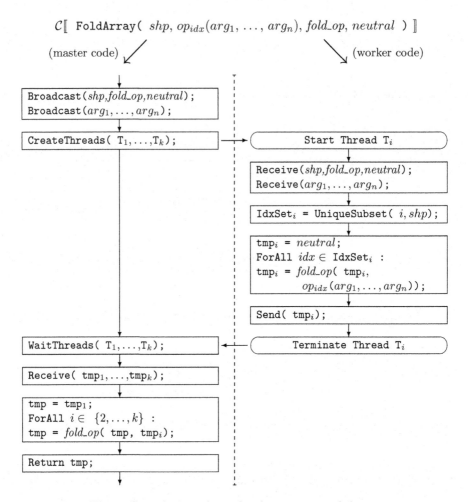

Fig. 2. Compilation scheme for the `FoldArray` skeleton.

Multithreaded code generated for the `FoldArray` skeleton, as shown in Fig. 2, is similar to the implementation of `GenArray`. The master thread broadcasts arguments of the skeleton's numerical operation along with the fold operation, its neutral element, and the corresponding shape and, subsequently, creates the worker threads. Having set up its individual execution environment, each worker thread identifies some unique iteration subspace, just as in the `GenArray` case. It then initializes a local accumulation variable tmp_i by the neutral element of the fold operation and then performs the specified computations restricted to the individual index subspace identified before. Hence, each worker thread computes a partial fold result, which it sends back to the master thread prior to its termination.

The master thread awaits the termination of all worker threads before it receives their partial fold results. Once again, necessary thread management operations are exploited to ensure proper synchronization upon send/receive communication. Finally, the master thread itself combines the various partial fold results to generate the overall result, which thereupon is returned to the surrounding context.

3   SPMD Optimization

Compiling each instance of the two array skeletons individually directly leads to a fork/join execution model, as illustrated in Fig. 3. Program execution repeatedly alternates between two different modes: sequential execution by the master thread and parallel execution by a given number of worker threads. Unfortunately, switching from one mode to the other inflicts significant runtime overhead:

- creation of worker threads,
- communication from master thread to worker threads,
- communication from worker threads to master thread (FoldArray only),
- termination of worker threads,
- synchronization of master thread with worker threads.

Since all this overhead is directly related to parallel program execution itself, it may severely reduce potential benefits in terms of reduced program runtimes.

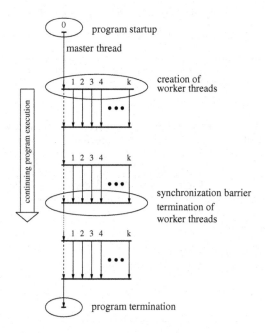

Fig. 3. Illustration of fork/join execution model.

As already pointed out before, array skeletons leave little opportunities for optimization, as they amalgamate directions for parallel program execution with potentially complex numerical operations. To overcome these limitations we adopt a two-level representation of array skeletons. On the outer level the new meta skeleton

spmd(*USE, MAP, FOLD, SKEL*)

represents the coordination behaviour, whereas — embedded as fourth parameter — variants of the array skeletons define the computations to be performed in parallel. The first three parameters *USE*, *MAP*, and *FOLD* are sets of program identifiers, which serve organizational purposes during subsequent optimization and compilation steps.

Fig. 4 contains the definition of a transformation scheme $\mathcal{SPMD}$, which introduces spmd meta skeletons around instances of original array skeletons. For reasons of simplicity, here and in the sequel of this paper it is assumed that code has been transformed into sequences of nested let-expressions with a single variable binding and a simple, unnested expression as definition.

To allow for compiling spmd skeletons independently from the array skeletons collected in the fourth parameter, additional information is gathered and maintained in the first three parameters. The first parameter *USE* contains the set of argument variables, characterizing the data which have to be broadcast to worker threads when switching to parallel program execution. The *MAP* and *FOLD* sets

$\mathcal{SPMD} \left[\!\left[\text{let } A = \text{GenArray}(\; shp, op_{idx}(arg_1, \ldots, arg_n)) \text{ in } Rest \right]\!\right]$
$\implies \text{let } A = \text{spmd}(\; \{ \; arg_1, \ldots, arg_n, shp \; \},$
$\qquad\qquad\qquad\quad \{ \; [\; \text{tmp}_A, \; shp \;] \; \},$
$\qquad\qquad\qquad\quad \{ \; \},$
$\qquad\qquad\qquad\quad \text{let tmp}_A = \text{GenArray'}(\; shp, \; op_{idx}(arg_1, \ldots, arg_n))$
$\qquad\qquad\qquad\quad \text{in [tmp}_A] \;)$
$\qquad \text{in } \; \mathcal{SPMD} \left[\!\left[Rest \right]\!\right]$

$\mathcal{SPMD} \left[\!\left[\text{let } A = \text{FoldArray}(\; shp, op_{idx}(arg_1, \ldots, arg_n), fop, neu) \text{ in } Rest \right]\!\right]$
$\implies \text{let } A = \text{spmd}(\; \{ \; arg_1, \ldots, arg_n, shp, fop, neu \; \},$
$\qquad\qquad\qquad\quad \{ \; \},$
$\qquad\qquad\qquad\quad \{ \; [\; \text{tmp}_A, \; fop \;] \; \},$
$\qquad\qquad\qquad\quad \text{let tmp}_A = \text{FoldArray'}(\; shp, \; op_{idx}(arg_1, \ldots, arg_n),$
$\qquad\qquad\qquad\qquad\qquad\qquad\qquad\qquad\quad fop, neu)$
$\qquad\qquad\qquad\quad \text{in [tmp}_A] \;)$
$\qquad \text{in } \; \mathcal{SPMD} \left[\!\left[Rest \right]\!\right]$

$\mathcal{SPMD} \left[\!\left[\text{let } A = expr \text{ in } Rest \right]\!\right]$
$\implies \text{let } A = expr \text{ in } \; \mathcal{SPMD} \left[\!\left[Rest \right]\!\right]$

$\mathcal{SPMD} \left[\!\left[expr \right]\!\right]$
$\implies expr$

Fig. 4. Embedding array skeletons within spmd skeletons.

collect pairs consisting of result variables of `GenArray` and `FoldArray` skeletons and of the associated shape or fold operation, respectively. This information suffices to generate appropriate code from `spmd` skeletons without identifying the individual array skeletons embedded inside. They are marked by a prime indicating that they differ from the original array skeletons in that they expect to be evaluated in a multithreaded execution environment which is already set up appropriately rather than doing so themselves.

$\mathcal{MERGE}[\![$ let A = spmd(USE_A, MAP_A, $FOLD_A$,
  let $assigns_A$ in vec_A)
 in let B = spmd(USE_B, MAP_B, $FOLD_B$,
  let $assigns_B$ in vec_B)
 in $Rest$ $]\!]$

$\Longrightarrow \mathcal{MERGE}[\![$ let A++B = spmd(USE_A $\cup$ USE_B,
  MAP_A $\cup$ MAP_B,
  $FOLD_A$ $\cup$ $FOLD_B$,
  let $assigns_A$
  in let $assigns_B$
   in vec_A++vec_B)
 in $Rest$ $]\!]$
| $A \cap USE_B$ = $\emptyset$ = $A \cap B$

$\Longrightarrow$ let A = spmd(USE_A, MAP_A, $FOLD_A$,
  let $assigns_A$ in vec_A)
 in $\mathcal{MERGE}[\![$ let B = spmd(USE_B, MAP_B, $FOLD_B$,
  let $assigns_B$ in vec_B)
 in $Rest$ $]\!]$
| $OTHERWISE$

Fig. 5. SPMD optimization scheme $\mathcal{MERGE}$.

Introducing `spmd` meta skeletons around individual array skeletons itself does not alter the generation of multithreaded code at all. It lays the foundation for a subsequent optimization step, which aims at merging several `spmd` skeletons into a single one. This is formalized by means of the transformation scheme $\mathcal{MERGE}$, shown in Fig. 5. It identifies pairs of `spmd` skeletons which are directly adjacent in the linear nesting of `let`-expressions and which are free of data dependencies. Such pairs are combined into a single `spmd` skeleton which is then characterized by multiple array skeletons and hence multiple return values. An example which illustrates both the introduction of `spmd` skeletons as well as the merging step is given in Fig. 6.

The SPMD optimization may lead to complex `spmd` skeletons containing many different compound array operations. Nevertheless, compilation schemes for individual array skeletons, as outlined in Section 2, can be carried over to the new `spmd` skeleton almost straightforwardly. As shown in Fig. 7, compiling `spmd` skeletons mostly combines elements from both previous compilation schemes.

```
let A = GenArray( shp_A, op_A( D, k, C))
in let B = GenArray( shp_B, op_B( C))
   in let d = FoldArray( shp_d, op_d( D), fun, neu)
      in ...
              ⇓                    ⇓                  ⇓
let A = spmd( {shp_A, D, k, C},
              {[tmp_A, shp_A]},
              { },
              let tmp_A = GenArray'( shp_A, op_A( D, k, C))
              in [tmp_A])
in let B = spmd( {shp_B, C},
                 {[tmp_B, shp_B]},
                 { },
                 let tmp_B = GenArray'( shp_B, op_B( C))
                 in [tmp_B] )
   in let d = spmd( {shp_d, fun, neu, D},
                    { },
                    {[tmp_d, fun]},
                    let tmp_d = FoldArray'( shp_d, op_d( D),
                                                     fun, neu)
                    in [tmp_d] )
      in ...
              ⇓                    ⇓                  ⇓
let [A,B,d] = spmd( {shp_A, shp_B, shp_d, fun, neu, C, D, k},
                    {[tmp_A, shp_A] , [tmp_B, shp_B]},
                    {[tmp_d, fun]},
                    let tmp_A = GenArray'( shp_A, op_A( D, k, C))
                    in let tmp_B = GenArray'( shp_B, op_B( C))
                       in let tmp_d = FoldArray'( shp_d, op_d( D),
                                                          fun, neu)
                          in [tmp_A, tmp_B, tmp_d] )
in ...
```

Fig. 6. Example illustrating SPMD optimization.

The evaluation of an spmd skeleton starts with the allocation of memory for the result arrays of its embedded GenArray skeletons. Both their identifiers as well as their shapes can directly be derived from the MAP set. Then, all variables of the USE and MAP sets are broadcast to the worker threads. After creation, each worker thread immediately sets up its local execution environment for all array skeletons within the spmd skeleton. They are still compiled individually, as indicated by the dashed box. For each skeleton, code is generated which first identifies a unique index subspace and then performs the given numerical operation in a way that restricts all computations to exactly this subspace. Before termination, each worker thread sends its partial fold results, i.e. the variables of the FOLD set, back to the master thread, which eventually folds them using

$\mathcal{C}[\![\ \mathtt{spmd}(\mathit{USE},\ \mathit{MAP},\ \mathit{FOLD},\ \mathtt{let}\ \mathit{assigns}\ \mathtt{in}\ \mathit{vec})]\!]$

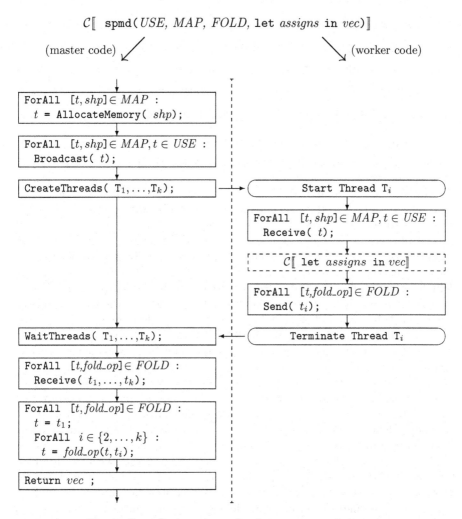

Fig. 7. Compilation scheme for the **spmd** meta skeleton.

the associated fold operations. Finally, the vector of results is returned to the surrounding context.

4 Array Skeletons and Scalar Code

The optimization scheme $\mathcal{MERGE}$, as introduced in the previous section, solely addresses **spmd** skeletons which occur directly adjacent in a linear nesting of **let**-expressions. However, even in programs dominated by array processing, this case is rather an exception. In fact, typical intermediate codes mix up array skeletons with scalar computations. Unfortunately, any scalar **let**-expression in between two skeletal ones prevents their optimization regardless of data dependencies.

```
let a = spmd( {u,c}, ... )
in let b = ... a ...
   in let c = ... d ...
      in let d = spmd( {b,d}, ...)
         in ...
```

Fig. 8. Example for restrictions on code reorganization.

In order to make the SPMD optimization more useful in practice, the $\mathcal{MERGE}$ scheme must be extended by a code restructuring component. Scalar let-expressions between two consecutive skeletons need to be moved either ahead of the first skeleton or behind the second one. However, the necessary code reorganization is restricted by data dependencies as well as by anti-dependencies. Fig. 8 illustrates some of these restrictions by means of an example. Ignoring the scalar let-expressions in between the two spmd skeletons makes them perfect candidates for merging. In fact, this is false as there is an indirect data dependency between the two skeletons via the scalar variable b. Also the let-expression defining c may not be moved. Although there are no data dependencies, as in the case of b, moving it either ahead of the first or behind the second skeleton would penetrate the binding structure of the entire code fragment.

Fig. 9 shows a refined version of the optimization scheme $\mathcal{MERGE}$, which — based on a thorough analysis of both direct and indirect dependencies and anti-dependencies — reorganizes the code as necessary to merge spmd skeletons whenever possible. Despite the restrictions discussed above, code reorganization is often feasible. To do so in a single sweep, three auxiliary parameters *store*, *use*, and *def* temporarily store scalar let-expressions and keep track of associated data dependencies and anti-dependencies; application of $\mathcal{MERGE}$ starts with all three being empty.

Leading scalar let-expressions are traversed by $\mathcal{MERGE}$ without alteration (3rd rule). The interesting case is encountered when the first skeletal let-expression is reached during code traversal. Let us assume, it is followed by a scalar one (2nd rule). If neither data dependencies nor anti-dependencies exist between them, the two let-expressions are simply exchanged, thus keeping the chance to merge the spmd skeleton with some subsequent one. Otherwise, it may still be possible to push the scalar let-expression further down behind a subsequent skeletal let-expression. However, whether or not this will be possible with respect to data dependencies or whether or not another spmd skeleton follows at all is currently undecidable. Therefore, this decision is postponed by temporarily appending the scalar let-expression to the auxiliary store. To keep track of all data dependencies involving such code, two variable sets *use* and *def* are maintained which provide those variables defined or needed by let-expressions currently residing in the auxiliary store.

Assuming another scalar let-expression follows, it becomes clear that the decision whether or not this can be moved ahead of the preceding skeletal one does not only depend on data dependencies between these two, but also involves all let-expressions in the auxiliary store.

(1) $\mathcal{MERGE}[\![$ let $A = $ spmd$(USE_A, MAP_A, FOLD_A,$
$\qquad\qquad$ let $assigns_A$ in $vec_A)$
$\qquad$ in let $B = $ spmd$(USE_B, MAP_B, FOLD_B,$
$\qquad\qquad\qquad$ let $assigns_B$ in $vec_B)$
$\qquad\qquad$ in $Rest$ $]\!]$
$\qquad$ $[\![store]\!][\![use]\!][\![def]\!]$

$\Longrightarrow \mathcal{MERGE}[\![$ let A++$B = $ spmd$(USE_A \cup USE_B,$
$\qquad\qquad\qquad\qquad MAP_A \cup MAP_B,$
$\qquad\qquad\qquad\qquad FOLD_A \cup FOLD_B,$
$\qquad\qquad\qquad\qquad$ let $assigns_A$
$\qquad\qquad\qquad\qquad$ in let $assigns_B$
$\qquad\qquad\qquad\qquad\qquad$ in vec_A++$vec_B)$
$\qquad\qquad\qquad$ in $Rest$ $]\!]$
$\qquad\qquad$ $[\![store]\!][\![use]\!][\![def]\!]$

$\qquad$ | $\quad (A \cup def) \cap USE_B = \emptyset = (A \cup def \cup use) \cap B$

$\Longrightarrow$ let $A = $ spmd$(USE_A, MAP_A, FOLD_A,$
$\qquad\qquad\qquad$ let $assigns_A$ in $vec_A)$
$\qquad$ in $store$
$\qquad\qquad \mathcal{MERGE}[\![$ let $B = $ spmd$(USE_B, MAP_B, FOLD_B,$
$\qquad\qquad\qquad\qquad\qquad$ let $assigns_B$ in $vec_B)$
$\qquad\qquad\qquad\qquad$ in $Rest$ $]\!]$
$\qquad\qquad\qquad$ $[\![\ ]\!][\![\ ]\!][\![\ ]\!]$

$\qquad$ | $\quad OTHERWISE$

(2) $\mathcal{MERGE}[\![$ let $A = $ spmd$(USE_A, MAP_A, FOLD_A,$
$\qquad\qquad\qquad$ let $assigns_A$ in $vec_A)$
$\qquad\qquad$ in let $B = expr$
$\qquad\qquad\qquad$ in $Rest$ $]\!]$
$\qquad\qquad$ $[\![store]\!][\![use]\!][\![def]\!]$

$\Longrightarrow$ let $B = expr$
$\qquad$ in $\mathcal{MERGE}[\![$ let $A = $ spmd$(USE_A, MAP_A, FOLD_A,$
$\qquad\qquad\qquad\qquad\qquad$ let $assigns_A$ in $vec_A)$
$\qquad\qquad\qquad\qquad$ in $Rest$ $]\!]$
$\qquad\qquad\qquad\qquad$ $[\![store]\!][\![use]\!][\![def]\!]$

$\qquad$ | $\quad (A \cup def) \cap USE_{expr} = \emptyset = (A \cup USE_{expr} \cup use) \cap B$

$\Longrightarrow \mathcal{MERGE}[\![$ let $A = $ spmd$(USE_A, MAP_A, FOLD_A,$
$\qquad\qquad\qquad\qquad$ let $assigns_A$ in $vec_A)$
$\qquad\qquad\qquad$ in $Rest]\!]$
$\qquad\qquad\qquad$ $[\![store$ let $B = expr$ in $]\!][\![use \cup USE_{expr}]\!][\![def \cup B]\!]$
$\qquad$ | $\quad OTHERWISE$

(3) $\mathcal{MERGE}[\![$ let $A = expr$ in $Rest$ $]\!]$ $[\![store]\!][\![use]\!][\![def]\!]$
$\qquad \Longrightarrow$ let $A = expr$ in $\mathcal{MERGE}[\![Rest]\!][\![store]\!][\![use]\!][\![def]\!]$

(4) $\mathcal{MERGE}[\![$ $expr$ $]\!][\![store]\!][\![use]\!][\![def]\!]$
$\qquad \Longrightarrow store\ expr$

Fig. 9. Code restructuring SPMD optimization scheme.

Two skeletal `let`-expressions which directly follow each other or which have been made so by preceding transformations may or may not be merged. Once again this does not only depend on data dependencies between them but also involves the auxiliary store (1st rule). In the absence of dependencies as well as of anti dependencies the two `spmd` skeletons are merged just as by the initial $\mathcal{MERGE}$ scheme. However, if merging is not possible, all scalar `let`-expressions from the auxiliary store are re-introduced into the nesting of `let`-expressions in between the two skeletons and the optimization scheme continues with the second skeletal `let`-expression. Last but not least, the auxiliary store also needs to be flushed whenever $\mathcal{MERGE}$ reaches the goal expression (4th rule).

Whereas data dependencies reflect the nature of the problem and, therefore, cannot be eliminated, anti-dependencies arise from accidentally giving two different variables the same name. Hence, anti-dependencies may completely be removed by consistent variable renaming. As a consequence, anti dependencies could completely be ignored by $\mathcal{MERGE}$ considerably simplifying its definition. However, such a more far-reaching code transformation is beyond the scope of this paper.

5   Preliminary Performance Investigations

To quantify the effect of the SPMD optimization on the runtime performance of compiled code some experiments have been made in the context of the functional array processing language SAC [23]. Its WITH-loops [15] in some sense represent concrete implementations of the `GenArray` and `FoldArray` skeletons discussed throughout this paper. The SAC compiler implicitly derives multithreaded host machine code for parallel program execution on shared memory multiprocessors using techniques similar to those described in Section 2 [13,14]. The SPMD optimization has not yet been fully implemented, but needed some manual adjustments in intermediate code, namely to realize some of the code reorganization described in Section 4. Test programs were run on a 6-processor SUN Enterprise E4500 as well as on 2 and on 4 identical such systems using a SUN WildFire[1] interconnect [17] to provide a global cache-coherent shared memory with non-uniform memory access times.

The first benchmark code consists of a loop containing a sequence of five `GenArray` skeletons which each initialize a vector of N integers by some trivial computation. In the absence of data dependencies, the SPMD optimization manages to transform the sequence of individual skeletons into a single `spmd` meta skeleton and therefore to remove four out of five synchronization barriers in the benchmark code.

---

[1]   "WildFire is Sun's internal code name for an advanced Server architecture that is under development. WildFire prototype systems have not been tested, optimized, or qualified for sale; they have been built for evaluative purposes only. Elements of the WildFire prototype may or may not be used in future Sun products. We obtained the WildFire used in this paper through participation in the WildFire Beta/Collaborative Research program."

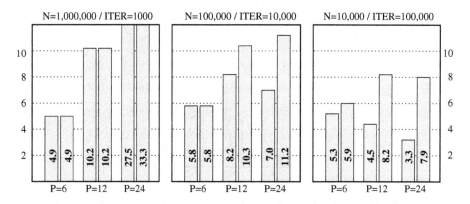

N=1,000,000 / ITER=1000   N=100,000 / ITER=10,000   N=10,000 / ITER=100,000

Fig. 10. Speedups with (right bar) and without (left bar) SPMD optimization.

Fig. 10 shows the effect on speedups achieved by parallel program execution for different vector sizes N, adjusted numbers of iterations ITER, and for the three architectural configurations mentioned before. For each setting the left bar indicates the speedup achieved without SPMD optimization, the right bar gives the speedup with SPMD optimization enabled. Note that between the experiment shown on the left-hand side and that shown on the right-hand side of Fig. 10 the ratio of computations to synchronizations decreases by two orders of magnitude. As expected, the impact of the SPMD optimization on runtime performance grows with program execution increasingly being dominated by synchronization overhead, which in turn grows with increasing processor counts.

However, runtime overhead inflicted by synchronization barriers does not only stem from additional instructions to be executed and from associated com-

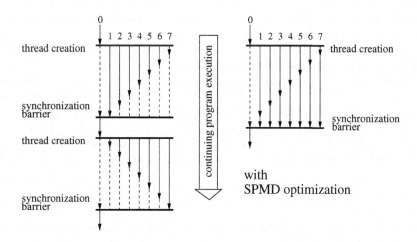

Fig. 11. Load imbalance compensation through SPMD optimization.

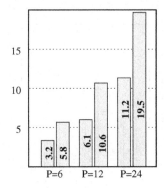

Fig. 12. Performance impact of load imbalance compensation.

munication requirements. Even more significant may be the fact that at each barrier program execution stalls until the very last processor has completed its share of work. Unlike the first experiment, workload distributions among processors are generally imperfect, thus reducing the potential benefits of parallel program execution. Eliminating synchronization barriers by means of the SPMD optimization is likely to result at least in a partial compensation of workload imbalances.

This effect is investigated in the second experiment which maps a complex numerical operation to an upper triangular matrix and, in a subsequent step, to a lower triangular matrix, both of which have 1000^2 elements. Assuming a standard horizontal block decomposition of the operation with respect to the entire matrix, the workload is poorly balanced among the cooperating processors in both individual steps, as illustrated in Fig. 11 for an example using eight processors. However, if the intermediate synchronization barrier can be eliminated, workload imbalances in the two steps are likely to compensate each other almost perfectly. Fig. 12 shows the outcome of this experiment in terms of speedups achieved with and without SPMD optimization. As expected, speedups almost double by SPMD optimization, although the frequency of synchronizations is insignificant due to the large size of the matrices involved.

Though the SAC programs used in the two experiments are rather simple, it is noteworthy that no optimization would have been possible at all by using only the simple $\mathcal{MERGE}$ scheme, introduced in Section 3. Preceding code transformations and optimizations performed by the SAC compiler, in all cases, introduce scalar code in between the array skeletons. This demonstrates the need for the extended optimization scheme introduced in Section 4.

6   Related Work

Research in the area of (parallel) functional programming languages prevailingly has concentrated on algebraic data structures like lists and trees rather than on flat, uniform arrays [18]. Partly due to this more irregular setting, the focus with respect to algorithmic skeletons has been on finding suitable abstractions [22], on expressing applications in terms of skeletons [8], and on constructing skeletons on top of more low-level constructs [25] rather than on optimizing interactions between multiple skeleton instances.

Although not specific to parallel execution, deforestation [9,26] may have a similar effect as the SPMD optimization described in this paper. Whenever explicit construction of intermediate data structures can be avoided, the same holds for associated organizational overhead inflicted by parallel execution. Similar to deforestation in its objective, though different in setting otherwise, WITH-loop-folding [24] condenses consecutive array operations in SAC into single ones. Overhead in case of parallel program execution is condensed incidentally. Nevertheless, both approaches are in some sense orthogonal to SPMD optimization. Whereas they glue together operations that are characterized by the result of one being the argument to the other, the SPMD optimization addresses operations which are unrelated to each other in terms of data dependencies.

With respect to data dependencies, the SPMD optimization is more similar to tupling [5,6]. Yet, once again the setting is very different. Tupling aims at avoiding repeated traversals of the same algebraic data structure by gathering a tuple of results in a single sweep. Similar to deforestation or WITH-loop-folding, tupling may improve the runtime performance of compiled code irrespective of whether it is executed sequentially or in parallel. However, its application is also more restricted making it difficult in general to find suitable candidates for tupling [21]. In contrast, the SPMD optimization solely addresses overhead inflicted by parallel execution. By separating organizational concerns from computational concerns it also needs no assumptions on concrete operations involved.

On the level of programming methodology, frameworks have been developed that combine meaning-preserving transformation rules on a fixed set of skeletons with a cost model guiding their application [10,11]. Code transformations always remain within the given set of user-level skeletons. Similar to deforestation and tupling, their effect in general is not specific to parallel program execution, and their application is also constrained in that concrete operations must meet certain conditions as prerequisites.

In the field of imperative parallel programming, the elimination of synchronization barriers has long been identified as vital for achieving high performance. However, the problem is usually addressed on a lower level of abstraction than in our approach. For instance, code written in the imperative array language ZPL [4] is compiled into sequences of loop nestings and collective data transfer and synchronization operations, so-called *factors* [3]. Subsequent optimizations aim at eliminating superfluous factors and combining (*"joining"*) others.

Similar optimizations have been proposed on the level of collective operations in MPI [16]. Certain combinations of adjacent collective operations are replaced by less expensive ones [12].

On an even lower level of abstraction, much research has been carried out on eliminating synchronization barriers in sequences of automatically parallelized FORTRAN-77-style loop nestings [19,20]. These approaches differ from our's not only in the imperative background. Automatic parallelization of loop nestings tends to introduce lots of barriers at first and subsequently applies optimization steps to reduce this number in the presence of dependencies that are often difficult to track. In contrast, high-level compound operations like array skeletons along with preceding transformations on that level already avoid explicit creation of most barriers when solving the same numerical problem. Moreover, the remaining barriers can be addressed with clear knowledge of dependencies.

7   Conclusions and Future Work

Array skeletons are a suitable approach for expressing concurrency in functional array processing both from a specificational as well as from an implementational point of view. Unfortunately, the individual compilation of each instance of an array skeleton generally introduces communication and synchronization overhead which could be avoided. The drawback of array skeletons is that they specify both a (potentially) complex numerical operation as well as the organization of parallel program execution. This often prevents optimizations on the level of array skeletons.

This paper proposes an optimization scheme which explicitly separates both aspects from each other by embedding array skeletons within so-called spmd meta skeletons. Whereas the former are mostly restricted to the numerical operation, the latter take responsibility for the organization of parallel execution. Based on a thorough analysis of data dependencies as well as of anti-dependencies, multiple array skeletons may be combined into a single spmd meta skeleton. This allows for optimizations on the organizational level regardless of concrete numerical operations involved.

Preliminary performance investigations based on partially hand-optimized multithreaded SAC code reveal considerable improvements whenever the organizational overhead of parallel program execution turns out to be significant. This observation motivates us to fully implement the code restructuring version of the SPMD optimization in the future. More thorough investigations of its performance impact, involving realistic benchmark codes and application programs, have to be undertaken.

Moreover, the SPMD optimization itself may further be improved. Currently, it aggressively seeks to merge array skeletons as far as possible in order to reduce synchronization overhead. Unfortunately, it may considerably increase memory requirements at the same time. Rather than allocating memory for target arrays one after the other in a sequence of GenArray skeletons, memory allocation is done for all arrays at once prior to computing their elements. Since it is guaranteed that no data dependencies exist within a merged spmd skeleton, this is no problem in itself, as allocated arrays are needed beyond the current context, anyways. However, to the same extent as memory allocations are moved ahead in the code, memory de-allocations are deferred til completion of an entire spmd skeleton. Both effects in conjunction may — in pathological cases — increase the overall memory consumption of a program beyond what is available and, hence, hinder a program from running to completion. In order to cope with this effect, the SPMD optimization should further be extended by a component that keeps track of such effects and — whenever necessary — prevents merging of spmd skeletons in unfavourable cases.

References

1. J.C. Adams, W.S. Brainerd, J.T. Martin, B.T. Smith, and J.L. Wagener. *Fortran-95 Handbook — Complete ANSI/ISO Reference*. Scientific and Engineering Computation. MIT Press, 1997.
2. G.H. Botorog and H. Kuchen. Efficient High-Level Parallel Programming. *Theoretical Computer Science*, 196(1-2):71–107, 1998.
3. B.L. Chamberlain, S.-E. Choi, E.C. Lewis, C. Lin, L. Snyder, and W.D. Weathersby. Factor-Join: A Unique Approach to Compiling Array Languages for Parallel Machines. In D.C. Sehr, U. Banerjee, D. Gelernter, A. Nicolau, and D.A. Padua, editors, *Proceedings of the 9th Workshop on Languages and Compilers for Parallel Computing (LCPC'96), San José, California, USA*, volume 1239 of *Lecture Notes in Computer Science*, pages 481–500. Springer-Verlag, 1997.
4. B.L. Chamberlain, S.-E. Choi, E.C. Lewis, C. Lin, L. Snyder, and W.D. Weathersby. The Case for High Level Parallel Programming in ZPL. *IEEE Computational Science and Engineering*, 5(3):76–86, 1998.
5. W. Chin. Towards an Automated Tupling Strategy. In *Proceedings of the ACM SIGPLAN Symposium on Partial Evaluation and Semantic-Based Program Manipulation (PEPM'97), Copenhagen, Denmark*, pages 119–132. ACM Press, 1993.
6. W. Chin. Fusion and Tupling Transformations: Synergies and Conflicts. In *Proceedings of the Fuji International Workshop on Functional and Logic Programming, Susono, Japan*, pages 106–125. World Scientific Publishing, 1995.
7. M.I. Cole. *Algorithmic Skeletons: Structured Management of Parallel Computation*. Reserach Monographs in Parallel and Distributed Computing. Pitman, 1989.
8. J. Darlington, A.J. Field, P.G. Harrison, P.H.J. Kelly, D.W.N. Sharp, Q. Wu, and R.L. While. Parallel Programming using Skeleton Functions. In *Proceedings of the Conference on Parallel Architectures and Reduction Languages Europe (PARLE'93)*, volume 694 of *Lecture Notes in Computer Science*, pages 146–160. Springer-Verlag, 1993.
9. A. Gill, J. Launchbury, and S.L. Peyton Jones. A Short Cut to Deforestation. In *Proceedings of the Conference on Functional Programming Languages and Computer Architecture (FPCA'93), Copenhagen, Denmark*, pages 223–232. ACM Press, 1993.
10. S. Gorlatch and C. Lengauer. (De)Composition Rules for Parallel Scan and Reduction. In *Proceedings of the 3rd International Working Conference on Massively Parallel Programming Models (MPPM'97), London, UK*, pages 23–32. IEEE Computer Society Press, 1997.
11. S. Gorlatch and S. Pelagatti. A Transformational Framework for Skeletal Programs: Overview and Case Study. In J. Rohlim et al., editors, *Parallel and Distributed Processing. IPPS/SPDP'99 Workshops Proceedings*, volume 1586 of *Lecture Notes in Computer Science*, pages 123–137. Springer-Verlag, 1999.
12. S. Gorlatch, C. Wedler, and C. Lengauer. Optimization Rules for Programming with Collective Operations. In M. Atallah, editor, *Proceedings of the 13th International Parallel Processing Symposium and the 10th Symposium on Parallel and*

Distributed Processing (IPPS/SPDP'99), San Juan, Puerto Rico, pages 492–499, 1999.

13. C. Grelck. Shared Memory Multiprocessor Support for SAC. In K. Hammond, T. Davie, and C. Clack, editors, *Proceedings of the 10th International Workshop on Implementation of Functional Languages (IFL'98), London, UK, selected papers*, volume 1595 of *Lecture Notes in Computer Science*, pages 38–54. Springer-Verlag, 1999.

14. C. Grelck. *Implicit Shared Memory Multiprocessor Support for the Functional Programming Language SAC — Single Assignment C*. PhD thesis, University of Kiel, Kiel, Germany, 2001. Logos Verlag, Berlin, 2001.

15. C. Grelck, D. Kreye, and S.-B. Scholz. On Code Generation for Multi-Generator WITH-Loops in SAC. In P. Koopman and C. Clack, editors, *Proceedings of the 11th International Workshop on Implementation of Functional Languages (IFL'99), Lochem, The Netherlands, selected papers*, volume 1868 of *Lecture Notes in Computer Science*, pages 77–94. Springer-Verlag, 2000.

16. W. Gropp, E. Lusk, and A. Skjellum. *Using MPI: Portable Parallel Programming with the Message Passing Interface*. MIT Press, Cambridge, Massachusetts, USA, 1994.

17. E. Hagersten and M. Koster. WildFire: A Scalable Path for SMPs. In *Proceedings of the 5th International Conference on High-Performance Computer Architecture (HPCA'99), Orlando, Florida, USA*, pages 172–181. IEEE Computer Society Press, 1999.

18. K. Hammond and G. Michaelson. *Research Directions in Parallel Functional Programming*. Springer-Verlag, 1999.

19. H. Han, C.-W. Tseng, and P. Keleher. Eliminating Barrier Synchronization for Compiler-Parallelized Codes on Software DSMs. *International Journal of Parallel Programming*, 26(5):591–612, 1998.

20. M.F.P. O'Boyle (HP), L. Kervella (HP), and F. Bodin. Sronisation Mininimisation in a SPMD Execution Mode. *Journal of Parallel and Distributed Computing*, 29(2):196–210, 1995.

21. Z. Hu, H. Iwasaki, M. Takeichi, and A. Takano. Tupling Calculation Eliminates Multiple Data Traversals. In *Proceedings of the ACM SIGPLAN International Conference on Functional Programming (ICFP'97), Amsterdam, The Netherlands*. ACM Press, 1997.

22. F.A. Rabhi. Exploiting Parallelism in Functional Languages: A "Paradigm-Oriented" Approach. In T. Lake and P. Dew, editors, *Abstract Machine Models for Highly Parallel Computers*. Oxford University Press, 1993.

23. S.-B. Scholz. On Defining Application-Specific High-Level Array Operations by Means of Shape-Invariant Programming Facilities. In S. Picchi and M. Micocci, editors, *Proceedings of the International Conference on Array Processing Languages (APL'98), Rome, Italy*, pages 40–45. ACM Press, 1998.

24. S.-B. Scholz. With-loop-folding in SAC — Condensing Consecutive Array Operations. In C. Clack, K.Hammond, and T. Davie, editors, *Proceedings of the 9th International Workshop on Implementation of Functional Languages (IFL'97), St. Andrews, Scotland, UK, selected papers*, volume 1467 of *Lecture Notes in Computer Science*, pages 72–92. Springer-Verlag, 1998.

25. P. Trinder, K. Hammond, H.-W. Loidl, and S.L. Peyton Jones. Algorithm + Strategy = Parallelism. *Journal of Functional Programming*, 8(1):23–60, 1998.

26. P. Wadler. Deforestation: Transforming Programs to Eliminate Trees. *Theoretical Computer Science*, 73(2):231–248, 1990.

Theorem Proving for Functional Programmers

SPARKLE: A Functional Theorem Prover

Maarten de Mol, Marko van Eekelen, and Rinus Plasmeijer

Department of Computer Science
University of Nijmegen, the Netherlands
{maartenm,marko,rinus}@cs.kun.nl

Abstract. SPARKLE is a new theorem prover written in and specialized for the functional programming language CLEAN. It is mainly intended to be used by programmers for proving properties of parts of programs, combining programming and reasoning into one process. It can also be used by logicians interested in proving properties of larger programs.

Two features of SPARKLE are in particular helpful for programmers. Firstly, SPARKLE is integrated in CLEAN and has a semantics based on lazy graph-rewriting. This allows reasoning to take place on the program itself, rather than on a translation that uses different concepts. Secondly, SPARKLE supports automated reasoning. Trivial goals will automatically be discarded and suggestions will be given on more difficult goals.

This paper presents a small example proof built in SPARKLE. It will be shown that building this proof is easy and requires little effort.

1 Introduction

It has often been stated that functional programming languages are well suited for formal reasoning. In practice, however, there is little support for reasoning about functional programs. Existing theorem provers, such as PVS[10], COQ[5] and ISABELLE[12], do not support the full semantics of functional languages and can only be used if the program is translated first, making them difficult to use.

Still, formal reasoning can be a useful tool for any programming language. To make reasoning about programs written in the functional programming language CLEAN[6] feasible, SPARKLE was developed. Work on SPARKLE started after a successful experiment with a restricted prototype[9]. SPARKLE is a semi-automatic theorem prover that can be used to reason about any CLEAN-program.

SPARKLE supports all functional concepts and has a semantics based on lazy graph-rewriting. It puts emphasis on tactics which are specifically useful for reasoning about functional programs and automatically provides suggestions to guide users in the reasoning process. SPARKLE is written in CLEAN; with approximately 130.000 lines of source code (also counting libraries and comments) it is one of the larger programs written in CLEAN. It has an extensive user interface which was implemented using the Object I/O library[1]. SPARKLE is prepared for CLEAN 2.0 and will be integrated in the new IDE. Currently, SPARKLE is a stand-alone application and can be downloaded at http://www.cs.kun.nl/Sparkle.

T. Arts and M. Mohnen (Eds.): IFL 2001, LNCS 2312, pp. 55–71, 2002.

The ultimate goal of the project is to include formal reasoning in the programming process, enabling programmers to easily state and prove properties of parts of programs. This *on-the-fly* proving can only be accomplished if reasoning requires little effort and time. This is already achieved by SPARKLE for smaller programs, mainly due to the possibility to reason on source code level and the support for automatic proving.

In this paper a global description of SPARKLE and its possibilities will be presented. For this purpose a desired property of a small CLEAN-program will be formulated. It will be shown that building a formal proof for this property is very easy in SPARKLE. The specialized features of SPARKLE that in particular assist programmers in building this proof will be highlighted.

The rest of this paper is structured as follows. First, the specification language of SPARKLE will be introduced and the example program will be expressed in it. A comparison with the specification languages of other theorem provers will be made. Then, the logical language of SPARKLE is introduced and the property to prove will be defined in it. Then, a detailed description is given of a proof for this property in SPARKLE. Finally, after the conclusions and related work, an appendix is given in which the tactics needed to build the proof are explained.

2 The Specification Language of SPARKLE

Although SPARKLE can be used to prove properties about arbitrary CLEAN-programs, the reasoning process itself takes place on a simplified representation of the CLEAN-program. In this section the CLEAN-program to reason about will be presented and its simplification for SPARKLE will be described. Then, the specification of functional programs in other theorem provers will be examined and compared to SPARKLE.

2.1 The CLEAN-Program

The proof that will be constructed in this paper relates the functions `take` and `drop` by means of the function `++`. These functions are defined in the standard environment of CLEAN. For this proof, however, the definitions of `take` and `drop` have been improved to handle negative arguments more consistently. The next distribution of CLEAN will use the improved definitions.

```
take :: Int ![a] -> [a]              drop :: Int ![a] -> [a]
take n [x:xs]                        drop n [x:xs]
    | n < 1    = []                      | n < 1    = [x:xs]
    | otherwise = [x:take (n-1) xs]      | otherwise = drop (n-1) xs
take n []                            drop n []
    = []                                 = []

++ :: ![a] [a] -> [a]                - :: infixl 6 !Int !Int -> Int
++ [x:xs] ys                         - x y = code inline {subI}
    = [x:xs++ys]
++ [] ys                             < :: infix 4 !Int !Int -> Bool
    = ys                             < x y = code inline {ltI}
```

These definitions are very straightforward, but it is important to take note of the use of *strictness*. Because there is no exclamation mark in front of the first argument type of `take` (or `drop`), the expression `take` ⊥ `[]` reduces to `[]` and not to ⊥. Adding an exclamation mark would change this behavior. The exclamation mark in front of the second argument of `take` (or `drop`), however, is superfluous, because a pattern match is carried out on this argument.

The functions above also make use of several *predefined* concepts: the integer type `Int`, the integer denotations 0 and 1, the list type `[a]`, the nil constructor `[]` and the cons constructor `[_:_]`. Furthermore, the auxiliary functions – and <, also from the standard environment of CLEAN, are defined in machine code.

2.2 Simplification for SPARKLE

Reasoning in SPARKLE takes place on CORE-CLEAN, which is a subset of CLEAN. CORE-CLEAN is a simple functional programming language, basically containing only application, sharing and case distinction. Its semantics is based on lazy graph-rewriting and it supports strictness annotations. Reductions leading to an error and non-terminating reductions are represented by the constant ⊥.

SPARKLE automatically translates each CLEAN-program to CORE-CLEAN. For this purpose functions from the source code of the new CLEAN-compiler are used. These functions transform CLEAN to a variant of CORE-CLEAN which is used internally in the compiler. Translating CLEAN to CORE-CLEAN is by no means an easy task and would require a huge effort by hand. Using the real compiler saves a lot of work and has an additional advantage as well: it is trivially guaranteed that the translation preserves the semantics of the program.

The program to reason about is a very basic CLEAN-program and can be expressed in CORE-CLEAN almost immediately. The only concept used that is not supported by CORE-CLEAN is pattern matching. The patterns in the functions therefore have to be transformed to case distinctions. The effect of this translation is minimal and is further reduced by SPARKLE, which is able to hide top-level case distinctions and present them as patterns.

The translation of predefined concepts is not a problem, because these are also made available by CORE-CLEAN. The semantics of the representation of numbers, however, is different. SPARKLE disregards overflow and rounding errors, because these would complicate the reasoning process too much. Instead, an idealized representation of numbers is assumed, resulting in an `Int` type without bounds and a `Real` type without bounds and with infinite precision.

Translating *delta rules*, which are functions written in machine code, to CORE-CLEAN is problematic, however. SPARKLE is not able to translate an arbitrary delta rule to CORE-CLEAN. Instead, a fixed set of delta rules occurring in the standard environment of CLEAN is recognized. The translation of recognized delta rules is hard-coded in the theorem prover, usually by referring to mathematical definitions working on idealized numbers. This is for example the case for the subtract function from the example program.

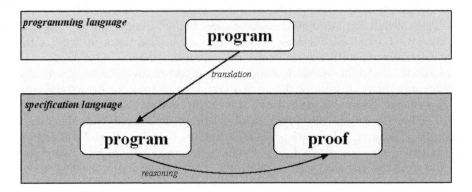

Fig. 1. Reasoning takes place in the specification language

2.3   Specification in Other Theorem Provers

In order to reason about a program in a theorem prover, it must first be translated to its *specification language*, which is CORE-CLEAN for SPARKLE. This language is a very important aspect of a theorem prover, because the reasoning process takes place on the translated program in the specification language.

For effective reasoning, a good understanding of the translated program is required. Programmers usually understand the programs they write very well, but this may not be the case for the translated version. If the differences are too big, knowledge of the original program is completely lost and proving will be a lot more difficult. Moreover, a new specification language must be mastered. These obstacles will likely lead to programmers giving up on formal reasoning.

Unfortunately, there is still a big gap between an executable (programming) language which is useful in practice and a formal (specification) language which is useful in theory. Differences between the specification language and the programming language are inevitable. The following differences can be distinguished, in decreasing order of importance:

1. *Differences in semantics.* These are quite serious, because understanding the translated program may become very difficult. Firstly, the concepts in the specification language may not be known to the programmer. Secondly, the relation between the original program and its translation may be lost, making it difficult to re-use the expertise of the original program.
2. *Differences in notational expressivity.* Sometimes complicated concepts have to be translated to simpler ones, such as translating notational sugar to ordinary function applications. These differences can again make it difficult to relate the translated program to the original program.
3. *Differences in syntax.* These are not so serious and can often be solved easily. However, it can still be very annoying to programmers.

The specification languages of existing theorem provers are very powerful but score badly on the points mentioned above. Most importantly, there are usually

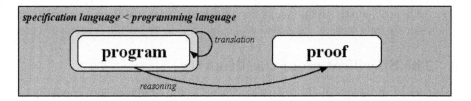

Fig. 2. Reasoning takes place in a subset of the programming language

many differences in semantics. For instance, COQ supports both reasoning about finite (inductive) and infinite (co-inductive) objects, but these objects can not be combined into one datatype. Strictness annotations are not supported by any existing theorem prover. Writing a translation from CLEAN to for instance the specification language of PVS would require a huge effort and may in fact be as difficult as developing a new theorem prover.

All in all, using an existing theorem prover to reason about CLEAN-programs is very problematic for programmers.

2.4   Suitability of CORE-CLEAN for Reasoning about CLEAN

Reasoning in SPARKLE takes place on CORE-CLEAN, which is not a *new* language but only a subset of CLEAN:

In contrast to the specification language of other theorem provers, CORE-CLEAN is very similar to CLEAN. There will not be many differences between a CLEAN-program and its simplification in CORE-CLEAN:

1. *Semantics.* CORE-CLEAN borrows its semantics from CLEAN[2], using a lazy term-graph rewriting system to reduce expressions. All programs written in CORE-CLEAN are valid CLEAN as well and will therefore easily be understood by experienced CLEAN-programmers. The only difference in semantics lies in the handling of numbers. This is only a problem for programs in which overflow or rounding occurs. If one wants to reason about these programs, a different representation of numbers must be chosen.
2. *Concepts.* In CORE-CLEAN all basic constructs of CLEAN are available. Notational sugar is translated to these basic concepts, including pattern matching (translated to case distinctions), overloading (translated to dictionaries), dot-dot-expressions (translated to functions) and comprehensions (translated to functions). The translated versions are usually recognized and understood easily by programmers, because they are not that different. There is, however, one exception: the translation of comprehensions to functions is not transparent at all. The functions created here are hard to understand and almost impossible to relate to the original program.
3. *Syntax.* CORE-CLEAN uses the same syntax as CLEAN.

Due to these similarities, CORE-CLEAN is a good specification language for reasoning about CLEAN-programs. The translation of comprehensions is, however, still problematic. This could be solved by using a different translation-scheme or by interpreting comprehensions; further investigation is required here.

3   The Specification of the Property

Properties can be specified in SPARKLE using a simple first-order propositional logic which is extended with equalities on expressions. The logical connectives $\neg, \rightarrow, \wedge, \vee, \leftrightarrow$ and the quantors $\forall, \exists$ are available. Quantification, either existential or universal, is possible over propositions and expressions of an arbitrary type. Predicates and quantification over predicates are not allowed.

A standard semantics for propositional logics is used. The semantics of the equality on expressions is defined using the operational reduction semantics of CLEAN. Two expressions are equal if for all reductions of one expression there exists a reduction of the other expression that produces the same constructors and basic values (and possibly more). This semantics covers both the equality between finite and infinite structures.

SPARKLE offers the following features to make the specification of properties as easy as possible:

- The same syntax may be used as in CLEAN, meaning that infix applications are allowed and no superfluous brackets have to be supplied.
- Top-level universal quantors may be omitted. For each free variable in the proposition, a top-level universal quantor will automatically be created by SPARKLE.
- It is optional to specify the types of the variables in a $\forall$ or $\exists$. If the type is left out, it will be inferred by the theorem prover. The property will always be type-checked.
- Quantification over type-variables is implicit and must not be specified. Properties will always be interpreted as polymorphic as possible.

The property that is going to be proved in this paper relates the functions **take** and **drop**. Using the described features it can be specified as follows:

$$\textbf{take} \; n \; xs \; \textbf{++} \; \textbf{drop} \; n \; xs = xs$$

There is, however, a problem with this property. If $n = \bot$ and $xs = [7]$, the left-hand-side of the equation will reduce to $\bot$ while the right-hand-side is $[7]$. These kind of problems with undefined expressions occur frequently and can be very hard to detect beforehand. They will always be revealed in the reasoning process, though. An easy solution is to simply demand that n is always defined:

$$n \neq \bot \rightarrow \textbf{take} \; n \; xs \; \textbf{++} \; \textbf{drop} \; n \; xs = xs$$

This property contains two free variables, n and xs, for which universal quantors will be created automatically by SPARKLE. The type of n will be inferred as **Int** and the type of xs will be inferred as **[a]**. A universal quantor for the type variable **a** will be omitted. This results in the following property, which will be the starting point of the proof:

$$\forall_{n \in \texttt{Int}} \forall_{xs \in [\texttt{a}]} [n \neq \bot \rightarrow \textbf{take} \; n \; xs \; \textbf{++} \; \textbf{drop} \; n \; xs = xs]$$

4   Building the Proof

In this section the process of building a proof for the given property in SPARKLE will be described. Before the proof itself is given, the reasoning style of SPARKLE (how proofs are constructed) and its hint mechanism (a mechanism to assist users in building proofs) will be explained.

4.1   Reasoning Style in SPARKLE

Reasoning in SPARKLE is similar to reasoning in other theorem provers and consists of the repeated application of tactics on goals until all goals are discarded.

A *goal* is a property that still has to be proven. Each goal is associated with a *goal context*. In a goal context variables are declared and local hypotheses are stored. The *proof state* consists of a list of goals. The active goal being manipulated is called the *current goal*; the others are called *subgoals*. Changing the active goal is always allowed.

A *tactic* is a function from a single goal to a list of goals. Applying a tactic on the current goal will lead to a new proof state, which consists of the created goals and the old subgoals. All tactics must be *sound* with respect to semantics, meaning that the validity of the created goals must logically imply the validity of the original goal.

SPARKLE implements a total of 42 tactics. Although all of these tactics can also be found, or expressed, in other theorem provers, their behavior is specifically geared towards proving properties of lazy functional programs. The Induction tactic, for example, can only be applied to admissible propositions (see [11]) and is valid for both finite and infinite structures.

A proof of the example property can be constructed using a subset consisting of eight tactics, which are: (1)**Contradiction**(proof by contradiction); (2)**Definedness**(use absurd hypotheses concerning $\perp$); (3)**Induction**(structural induction); (4)**Introduce**(elimination of $\forall$ and $\rightarrow$); (5)**Reduce**(reduction to root-normal-form); (6)**Reflexive**(prove reflexive equality); (7)**Rewrite**(rewrite according to a hypothesis); (8)**SplitCase**(case distinction). See the appendix for a more detailed description of these tactics.

4.2   The Hint Mechanism

Successfully building a proof in SPARKLE depends on the selection of the right tactics. For this, knowledge of the available tactics and their effect is needed, as well as expertise in proving. To make the selection of tactics easier, a hint mechanism is available in SPARKLE.

The hint mechanism is activated each time the current goal changes. It automatically produces a list of applicable tactics. Based on built-in heuristics only the most important applicable tactics are suggested. Each tactic is assigned a score between 1 and 100 that indicates the likelihood of that tactic being helpful in the proof. A score of 100 is reserved for tactics that prove the current goal in one step. The assignment of scores to tactics is hard-coded in SPARKLE.

The hint mechanism is a valuable tool, especially for those with little expertise in proving. However, it is by no means a failsafe feature. Sometimes the right tactic is not suggested or several wrong tactics get high scores. Programmers can use the mechanism to their advantage but should not completely rely on it. Future work will concentrate on improving the hint mechanism.

On top of making users aware of useful applicable tactics, there are two additional advantages offered by the hint mechanism:

1. Suggested tactics are assigned a hot-key and can be applied instantly. This reduces the typing (or clicking) effort for building proofs considerably.
2. A threshold for automatic application can be set. If the best applicable tactic has a score higher than this threshold, it will be applied automatically. This process continues until no tactic with a high enough score can be found. A low threshold can be used for automatic proving; a medium threshold for semi-automatic proving and a high threshold for manual proving.

4.3   Proof of the Example Program

In this subsection a proof of the example property built with SPARKLE will be presented. The description will focus on the goals that have to be proved. At each goal, a tactic to be applied is chosen. An argument for this choice will be given. The description then continues with the first goal that is created; if several goals are created, they will be proved later. The order in which the goals are proved is the same as in SPARKLE. (to be more precise: all unproved goals are stored in a proof tree, which is traversed from left to right and top-down). A numbering system is used to keep track of the goals.

The initial goal is simply the property to be proven. It has an empty context.

$$\dfrac{-}{\forall_{n\in\text{Int}}\forall_{xs\in[\text{a}]}\,[n \neq \perp \rightarrow \textbf{take}\ n\ xs \ \texttt{++}\ \textbf{drop}\ n\ xs = xs]} \quad (1)$$

Because of the definitions of **take** and **drop**, which are tail-recursive in the list argument, structural induction on xs is likely to be useful here. This is accomplished by applying the tactic $\boxed{\texttt{Induction xs}}$. Three new goals(1.1,1.2,1.3) are created: one for the case that xs is $\perp$; one for the case that xs is $[]$ and one for the case that xs is a non-empty list. Note that $\perp$ is treated as a constructor for all algebraic types; therefore induction creates three new goals instead of two.

$$\dfrac{-}{\forall_{n\in\text{Int}}\,[n \neq \perp \rightarrow \textbf{take}\ n\ \perp \ \texttt{++}\ \textbf{drop}\ n\ \perp = \perp]} \quad (1.1)$$

The *goal context* is used to store introduced variables and hypotheses. It is actually just a prettier representation of a chain of $\forall$'s and $\rightarrow$'s, which allows the reasoning to focus on the interesting part of the goal. Another induction is not needed in the current goal. The variable n and the hypothesis $n \neq \perp$ can therefore safely be moved to the goal context using the tactic $\boxed{\texttt{Introduce n H1}}$.

$$\frac{\begin{array}{c} n \in \text{Int} \\ \textbf{H1: } n \neq \bot \end{array}}{\text{take } n \perp \text{ ++ drop } n \perp = \perp} \quad (1.1')$$

Due to the strictness of `take` and `++` and the presence of $\perp$ arguments, redexes are present in the current goal. The tactic Reduce NF All can be used to reduce all redexes in the current goal to normal form (eager reduction). With other parameters, the tactic `Reduce` can also be used for stepwise reduction, lazy reduction, reduction of one particular redex and reduction in the goal context.

$$\frac{\begin{array}{c} n \in \text{Int} \\ \textbf{H1: } n \neq \bot \end{array}}{\bot = \bot} \quad (1.1'')$$

This is clearly a trivial goal, because equality is a reflexive relation. Such reflexive equalities are proved immediately with the tactic Reflexive.

$$\frac{-}{\forall_{n \in \text{Int}}[n \neq \bot \rightarrow \text{take } n\ [] \text{ ++ drop } n\ [] = []]} \quad (1.2)$$

This is the second case of the induction, created for the case that $xs = []$. Again, introduction in the context should be done first: Introduce n H1.

$$\frac{\begin{array}{c} n \in \text{Int} \\ \textbf{H1: } n \neq \bot \end{array}}{\text{take } n\ [] \text{ ++ drop } n\ [] = []} \quad (1.2')$$

There are again redexes present in the current goal, due to the pattern matching performed by `take` and `drop`. Therefore: Reduce NF All.

$$\frac{\begin{array}{c} n \in \text{Int} \\ \textbf{H1: } n \neq \bot \end{array}}{[] = []} \quad (1.2'')$$

This is another example of a reflexive equality; therefore Reflexive.

$$\frac{-}{\begin{array}{l} \forall_{x \in a} \forall_{xs \in [a]}[\\ \quad \forall_{n \in \text{Int}}[n \neq \bot \rightarrow \text{take } n\ xs \text{ ++ drop } n\ xs = xs] \\ \quad \rightarrow \forall_{n \in \text{Int}}[n \neq \bot \rightarrow \text{take } n\ [x{:}xs] \text{ ++ drop } n\ [x{:}xs] = [x{:}xs]\ ]] \end{array}} \quad (1.3)$$

This is the third goal created by the induction; the induction step. The current goal looks quite complicated, but introduction can make things a lot clearer. For reasons of clarity, the first hypothesis will be called IH (induction hypothesis) and the variable n will be introduced as m (to avoid name conflicts with the n already present in the induction hypothesis): Introduce x xs IH m H1.

$$\frac{\begin{array}{c} x \in \mathtt{a}, xs \in [\mathtt{a}], m \in \mathtt{Int} \\ \textbf{IH: } \forall_{n \in \mathtt{Int}} [n \neq \bot \rightarrow \mathtt{take}\ n\ xs\ \texttt{++}\ \mathtt{drop}\ n\ xs = xs] \\ \textbf{H1: } m \neq \bot \end{array}}{\mathtt{take}\ m\ [x\text{:}xs]\ \texttt{++}\ \mathtt{drop}\ m\ [x\text{:}xs] = [x\text{:}xs]} \quad (1.3')$$

Again, the current goal contains redexes that can be removed by applying the tactic $\boxed{\mathtt{Reduce\ NF\ All}}$. Note that a lazy reduction (to root-normal-form) will not suffice here, because $\texttt{++}$ is lazy in its second argument and therefore $\mathtt{drop}\ m$ $[x\text{:}xs]$ as a whole will not be reduced at all.

$$\frac{\begin{array}{c} x \in \mathtt{a}, xs \in [\mathtt{a}], m \in \mathtt{Int} \\ \textbf{IH: } \forall_{n \in \mathtt{Int}} [n \neq \bot \rightarrow \mathtt{take}\ n\ xs\ \texttt{++}\ \mathtt{drop}\ n\ xs = xs] \\ \textbf{H1: } m \neq \bot \end{array}}{\left(\begin{array}{l} \mathtt{case}\ (m < 1)\ \mathtt{of} \\ \quad \mathtt{True} \quad \rightarrow\ [] \\ \quad \mathtt{default} \rightarrow [x\text{:}\mathtt{take}\ (m\text{-}1)\ xs] \end{array}\right) \texttt{++} \left(\begin{array}{l} \mathtt{case}\ (m < 1)\ \mathtt{of} \\ \quad \mathtt{True} \quad \rightarrow [x\text{:}xs] \\ \quad \mathtt{default} \rightarrow \mathtt{drop}\ (m\text{-}1)\ xs \end{array}\right) = [x\text{:}xs]}$$

(This proof state is also shown in Fig. 3.)

The natural next step is a case distinction on $m < 1$, because that will allow the reduction of both case-expressions in the current goal. A special tactic is used for

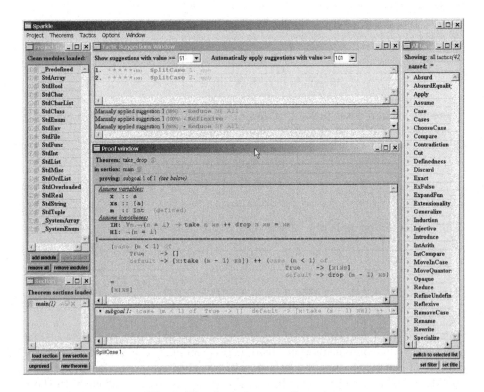

Fig. 3. The theorem prover in action

this purpose: SplitCase 1 . This tactic will examine the first case-expression in the current goal. Three cases are distinguished: (1) $\perp$ (for when $m < 1$ can not be properly evaluated); (2) True (for the first alternative); (3) False (for the default alternative). For each case a new goal(1.3.1,1.3.2,1.3.3) is created, in which the appropriate alternatives of the case-expressions are chosen. Also, in each goal hypotheses are introduced to reflect the case chosen.

$$
\begin{array}{c}
x \in \mathtt{a}, xs \in [\mathtt{a}], m \in \mathtt{Int} \\
\textbf{IH: } \forall_{n \in \mathtt{Int}} [n \neq \perp \rightarrow \textbf{take } n \ xs \textbf{ ++ drop } n \ xs = xs] \\
\textbf{H1: } m \neq \perp \\
\textbf{H2: } (m < 1) = \perp \\
\hline
\perp \textbf{ ++ } \perp = [x{:}xs]
\end{array}
\qquad (1.3.1)
$$

This is the goal created by SplitCase for the case that $m < 1 = \perp$. This goal can be proved in one step, because hypotheses H1 and H2 are contradictory. This is due to the totality of $<$, which ensures that $x < y$ can only be $\perp$ if either $x = \perp$ or $y = \perp$. Hypothesis H2 states that $m < 1 = \perp$, thus either $m = \perp$ or $1 = \perp$. Of course, $1 = \perp$ is not true, thus from hypothesis H2 it may be concluded that $m = \perp$. This contradicts with hypothesis H1. In SPARKLE, a specialized tactic is available to handle these cases: Definedness . This tactic searches for expressions (most notably, variables) that are *defined* (known to be unequal to $\perp$) and expressions that are *undefined* (known to be equal to $\perp$). The analysis makes use of the hypotheses, the ordinary strictness information of functions and the totality of functions such as $-$ and $<$. If an expression is found which is both defined and undefined, the goal is proved by contradiction.

$$
\begin{array}{c}
x \in \mathtt{a}, xs \in [\mathtt{a}], m \in \mathtt{Int} \\
\textbf{IH: } \forall_{n} [n \neq \perp \rightarrow \textbf{take } n \ xs \textbf{ ++ drop } n \ xs = xs] \\
\textbf{H1: } m \neq \perp \\
\textbf{H2: } (m < 1) = \mathtt{True} \\
\hline
[] \textbf{ ++ } [x{:}xs] = [x{:}xs]
\end{array}
\qquad (1.3.3)
$$

This is the goal created by SplitCase for the case that $m < 1 = $ True. The appropriate case alternatives have been chosen and the resulting goal is clearly a trivial one. It can be proved by a reduction followed by an application of Reflexive. These two can be combined by Reduce NF All; Reflexive .

$$
\begin{array}{c}
x \in \mathtt{a}, xs \in [\mathtt{a}], m \in \mathtt{Int} \\
\textbf{IH: } \forall_{n \in \mathtt{Int}} [n \neq \perp \rightarrow \textbf{take } n \ xs \textbf{ ++ drop } n \ xs = xs] \\
\textbf{H1: } m \neq \perp \\
\textbf{H2: } (m < 1) = \mathtt{False} \\
\hline
[x{:}\textbf{take } (m{-}1) \ xs] \textbf{ ++ drop } (m{-}1) \ xs = [x{:}xs]
\end{array}
\qquad (1.3.3)
$$

This is the goal created by SplitCase for the case that $m < 1 = $ False. Filling in the proper case alternatives has resulted in a goal which contains a redex (++ can be reduced); therefore: Reduce NF All .

$$\frac{\begin{array}{c} x \in \mathtt{a}, xs \in [\mathtt{a}], m \in \mathtt{Int} \\ \textbf{IH:}\ \forall_{n \in \mathtt{Int}}[n \neq \bot \rightarrow \mathtt{take}\ n\ xs\ \texttt{++}\ \mathtt{drop}\ n\ xs = xs] \\ \textbf{H1:}\ m \neq \bot \\ \textbf{H2:}\ (m < 1) = \mathtt{False} \end{array}}{[x\mathtt{:take}\ (m\text{-}1)\ xs\ \texttt{++}\ \mathtt{drop}\ (m\text{-}1)\ xs] = [x\mathtt{:}xs]} \qquad (1.3.3')$$

In this goal it is finally possible to use the induction hypothesis, using $(m-1)$ as value for n. This results in the substitution of $\mathtt{take}\ (m-1)\ xs\ \texttt{++}\ \mathtt{drop}\ (m-1)$ xs by xs in the current goal. This is accomplished in SPARKLE by the tactic $\boxed{\mathtt{Rewrite\ IH}}$. This tactic will create two new goals, one for the goal after substitution (1.3.3.1) and one for the condition $m-1 \neq \bot$ (1.3.3.2).

$$\frac{\begin{array}{c} x \in \mathtt{a}, xs \in [\mathtt{a}], m \in \mathtt{Int} \\ \textbf{IH:}\ \forall_{n \in \mathtt{Int}}[n \neq \bot \rightarrow \mathtt{take}\ n\ xs\ \texttt{++}\ \mathtt{drop}\ n\ xs = xs] \\ \textbf{H1:}\ m \neq \bot \\ \textbf{H2:}\ (m < 1) = \mathtt{False} \end{array}}{[x\mathtt{:}xs] = [x\mathtt{:}xs]} \qquad (1.3.3.1)$$

This trivial goal is proved immediately by $\boxed{\mathtt{Reflexive}}$.

$$\frac{\begin{array}{c} x \in \mathtt{a}, xs \in [\mathtt{a}], m \in \mathtt{Int} \\ \textbf{IH:}\ \forall_{n \in \mathtt{Int}}[n \neq \bot \rightarrow \mathtt{take}\ n\ xs\ \texttt{++}\ \mathtt{drop}\ n\ xs = xs] \\ \textbf{H1:}\ m \neq \bot \\ \textbf{H2:}\ (m < 1) = \mathtt{False} \end{array}}{(m - 1) \neq \bot} \qquad (1.3.3.2)$$

This goal is proved by contradiction: the negation of the current goal will lead to an absurd situation. This action is performed by the tactic $\boxed{\mathtt{Contradiction}}$, which creates a hypothesis that is the negation of the current goal and replaces the current goal by the proposition *False*.

$$\frac{\begin{array}{c} x \in \mathtt{a}, xs \in [\mathtt{a}], m \in \mathtt{Int} \\ \textbf{IH:}\ \forall_{n \in \mathtt{Int}}[n \neq \bot \rightarrow \mathtt{take}\ n\ xs\ \texttt{++}\ \mathtt{drop}\ n\ xs = xs] \\ \textbf{H1:}\ m \neq \bot \\ \textbf{H2:}\ (m < 1) = \mathtt{False} \\ \textbf{H3:}\ (m - 1) = \bot \end{array}}{\mathit{False}} \qquad (1.3.3.2')$$

This goal is similar to goal 1.3.1. Here, a contradiction can be found by examining hypotheses H1 and H3 and using the totality of $-$. An application of $\boxed{\mathtt{Definedness}}$ will therefore prove the current goal and finish the proof!

4.4   Remarks Concerning the Reasoning Process

The presented proof was not difficult to build. An examination of the current goal always resulted in a tactic to apply; no overview of the proof as a whole was ever required. This actually turns out to be the case for many small proofs about functional programs.

The hint mechanism is especially useful for building such 'goal-directed' proofs. In fact, *all steps in the presented proof were given as hints by* SPARKLE. Building the proof is therefore reduced to selecting hints, which is a lot easier than selecting tactics, simply because there are far less options to choose from. Right now, there are 42 different tactics which can have arguments as well, whereas there are typically less than 15 hints given for a small-sized goal.

Automatic proving is possible in SPARKLE by letting it automatically apply the hint with the highest score. *The example property can be proved automatically with the hint mechanism.* Of course, larger and more difficult proofs can not be built automatically, although often suggestions given by SPARKLE can be used successfully. Further improving the hint mechanism will be one of the spearheads in the further development of SPARKLE.

A proof of (almost) the same property is also presented in Bird's Introduction to Functional Programming[3]. The proof presented there only takes positive integer arguments into account, but is otherwise quite similar. Note that building such a formal proof with the aid of a theorem prover is much easier than doing it on paper. In [3], a lot of proofs of properties about functional programs are given. A lot of these proofs (about 80%) have already been translated to SPARKLE without difficulties. No problems are expected for translating the others.

5   Conclusions and Further Work

Building the proof required little effort and little expertise. The proving action could always be found by examining the current goal and following a few ground rules. The theorem prover is able to follow these same ground rules and suggest the correct tactics to users, reducing the required expertise even more. All in all, a programmer can build this proof in a short time and without many difficulties.

The two features of SPARKLE that contribute the most to this are:

- The possibility to reason about the source program. Starting with proving is trivial: state what you want to prove and run the theorem prover.
- The hint mechanism. Selecting suggested hints is very easy. An application of a hint can easily be undone, making playing with hints possible. This is not only a fast way of learning how to use the system, but also a fast way of actually constructing the proof.

There are, however, lots of things that still need to be done. Although SPARKLE can already be used to build proofs, it is by no means finished. For instance, documentation must still be added to the system. Furthermore, the hint mechanism must be compared to the automatic reasoning abilities of other theorem provers and possibilities to improve the mechanism must be researched.

Also, work needs to be done on the formal framework of the theorem prover. The effect of the tactics must be described formally in this framework and their soundness with respect to the semantics of CLEAN must be proved. Of particular importance is the soundness of `Induction` for all lazy structures.

6   Related Work

In many textbooks (for instance [3]) properties about functional programs are proved by hand. Also, several articles (for instance [4]) make use of reasoning about functional programs. It seems worthwhile to attempt to formalize these proofs in SPARKLE. In programming practice, however, reasoning about functional programs is scarcely used.

Widely used generic theorem provers are PVS[10], COQ[5] and ISABELLE[12]. They are not tailored towards a specific programming language. Reasoning in these provers requires using a syntax and semantics that are different from the ones used in the programming language. For instance, strictness annotations as in CLEAN are not supported by any existing theorem prover. This makes it rather hard for a programmer to use. On the other hand, these well established theorem provers offer features that are not available in SPARKLE. Most notably, the tactic language and the logic are much richer than in SPARKLE.

Somewhat closer related work is described in [8], in which a description is given of a proof tool which is dedicated to HASKELL[13]. It supports a subset of HASKELL and needs no guidance of users in the proving process. The user can however not manipulate a proof state by the use of tactics to help the prover in constructing a proof, and induction is only applied when the corresponding quantifier has been explicitly marked in advance.

Further related work concerns a proof tool specialized for HASKELL, called ERA, which stands for Equational Reasoning Assistant. This proof tool is still in development, although a working prototype is available. ERA, however, is intended to be used for equational reasoning, and not for theorem proving in general. Additional proving methods, including induction or any logical tactics, are not supported. ERA is a stand-alone application.

Another theorem prover which is dedicated to a functional programming language is EVT[7], the Erlang Verification Tool. It differs from SPARKLE because ERLANG is a strict, untyped language which is mainly used for developing distributed applications. EVT has been applied in practice to larger examples.

We do not know of any other theorem prover than SPARKLE that is integrated, tailored towards a lazy functional language and semi-automatic.

References

1. P. Achten and M. Wierich. *A Tutorial to the CLEAN Object I/O Library (version 1.2)*, Nijmegen, February 2000. CSI Technical Report, CSI-R0003.
2. E. Barendsen and S. Smetsers. *Strictness Typing*, Nijmegen, 1998. In proceedings of the 10th International Workshop on Implementation of Functional Languages (IFL'98), London, 1998, pages 101-116.
3. R. Bird. *Introduction to Functional Programming using Haskell, second edition*, Prentice Hall Europe, 1998, ISBN 0-13-484346-0.
4. A. Butterfield and G. Strong. *Proving Correctness of Programs with I/O - a paradigm comparison*, Dublin, 2001. In proceedings of the 13th International Workshop on Implementation of Functional Languages (IFL'01), Stockholm, 2001, pages 319-334.

5. The Coq Development Team. *The Coq Proof Assistant Reference Manual (version 7.0)*, Inria, 1998. http://pauillac.inria.fr/coq/doc/main.html
6. M. van Eekelen and R. Plasmeijer. *Concurrent Clean Language Report (version 1.3)*, Nijmegen, June 1998. CSI Technical Report, CSI-R9816. http://www.cs.kun.nl/ clean/Manuals/manuals.html
7. T. Noll, L. Fredlund and D. Gurov. *The EVT Erlang Verification Tool*, Stockholm, 2001. In proceedings of the 7th International Conference on Tools and Algorithms for the Construction and Analysis of Systems (TACAS'01), Lecture Notes in Computer Science, Vol. 2031, Springer, 2001, ISBN 3-540-41865-2, pages 582-585.
8. S. Mintchev. *Mechanized reasoning about functional programs*, Manchester, 1994. In K. Hammond, D.N. Turner and P. Sansom, editors, *Functional Programming, Glasgow 1994*, pages 151-167. Springer-Verlag.
9. M. de Mol and M. van Eekelen. *A proof tool dedicated to Clean - the first prototype*, 1999. In proceedings of Applications of Graph Transformations with Industrial Relevance 1999, Lecture Notes in Computer Science, Vol. 1779, Springer, 2000, ISBN 3-540-67658-9, pages 271-278.
10. S. Owre, N.Shankar, J.M. Rushby and D.W.J. Stringer-Calvert. *PVS Language Reference (version 2.3)*, 1999. http://pvs.csl.sri.com/manuals.html
11. L. C. Paulson. *Logic and Computation*, Cambridge University Press, 1987. ISBN 0-52-134632-0.
12. L. C. Paulson. *The Isabelle Reference Manual*, Cambridge, 2001. http://www.cl.cam.ac.uk/Research/HVG/Isabelle/docs.html
13. S. Peyton Jones(editor), J. Hughes(editor) et al. *Report on the programming language Haskell 98*, Yale, 1999. http://www.haskell.org/definition/
14. N. Winstanley. *Era User Manual, version 2.0*, Glasgow, 1998. http://www.dcs.gla.ac.uk/ nww/Era/Era.html

A   A Short Description of 8 Tactics (Appendix)

This appendix provides a short description of the tactics used in the example proof. In this description the following categorization of tactics is used:

Safe/Unsafe - A tactic is safe if its inverse is also a valid tactic. This can only be the case if the created goals are logically equivalent to the original goal, whereas an unsafe tactic creates goals which are logically stronger.

Forwards/Backwards - Forwards reasoning brings hypotheses closer to the current goal (top-down), while backwards reasoning brings the current goal closer to the hypotheses (bottom-up).

Instantaneous - An instantaneous tactic proves a goal in one single step. Such a tactic will not be categorized as safe/unsafe or forwards/backwards.

Programming/Logic - Logic tactics are based on the semantics of the logical connectives. Programming tactics are based on the semantics of CLEAN.

Contradiction.

Type: Safe; backwards; logic.
Info: Builds a proof by contradiction.
Effect: Replaces the current goal by the absurd proposition *False* and adds its negation as a hypothesis in the context. If a double negation is produced, it will be removed automatically.

Example: $xs \vdash xs \mathbin{++} [] \neq xs$
$\Longrightarrow$ `Contradiction` $\Longrightarrow$
(1) $xs, \langle xs \mathbin{++} [] = xs \rangle \vdash False$

`Definedness.`

Type: Instantaneous; logic.

Info: Determines two sets of expressions: (1) the set of defined expressions, which are expressions that are unequal to $\perp$; (2) the set of undefined expressions, which are expressions that are equal to $\perp$. These sets are determined by examining equalities in hypotheses and using strictness information. In addition, the totality of certain predefined functions is used.

Effect: If an expression is found that is both defined and undefined, the goal is proved instantaneously. Otherwise nothing happens.

Example: $xs, ys, zs, \langle xs = \perp \rangle, \langle xs \mathbin{++} ys = [1{:}zs] \rangle \vdash False$
$\Longrightarrow$ `Definedness` $\Longrightarrow$
$\square$

`Induction <variable>.`

Type: Unsafe; backwards; programming.

Info: Performs structural induction on a variable. A goal is created for each root-normal-form the variable may have, including $\perp$. The type of the variable must be `Int`, `Bool` or algebraic. The root-normal-forms of an algebraic type are determined by its constructors.

Effect: In each created goal the variable is replaced by its root-normal-form. Universal quantors are created for new variables. Additionally, induction hypotheses are added (as implications) for all recursive variables.

Example: $\vdash \forall_{xs}[xs \mathbin{++} [] = xs]$
$\Longrightarrow$ `Induction xs` $\Longrightarrow$
(1) $\vdash \perp \mathbin{++} [] = \perp$
(2) $\vdash [] \mathbin{++} [] = []$
(3) $\vdash \forall_x \forall_{xs}[xs \mathbin{++} [] = xs \rightarrow [x{:}xs] \mathbin{++} [] = [x{:}xs]]$

`Introduce <name(1)> <name(2)> ... <name(n)>.`

Type: Safe; backwards; logic.

Info: Moves as many universally quantified variables and hypotheses to the goal context as there are names given.

Effect: The current goal must be of the form $\forall_{x_1} \ldots \forall_{x_a}[P_1 \rightarrow \ldots P_b \rightarrow Q]$, where $a + b = n$. The quantors and implications may be mixed. The variables $x_1 \ldots x_a$ and the hypotheses $P_1 \ldots P_b$ are deleted from the current goal and are added to the goal context using the names given.

Example: $\vdash \forall_x[x = 7 \rightarrow \forall_y[y = 7 \rightarrow x = y]]$
$\Longrightarrow$ `Introduce p H1 q H2` $\Longrightarrow$
(1) $p, q, \langle \text{H1}{:}\ p = 7 \rangle, \langle \text{H2}{:}\ q = 7 \rangle \vdash p = q$

`Reduce NF All.`

Type: Safe; backwards; programming.

Info: Reduces all expressions in the current goal to normal form. This is accomplished by a reduction to root-normal-form, followed by the recursive reduction to normal form of all top-level lazy arguments. The functional reduction strategy is used. An artificial limit on the maximum number of reduction steps is imposed in order to safely handle non-terminating reductions. Replacing the `NF` by `RNF` results in reduction to root-normal-form only.

Effect: All redexes are replaced by their reducts.

Example: $x, xs, ys, zs \vdash [x{:}xs] \,{+\!\!+}\, ys = \texttt{reverse } zs$
$\Longrightarrow$ `Reduce NF All` $\Longrightarrow$
(1) $x, xs, ys, zs \vdash [x{:} \; xs \,{+\!\!+}\, ys] = \texttt{reverse } zs$

`Reflexive.`

Type: Instantaneous; logic.

Info: Proves any reflexive equality instantaneously.

Effect: Proves any goal of the form $E = E$. Additional quantors and implications are allowed in front of the equality.

Example: $\vdash \forall_{xs} \exists_{ys} [xs = ys \rightarrow xs \,{+\!\!+}\, ys = xs \,{+\!\!+}\, ys]$
$\Longrightarrow$ `Reflexive` $\Longrightarrow$
$\square$

`Rewrite <hypothesis>.`

Type: Safe; backwards/forwards; logic.

Info: Rewrites the current goal using an equality in a hypothesis.

Effect: The hypothesis must be of the form $\forall_{x_1} \ldots \forall_{x_n} [P_1 \rightarrow \ldots P_m \rightarrow E_1 = E_2]$. For all substitutions $\overrightarrow{x_i} = \overrightarrow{e_i}$ such that $E_1[\overrightarrow{x_i} := \overrightarrow{e_i}]$ occurs in the current goal, $E_1[\overrightarrow{x_i} := \overrightarrow{e_i}]$ is replaced by $E_2[\overrightarrow{x_i} := \overrightarrow{e_i}]$. Variables in the context are treated as constants. Additionally, goals are created for all conditions $P_1 \ldots P_m$.

Example: $xs, \langle \texttt{H1}{:} \; xs = [] \rangle \vdash xs \,{+\!\!+}\, xs = xs$
$\Longrightarrow$ `Rewrite H1` $\Longrightarrow$
(1) $xs, \langle \texttt{H1}{:} \; xs = [] \rangle \vdash [] \,{+\!\!+}\, [] = []$

`SplitCase <number>.`

Type: Unsafe; backwards; programming.

Info: Performs a case distinction based on the case-expression in the current goal that is indicated by the argument number. For each alternative a goal will be created. Two goals are always created: (1) for the case that evaluation of the condition produces an error; (2) for the case that no alternative matches (replaced by the default alternative if one is available).

Effect: In each created goal, the case-expression is replaced by the result of the alternative chosen (or $\perp$ for the erroneous case). Hypotheses are introduced in the context to reflect which alternative was chosen. The goal for the default alternative is optimized: a negation of all other alternatives is transformed to an ordinary alternative if possible.

Example: $xs \vdash (\texttt{case } xs \texttt{ of } [y{:}ys] \rightarrow y; \texttt{default} \rightarrow 12) = 0$
$\Longrightarrow$ `SplitCase 1` $\Longrightarrow$
(1) $xs, \langle xs = \perp \rangle \vdash \perp = 0$
(2) $xs, y, ys, \langle xs = [y{:}ys] \rangle \vdash y = 0$
(3) $xs, \langle xs = [] \rangle \vdash 12 = 0$

Proving Correctness of Programs with IO — A Paradigm Comparison

Andrew Butterfield and Glenn Strong

Trinity College, Dublin University
{Andrew.Butterfield, Glenn.Strong}@cs.tcd.ie

Abstract. This paper discusses reasoning about IO operations in Haskell, Clean and C and compares the effect on ease of reasoning of the different approaches taken to IO in these languages. An IO system model is built using VDM♣ and is used to prove a basic property of a program written in each of the three languages. We tentatively draw the conclusions that functional languages are easier to reason about and that Monads can make the reasoning process slightly more difficult, but note that much future work is needed.

1   Introduction

An often cited advantage of functional programming languages is that they are supposed to be easier to reason about than imperative languages [PJ87, p1],[Bd87, p23],[BJLM91, p17],[Hen87, pp6–7] with the property of *referential transparency* getting a prominent mention and the notion of *side-effect* being deprecated all round. For a long time, a major disadvantage of functional programming languages was their inability to adequately handle features where side-effects are an intrinsic component, such as file or other IO operations [BJLM91, p139],[Gor94, p-xi]. However, two methodologies have emerged in the last decade to combine the side-effect world of IO with the referentially transparent world of functional programming, namely the *uniqueness type system* of the programming language Clean [BS00] and the use of *monads* in the Haskell language [Gor94][Bir98, Chp 10, pp326–359].

Question 1. Has the technical machinery necessary to handle IO in pure functional languages, led to a situation where correctness proofs have the same difficulty as those found in imperative programs ?

A second issue concerns the relative ease of reasoning when using either of the two technical alternatives, namely uniqueness typing and/or monads. The uniqueness typing approach uses the type-system to ensure that the external "world" is accessed in an single-threaded fashion, so that an underlying implementation can safely implement operations on the world using side-effects, while still maintaining referential transparency. From the programmer's perspective nothing changes in the program, except that it must satisfy the type-checker. The monadic approach uses an abstract datatype which enforces single-threaded

T. Arts and M. Mohnen (Eds.): IFL 2001, LNCS 2312, pp. 72–87, 2002.
© Springer-Verlag Berlin Heidelberg 2002

use of world resources, but which also requires the programmer to explicitly make use of this datatype and its operations. In effect, the monad acts as a wrapper around the potentially dangerous operations.

Question 2. Does the explicit monadic wrapper and its laws make the monadic IO program harder to reason about when compared to a similar uniquely typed program ?

This paper describes a first step towards resolving these issues. In §2 we describe our overall methodology, and then in §3,§4, §5, and §6 we present excerpts from the programs, IO model, semantics, and proofs. Finally we give our conclusions in §7, discuss some issues raised, and discuss future work in §8.

2   Methodology

The key aim of this work is to establish the effect the choice of paradigm has on the ease of reasoning. In particular we wish to avoid differences introduced by idiosyncrasies associated with real world instances of these paradigms. The paradigms under study, and well-known real world instances are:

Imperative: explicit side-effects with sequencing and assignment (C [KR88]).
Uniquely-Typed: referentially transparent with side-effects guaranteed single-threaded by a type-system dealing with uniqueness (Clean [PvE98]).
Monadic: referentially transparent with side-effects guaranteed single-threaded by embedding them within monads (Haskell [PH+99]).

We compared the proofs based on the length and number of reasoning steps required.

We wanted a small case-study to start, in order that we did not get swamped in too much messy detail. The key requirement was that the program performed some IO and that the desired property would refer both to the external world and to some property of the data involved. The property to be checked was:

Proposition 1. *Given the existence of a file called "a" with at least one integer, that the same file would end up with only one integer value, being the square of the original value.*

Real programs were written in C, Clean and Haskell, compiled and run. As a common background to the three cases, we developed a uniform model of file IO to be used in all proofs. The programming languages were re-designed to minimise the differences between them, apart from the paradigm difference under study. Initially it was decided to develop and use a denotational semantics [Sch88], but proofs based on this rapidly became unwieldy, so it was decided to abandon them. However, some of the domains developed for the denotational semantics did prove very useful in the later semantic models. In all three cases, we integrated the IO model with the semantics being developed. For each paradigm, we stated in the property to be proved in the appropriate manner. We then proceeded to do the proofs, ensuring that they were complete, all necessary

lemmas were handled, and paying particular attention to the pre-conditions of
the operations. All the details are to be found in a technical report [BS01]. This
paper only contains selected extracts from it, plus explanation of the motivation
and results.

3   The Programs

The real world programs were abstracted to remove unnecessary detail and also
give uniform names to the IO operations. The kind of detail removed includes
variable declaration in the C program, and error-checking in both the C and
Clean programs. There is no explicit error checking code in the Haskell program,
largely because Haskell relies on an exception mechanism to deal with this.
For brevity, we do not list the original programs here, but instead give their
abstracted counterparts.

We chose a simple task which involved opening a file with a fixed filename
("a"), reading an integer from it, closing and re-opening it, and writing the
square of that integer back.

3.1   The Abstracted C Program

We renamed functions as appropriate, and discard variable declarations and
error checking.

```
main()
{ f = fopen("a",FRead);
  x = freadi(f);
  fclose(f);
  f = fopen("a",FWrite);
  fwritei(f,x*x);
  fclose(f); }
```

3.2   The Abstracted Clean Program

We remove return condition values

```
main w # (f,w) = fopen ''a" FRead w
       # (x,f) = freadi f
       # w     = fclose f w
       # (f,w) = fopen ''a" FWrite w
       # f     = fwritei (x*x) f
       # w     = fclose f w
       = w
```

3.3   The Abstracted Haskell Program

We use slightly different names here, mainly because it will make it easier to
distinguish the Haskell functions from the underlying IO model functions.

```
main
  = do h <- openFile ''a" ReadMode
       x <- hreadi h
       hclose h
       h <- openFile ''a" WriteMode
       hwritei h (x*x)
       hclose h
```

Note that the real world Haskell program had auxiliary definitions of `hreadi` and `hwritei`. For this exercise we assume these are part of the standard IO package.

4   The IO Model

We developed an IO model to suit the case-study. This model is common to all three proofs and is presented using the notation of the "Irish School" of the VDM ($VDM^{\clubsuit}$) [Mac90],[Hug00]. This is a variant of VDM [Jon90] which concentrates on using algebraic structures and morphisms as an organising and foundational principle, resulting in a formal methodology that is very functional in character. For the purposes of this paper, view $VDM^{\clubsuit}$ as a functional language extended with set and map types and their associated operations.

4.1   The World and the File-System

We posit a 'world' where everything of interest happens:

$$\mathcal{W} \in World \cong FS \times \dots$$

The world contains interesting sub-systems such as the file-system of the local machine, as well as other aspects of interest. We shall only be interested here in the file system component (FS). For this experiment we assume that there are no changes made to the filesystem other than those made explicit in the program under analysis (that is, there are no other programs accessing the filesystem).

The file system maps filenames to files, where files "contain" both state and data:

$$\Phi \in FS \cong FName \xrightarrow{m} File$$
$$n \in FName \cong \mathbb{A}^{\star}$$
$$f \in File \cong FState \times FData$$

We shall simply view data as sequences of integers

$$\delta \in FData \cong \mathbb{Z}^{\star}$$

A file can be opened many times for reading, but only once for writing, and never for both simultaneously.

$$\Sigma \in FState \cong \text{CLOSED} \mid \text{WRITE} \mid \text{READ } \mathbb{N}$$

Once a file is opened, we use a file status block, which tracks the state of the open file — it contains the filename as a "back-link" in order to facilitate file closing.

$$f \in \textit{FStatus} \mathrel{\widehat{=}} \mathrm{HWRITE}\ \textit{FName}\ \textit{FData} \mid \mathrm{HREAD}\ \textit{FName}\ \textit{FData}\ \textit{FData}$$

We need to define a file mode in order to be able to specify what kind of file status is required:

$$m \in \textit{FMode} \mathrel{\widehat{=}} \{\mathrm{FREAD}, \mathrm{FWRITE}\}$$

For some of the paradigms, we will need to hand around handles or references to information structures to allow side-effects to occur. The need for this become very obvious when trying to give a denotational semantics to an imperative language, and is also necessary for monadic IO. We shall view a handle as a natural number, and map this to the appropriate structures. Handles and instances of the relevant structure are then allocated and freed as required. We adopt a very simple approach to handle allocation, as evidenced by the formal definitions. We shall parameterise both handles and the handle mapping by the type (T) of the information structure:

$$h \in \textit{Handle}\ T \mathrel{\widehat{=}} \mathbb{N}$$
$$\varrho \in \textit{HMap}\ T \mathrel{\widehat{=}} \mathbb{N} \xrightarrow{m} T$$
$$\mathrm{hAlloc}\ :\ T \to \textit{HMap}\ T \to \textit{Handle}\ T \times \textit{HMap}\ T$$
$$\mathrm{hAlloc}[t]\varrho \mathrel{\widehat{=}} (h, \varrho \sqcup \{h \mapsto t\})\ \textbf{where}\ h = \max(\mathrm{dom}\ \varrho) + 1$$
$$\mathrm{hFree}\ :\ \textit{Handle}\ T \to \textit{HMap}\ T \to \textit{HMap}\ T$$
$$\mathrm{hFree}[h]\varrho \mathrel{\widehat{=}} \vartriangleleft [h]\varrho$$

4.2   The Operations

We defined four semantic operations (fopen,fclose,fwritei,freadi) one for each of the file operations used in the programs. Each operation has an associated pre-condition and an explicit functional description of its effect on the IO world. The four operations have the following signatures:

$$\mathrm{fopen} : \textit{FName} \times \textit{FMode} \to \textit{FS} \to \textit{FStatus} \times \textit{FS}$$
$$\mathrm{fclose} : \textit{FStatus} \to \textit{FS} \to \textit{FS}$$
$$\mathrm{fwritei} : \mathbb{Z} \to \textit{FStatus} \to \textit{FStatus}$$
$$\mathrm{freadi} : \textit{FStatus} \to \mathbb{Z} \times \textit{FStatus}$$

We shall only consider the freadi operation in detail in this paper — it's formal definition is:

$$\mathrm{pre\text{-}freadi}(\mathrm{HWRITE}\ \_) \mathrel{\widehat{=}} \mathrm{FALSE}$$
$$\mathrm{pre\text{-}freadi}(\mathrm{HREAD}\ \_\ \_\ \delta) \mathrel{\widehat{=}} \delta \neq \Lambda$$
$$\mathrm{freadi}(\mathrm{HREAD}\ n\ \delta_r\ (i : \delta_w)) \mathrel{\widehat{=}} (i, (\mathrm{HREAD}\ n\ (\delta_r \frown \langle i \rangle)\ \delta_w))$$

5   The Semantics

We now discuss the programming language semantics used in the proofs. An overarching theme here is the idea of a programming language as simply being a (readily) executable subset of a broader specification/semantic modelling language. This idea, common in work on program derivation [Mor94], avoids the need to deal with multiple notations.

5.1   C Semantics

We used Hoare-triples [HJ98, pp64–5] to give the semantics of the C program. The pre- and post-condition predicates will make assertions about the values of various components of the IO world $\mathcal{W} : World$, $\Phi : FS$, the runtime system $\varrho : HMap\ FStatus$ and program variables. The C-program mainline initialises ϱ. We define the meaning of

$$\{P\}\mathtt{main}()\{\mathtt{cstmts}\}\{Q\} \quad \text{as being} \quad \{P \wedge \varrho = \theta\}\mathtt{cstmts}\{Q\}$$

We then gave definitions of the file IO operations using this technique. The semantics of the freadi operation is given by the Hoare triple:

$$\{\ h \in \varrho \wedge \varrho(h) = (\mathrm{HREAD}\ n\ \delta_r\ J : \delta_w)\ \}$$

```
  i = freadi(h)
```
$$\{\ i' = J \ \wedge\ \varrho' = \varrho \dagger \{h \mapsto (\mathrm{HREAD}\ n\ \delta_r \frown \langle J \rangle\ \delta_w)\}\ \}$$

The method by which this definition was obtained is described in [BS01] but space does not allow us to explain it here.

5.2   Clean Semantics

For the Clean program we use a natural semantics and apply rewrite rules (detailed in [BS01]), as well as functional descriptions of the IO operations. Effectively, we have expanded the language to include an explicit view of the world. So, we give the semantics of the program function **freadi** as:

```
pre_freadi (HWrite _)        = False
pre_freadi (HRead n rd rem)  = rem <> []

freadi (HRead n rd [i:rest]) = (i,Hread n (rd++[i]) rest)
```

We have a definition of the precondition in the language and we give the effect as a function that manipulates the file status block as if we had these features in the language. Note that we can manipulate the file-status block directly in Clean, whereas this was not possible in either C or Haskell.

5.3   Haskell Semantics

The Haskell semantics used similar laws to that of Clean as well as some rules to handle do-notation. We do not attempt to reason using the well-known monad laws because we are unable to state the desired property in that system.

The `fopen`, `fclose`, `freadi` and `fwritei` functions have semantics identical to the Clean semantics.

"Handle" versions of the file operations also needed to encode the Haskell IO system.

```
:: IO a = (W,Hmap) -> (a, (W,Hmap))
:: Hmap = Int -> FStatus
```

We introduce map manipulation operations such as **override**. The semantics of `hreadi` is then given as:

```
hreadi h = \(w,l) -> (the_int, (w, override l h fs'))
           where   (the_int,fs') = freadi fs
                   fs             = lookup h l
```

6   The Proofs

We only present excerpts from the proofs here. The proposition to be proved was stated in section 2. We show the formal statement in each case of what is to be proved. We show how the proof starts, which illustrates how the programs are "started up", form a formal semantics perspective. Finally we show a fragment of each proof, namely that having to do with the integer read statement (`freadi`, `hreadi`).

6.1   Formal Statements of the Proposition

Formal Statement for C.

$$\{ \mathcal{W} = (\Phi_0 \sqcup \{"a" \mapsto (\text{CLOSED}, J : \_)\}), \_) \}$$

```
main() { Cstmts }
```

$$\{ \mathcal{W} = (\Phi_0 \sqcup \{"a" \mapsto (\text{CLOSED}, \langle J^2 \rangle)\}), \_) \}$$

We use the notation $\Phi_0 \sqcup \phi$ to denote a file system that contains at least the mapping ϕ. In all cases we use underlines $(\_,\_)$ to denote parts of the world that are not of relevance.

Formal Statement for Clean.

```
lookup phi' ''a" = (Closed,[J*J])
where (phi',_) = main (extend phi ''a" (Closed,J:_),_)
```

Formal Statement for Haskell.

```
lookup phi' ''a" = (Closed,[J*J])
where ((phi',_),_) = main ((extend phi ''a" (Closed,J:_),_),_)
```

For the functional programs we capture the pre-condition by denoting the initial world directly, rather than by asserting that a variable has that value. We use underlines (_,_) to denotes parts of the world that are not of relevance. Note that the Haskell world has more structure than the Clean world. This is because the IO monad covers not only the external world, but also any hidden parts of the program runtime system. In Clean, these are created and reference explicitly by the program we open and manipulate files.

6.2 The Overall Structure of the Proofs

The Structure of C Proof. The C proof started by initialising the runtime and expanding the program text:

$$\{ P_0 \equiv \mathcal{W} = (\Phi_0 \sqcup \{"a" \mapsto (\text{CLOSED}, J : \_)\}), \_) \wedge \varrho = \theta \}$$

```
f = fopen("a",FRead)
```
$\{ P_1 \}$
```
x = freadi(f)
```
$\{ P_2 \}$
```
fclose(f)
```
$\{ P_3 \}$
```
f = fopen("a",FWrite)
```
$\{ P_4 \}$
```
fwritei(f,x*x)
```
$\{ P_5 \}$
```
fclose(f)
```
$\{ P_6 \}$

We then show that $P_6 \Rightarrow \mathcal{W} = (\Phi_0 \sqcup \{"a" \mapsto (\text{CLOSED}, \langle J^2 \rangle)\}), \_)$

The proof for statement i (s_i) proceeded by showing that $P_i \Rightarrow pre$-s_i, having identified the substitution that made this so, then using this to generate P_{i+1}

The proof ended showing that P_6 was:

$$\mathcal{W} = (\Phi_0 \sqcup \{"a" \mapsto (\text{CLOSED}, \langle J^2 \rangle)\}), \_)$$
$$\varrho = \theta \wedge f = 1 \wedge x = J$$

which must imply

$$\{ \mathcal{W} = (\Phi_0 \sqcup \{"a" \mapsto (\text{CLOSED}, \langle J^2 \rangle)\}), \_) \}$$

This is trivially the case   ♣

The Structure of Clean Proof. The Clean proof commenced by re-writing the clean program, using the Hash Syntactic Sugar rule. The result will not be a syntactically correct Clean program, and so we must proceed by textual substitution, using the rules stated in [BS01].

```
main =\ w -> h1
h1 = letb (f,w)=fopen ''a" FRead w in h2
h2 = letb (i,f) = freadi f in h3
h3 = letb w = fclose f w in h4
h4 = letb (f,w)=fopen ''a" Fwrite w in h5
h5 = letb f =fwritei (x*x) f in h6
h6 = letb w = fclose f w in w
```

In this rewriting we use `letb` to indicate a non-recursive local definition (similar to the let-before structure in Clean). The non-recursive let can be rewritten by the *let-evaluation* rule:

```
letb v = e1 in e2
= ⟨ Let Evaluation ⟩
e2[v -> e1]
```

We then evaluated

```
main (extend phi ''a" (Closed,J:_),w)
```

reducing it down to

```
(override phi ''a" (Closed,[J*J]),_)
```

Now we evaluate our property:

```
lookup phi' ''a"
where (phi',_) = (override phi ''a" (Closed,[J*J]),_)
```

which reduced down to

```
(Closed,[J*J])
```

Proof is complete   ♣

The Structure of Haskell Proof. The Haskell proof started by transforming the Haskell program to a monad-free form using a similar set of transformations to the Hash Syntactic Sugar rule used in the Clean proof:

```
main = h1
    h1 = \w -> letb (h,w') = openFile ''a" ReadMode w in h2 w'
    h2 = \w -> letb (x,w') = hreadi h w in h3 w'
    h3 = \w -> letb w'      = hclose h w in h4 w'
    h4 = \w -> letb (h,w') = openFile ''a" WriteMode w in h5 w'
    h5 = \w -> letb w'      = hwritei h (x*x) w in h6
    h6 = \w -> hclose h w
```

This was done in order to have an explicit identifier referring to the world. We then evaluated the expression:

```
main ((extend phi ''a" (Closed,J:_),W),[])
```

Note that we started off the program by giving the world, *and an initialised runtime system* (namely the initially empty file handle mapping, denoted here as []). This reduced eventually down to

```
((override phi ''a" (Closed, [J*J]),W),[])
```

As for the Clean proof, we could then use lookup to establish the property.

6.3 Details of the Proof Surrounding freadi

Proving freadi in C. In the C program, this point was reached once we had determined P_1, as:

$$\mathcal{W} = (\Phi_0 \sqcup \{"a" \mapsto (\text{READ } 1, J : \_)\}, \_)$$
$$\varrho = \{1 \mapsto (\text{HREAD } "a" \; \Lambda \; J : \_)\}$$
$$f = 1$$

The next step was to handle the statement $s_2 : \mathtt{x} = \mathtt{freadi(f)}$. We showed that P_1 implies the pre-condition for this instance of $\mathtt{freadi}$, which is

$$f \in \varrho \wedge \varrho(f) = (\text{HREAD } n \; \delta_r \; J : \delta_w)$$

We don't give the details here, but this resulted in an assertion that the implication held, subject to the following variable binding:

$$n = "a" \; \wedge \; \delta_r = \Lambda \; \wedge \; \delta_w = \_$$

We then used these as substitutions on the pre-condition to obtain

$$x' = J \; \wedge \; \varrho' = \varrho \dagger \{1 \mapsto (\text{HREAD } "a" \; \Lambda \frown \langle J \rangle \; \_)\}$$

We then evaluated each term, keeping P_1 as an assumption:

$$x' = J$$

$$\varrho' = \varrho \dagger \{1 \mapsto (\text{HREAD } "a" \; \Lambda \frown \langle J \rangle \; \_)\}$$
$$= \quad \langle \text{defn. of conc.} \rangle$$
$$\varrho' = \varrho \dagger \{1 \mapsto (\text{HREAD } "a" \; \langle J \rangle \; \_)\}$$
$$= \quad \langle \text{val. of } \varrho \rangle$$
$$\varrho' = \{1 \mapsto (\text{HREAD } "a" \; \Lambda \; J : \_)\} \dagger \{1 \mapsto (\text{HREAD } "a" \; \langle J \rangle \; \_)\}$$
$$= \quad \langle \text{defn. of override} \rangle$$
$$\varrho' = \{1 \mapsto (\text{HREAD } "a" \; \langle J \rangle \; \_)\}$$

The postcondition became:

$$x' = J \,\wedge\, \varrho' = \{1 \mapsto (\text{HREAD } "a" \,\langle J \rangle \, \_)\}$$

We merged this with P_1, dropping primes, to get P_2:

$$P_2 \equiv \begin{cases} \mathcal{W} = (\Phi_0 \sqcup \{"a" \mapsto (\text{READ } 1, J : \_)\}, \_) \\ \varrho = \{1 \mapsto (\text{HREAD } "a" \,\langle J \rangle \, \_)\} \\ f = 1 \,\wedge\, x = J \end{cases}$$

The proof steps are mainly calculational in nature, but there is a lot of disjointedness. By contrast, the functional language proofs had a much more linear 'flow' to them, which made them easier to manage.

Proving freadi in Clean. The section of the Clean proof dealing with the integer read was as follows:

```
letb (f,w)=(Hread ''a" [] (J:_) ,(override phi ''a"
(Read 1,J:_),_)) in h2
=   ⟨ expand h2 ⟩
letb (f,w)=(Hread ''a" [] (J:_) ,(override phi ''a"
(Read 1,J:_),_)) in letb (x,f) = freadi f in h3
=   ⟨ partial let evaluation on f ⟩
letb w = (override phi ''a" (Read 1,J:_),_)
in letb (x,f) = freadi (Hread ''a" [] (J:_)) in h3
=   ⟨ Lemma K.4, defn of freadi ⟩
letb w = (override phi ''a" (Read 1,J:_),_)
in letb (x,f) = (J,Hread ''a" [J] _) in h3
```

It is a fairly straightforward proof segment, with a Lemma (referred to as K.4), which checked that the pre-condition was satisfied.

Proving freadi in Haskell. The section of the Haskell proof dealing with the integer read was as follows:

```
letb h = 1 in h2
   ((override phi ''a" (Read 1,J:_),W), override [] 1
   (Hread ''a" [] (J:_)))
=   ⟨ expansion of h2 ⟩
letb h = 1 in
   \w -> letb (x,w') = hreadi h w in h3 w'
   ((override phi ''a" (Read 1,J:_),W), override [] 1
   (Hread ''a" [] (J:_)))
=   ⟨ β-reduction ⟩
letb h = 1 in
   letb (x,w') = hreadi h ((override phi ''a" (Read 1,J:_),W),
                           override [] 1 (Hread ''a" [] (J:_)))
   in h3 w'
=   ⟨ Lemma H.2 ⟩
```

```
  letb h = 1 in letb (x,w') = (J, (override phi ''a"
                (Read 1,J:_),W), override [] 1 (Hread ''a" [J] _))
                in h3 w'
= ⟨ partial let evaluation ⟩
  letb h = 1 in letb x = J
  in h3 ((override phi ''a" (Read 1,J:_),W),
          override [] 1 (Hread ''a" [J] _))
= ⟨ expansion of h3 ⟩
  letb h = 1 in letb x = J in \w -> letb w' = hclose h w in h4 w'
                ((override phi ''a" (Read 1,J:_),W),
                 override [] 1 (Hread ''a" [J] _))
```

The proof is straightforward, using a lemma (Lemma H.2) to capture the behaviour of the read operation as well as to check its pre-condition. There are two aspects of this proof segment that make it more verbose than the corresponding Clean fragment, discussed below.

7   Conclusions and Observations

The C proof was more complex and involved, as the fragments above show. The Clean and Haskell proofs were much more straightforward, having a much better flow. However, the example chosen (freadi) shows a clear difference between the Clean IO and the monadic IO approaches. The Clean IO system works on the principle of breaking the world apart into smaller and smaller pieces. So, when we are reasoning about freadi, the only things of concern are the file-status block of the open file, and the integer being returned. By contrast, in Haskell, all IO is hidden inside the IO monad, which "contains" the entire world. So any proof segment dealing with any IO operation, requires us to explicitly reason about pulling out the relevant component from the whole world, and about inserting changed values back in. This happens no matter how small a part of the world is being affected. Also, the Haskell program results in some variables (notably h) having a larger scope than in the Clean program (c.f. f), necessitating the continual presence of enclosing letb-expressions. This leads to file handles still being in scope in the Haskell program after fclose has been applied. In Clean, any attempt to use a stale file handle after it is closed results in a uniqueness typing error.

Another key difference between Clean and Haskell is that the relevant part of the world is explicitly named in the Clean program, whereas it is all hidden in the monad in the Haskell programs. This means that Haskell programs have less 'plumbing' (an oft-cited advantage of monads [Wad92]), but it makes reasoning much more difficult.

The first main conclusion is that the proof for the C-like program is more difficult than for either of the functional programs. The main issue here is that the side-effects mandate the use of the triples of pre-condition, program fragment and post-condition. This is in order to capture any side-effects which might have happened during execution of the fragment, which can be global in scope. In particular, any program statement can alter values associated with entities that may not be explicitly mentioned in the program text, such as the underlying file-system or file status block. It is worth pointing out however, that computing a post-state given a pre-state satisfying the required pre-condition and the program fragment is quite straightforward, being mainly a series of reduction steps, in manner similar to that used in the functional language proofs. The difficulty in this proof may be attributable to the approach taken; a monadic proof may yield better results. Such a proof should be attempted in the future.

The second conclusion is that in the study the Clean proof appeared simpler. We observed a possible reason for the added complexity of the monadic proof which was that state changes are occurring to the world which is not explicitly mentioned in the program text — the world is hidden inside the IO monad abstract data-type. This is why one of the first steps we perform is to replace the do-notation by equivalent bind forms, and thence into let-notation, in order to make the world explicit. Thereafter, the Haskell proof is slightly more complicated because of the continual need to project out a component of the world, modify it and return it, for every invocation of a monadic IO operation. Due to the small sample size it is clear that further work is needed to see if these additional steps can be avoided.

Both conclusions can only be drawn tentatively from this case study until we have examined larger programs and applied some other reasoning methods.

An interesting observation concerns a demarcation between three classes of entities, namely: those denoted by program identifiers; those not mentioned explicitly, but forming part of the program runtime; and the entities making up the external world. The program identifiers and runtime entities only exist while the program is running, whereas the external world entities are persistent, existing before, during and after program execution. The Clean and C semantics allow these to be kept distinct, whereas the Haskell semantics lumps the volatile runtime and persistent external world together in the IO monad. In particular, in Haskell, the runtime initialisation has to be viewed as part of the world state before the program starts execution.

The key advantage that Clean's IO system appears to possess over the others, from a semantic viewpoint, is the ability to decompose the world into separate components, such a the filesystem, or even an individual opened file. This allows a segment of proof dealing with a file access, for instance, to focus solely on the relevant sub-part of the world. The other two paradigms keep requiring us to deal with the whole world, albeit in an often trivial way. This suggests that the Haskell proof might be improved considerably by a collection of laws that in some sense encapsulate the process of project/modify/update.

The Haskell proof is still considerably ahead of the C proof, which suggest that having single-threaded access to mutable entities in the first place gains much more than the precise mechanism employed — monads or uniqueness types. It does raise the interesting idea that monads might be a way of structuring a semantics for imperative languages that would make them easier to reason about.

A criticism that could be levelled at this work is that the (albeit slightly) favourable outcome for Clean is a consequence of our using a IO semantic model that is very Clean-like in nature. Maybe a different result would emerge if we started with an initial IO model based around monads ? However, we find that trying to give a semantics to Clean that incorporates the monadic IO model is very difficult. This arises because Clean allows the world to be split apart, with each part being processed in a single-threaded manner quite independently of the others, until time comes to merge them to form the final world value. A monadic IO approach would require any change in each part to be written back into the single world. At the very least, it seems that the resulting proof complexity would rise up to that of the Haskell program.

Another issue is the concern about how well all this will scale up, both to larger more complex programs, and larger more complex IO models, for instance models that include concurrency. It present, it certainly seems that any proof system that allows the world to be partitioned in order to focus attention on sub-parts, is going to show a better potential for scaling up. However we accept that much more work is required before we can say this for certain. What would be very interesting would be some way to decompose monads into partitions (as monads themselves), with a means of integrating them back together again. This would facilitate scaling up of proofs based on monadic IO.

8   Summary and Future Work

Future work will need to look at more complex programs and properties, as well as more complex IO models. In particular, case studies that look at reasoning about Peyton Jones' "awkward squad" [PJ01] will become very important. A key issue there will be how the kind of operational semantics presented there, in terms of labelled transitions, will affect proofs of the Haskell programs, and how they will be fit in with the Clean approach to similar issues [AW00]. Recent work on verification of temporal or dynamic properties in Clean [H+99a] show a considerable increase in the complexity of the reasoning process.

The IO model must be expanded to cover concurrency so that interaction with the world by processes outside the program can be considered. This will necessarily require error handling to be included in the IO model.

Another key point made there is that the IO monad is very useful in preventing the non-determinism associated with exceptions from contaminating the entire language [PJ01, p41]. As reasoning about non-determinism is a considerable complication, this is a very important aspect which needs serious investigation. The key question is to ask how well Clean can handle this particular member of the awkward squad, given that it does not provide exceptions, but instead relies upon returned error values, that a user is free to ignore.

Finally we note that there exists an interesting hybrid language which has a functional core, but gets non-functional when dealing with aspects of the awkward squad like IO and process forking, namely ERLANG [A+96]. Can the use of a well-designed hybrid language result in programs that are easier to reason with than those belonging to either extreme (i.e. pure functional or fully imperative) ?

We have done a comparative case study concerning the ease of reasoning about IO in three programming paradigms. Despite the highly simplified nature of our case-study, we can see clear distinctions between the three paradigms, including a clear trade-off between lack of 'plumbing' and ease of reasoning in program texts. The results to date suggest that it is worth exploring this area further, and that the results may help to improve the ability to reason about all three paradigms, by suggesting suitable programming styles, and IO models.

In [PJ01, p56], Peyton-Jones expresses concern about the complexity of Haskell, when dealing with the awkward squad, and finishes with

"I would be delighted to find a way to make it simpler and more declarative."

Our work is inspired by this motivation, a desire to see techniques emerge that make it possible to have the simplicity of functional reasoning married with the real world in a natural and straightforward manner.

References

A+96. Joe Armstrong et al. *Concurrent Programming in ERLANG*. Prentice Hall Europe, London, 2nd edition edition, 1996.

AW00. Peter Achten and Martin Wierich. A Tutorial to the Clean Object I/O Library — Version 1.2. Technical report, Dept. of Functional Programming, University of Nijmegen, The Netherlands, February 2000.

Bd87. Richard Bird and Oege de Moor. *Algebra of Programming*. Series in Computer Science. Prentice Hall International, London, 1987.

Bir98. Richard Bird. *Introduction to Functional Programming using Haskell*. Series in Computer Science. Prentice Hall, second edition edition, 1998.

BJLM91. J.-P. Banâtre, S.B. Jones, and D. Le Métayer. *Prospects for Functional Programming in Software Engineering*, volume 1 of *ESPRIT Research Reports, Project 302*. Springer-Verlag, Berlin, 1991.

BS00. Erik Barendsen and Sjaak Smetsers. Uniqueness typing for functional languages with graph rewriting semantics. *Mathematical Structures in Computer Science*, 00:pp1–36, 2000.

BS01. Andrew Butterfield and Glenn Strong. Comparing I/O Proofs in Three Programming Paradigms: a Baseline. Technical Report TCD-CS-2001-31, Dublin University, Computer Science Department, Trinity College, Dublin, August 2001.

Gor94. Andrew D. Gordon. *Functional Programming and Input/ Output*. Distinguished Dissertations in Computer Science. Cambridge University Press, 1994.

H+99a. Zoltan Horvath et al. Proving the temporal properties of the unique world. In *Software Technology, Fenno-Ugric Symposium FUSST'p99 Proceedings*, pages pp113–125, Technical Report CS 104/99, Tallin, 1999.

Hen87. M.C. Henson. *Elements of Functional Languages*. Computer Science Texts. Blackwell Scientific Publications, 1987.

HJ98. C. A. R. Hoare and He Jifeng. *Unifying Theories of Programming*. Series in Computer Science. Prentice Hall International, London, 1998.

Hug00. Arthur Hughes. *Elements of an Operator Calculus*. Ph.D. dissertation, University of Dublin, Trinity College, Department of Computer Science, 2000.

Jon90. Cliff B. Jones. *Systematic Software Development using VDM*. Series in Computer Science. Prentice Hall International, London, 2nd edition, 1990.

KR88. Brian W. Kernighan and Dennis M. Ritchie. *The C Programming Language*. Software Series. Prentice Hall, 2nd edition, 1988.

Mac90. Mícheál Mac an Airchinnigh. *Conceptual Models and Computing*. Ph.D. dissertation, University of Dublin, Trinity College, Department of Computer Science, 1990.

Mor94. Carroll Morgan. *Programming from Specifications*. Series in Computer Science. Prentice-Hall International, London, 2nd. edition, 1994.

PH$^+$99. Simon Peyton Jones, John Hughes, et al. Haskell 98. Technical report, www.haskell.org, 1999. URL: http://www.haskell.org/onlinereport/.

PJ87. S.L. Peyton-Jones. *The Implementation of Functional Programming Languages*. Series in Computer Science. Prentice Hall International, London, 1987.

PJ01. Simon Peyton-Jones. Tackling the awkward squad. Technical report, Microsoft Research, Cambridge, 2001.

PvE98. Rinus Plasmeijer and Marko van Eekelen. Concurrent clean (version 1.3). Technical report, High Level Software Tools B.V. and University of Nijmegen, 1998. URL:

Sch88. David A. Schmidt. *Denotational Semantics*. William C. Brown, Dubuque, Iowa, 1988.

Wad92. Philip Wadler. Monads for functional programming. Lecture Notes for Marktoberdorf Summer School on Program Design Calculi, Springer-Verlag, August 1992.

Proving the Correctness of the STG Machine[*]

Alberto de la Encina and Ricardo Peña

Departamento de Sistemas Informáticos y Programación
Universidad Complutense de Madrid, Spain
{albertoe,ricardo}@sip.ucm.es

Abstract. J. Launchbury gave an operational semantics for lazy evaluation and showed that it is sound and complete w.r.t. a denotational semantics of the language. P. Sestoft then introduced several abstract machines for lazy evaluation and showed that they were sound and complete w.r.t. Launchbury's operational semantics. We go a step forward and show that the *Spineless Tagless G-machine* is complete and (almost) sound w.r.t. one of Sestoft's machines. In the way to this goal we also prove some interesting properties about the operational semantics and about Sestoft's machines which clarify some minor points on garbage collection and on closures' local environments. Unboxed values and primitive operators are excluded from the study.

1 Introduction

One of the most successful abstract machines for executing lazy functional languages is the *Spineless Tagless G-machine* (STG machine) [6] which is at the heart of the *Glasgow Haskell Compiler* (GHC) [7]. The compiler receives a program written in Haskell [8] and, after some steps and intermediate transformations, produces a program in a very simple functional language called the STG language. This is the input for the STG machine. The back-end then generates imperative code emulating the transitions of the machine.

The STG machine has proved to be efficient compared with some other machines for lazy languages such as the G-machine [3] or the TIM (*Three Instructions Machine*) [2]. But until now there was no formal proof of its correctness. A semi-formal one was provided by J. Mountjoy in [5]. There, the author starts from Launchbury's natural semantics for lazy evaluation [4] and transforms it to successive more elaborated semantics. From these semantics he 'derives' a STG-like machine with a single stack. Additionally, he proves that his first semantics is in fact equivalent to Launchbury's. In Section 6 we criticize Mountjoy's work in more detail.

Launchbury's semantics is a good starting point because it has been accepted by many people as the reference for defining the meaning of lazy evaluation. We accept Launchbury's semantics as *the* specification and we continue with the abstract machines developed by Sestoft in [10] which were shown to be sound and complete w.r.t. Launchbury's semantics. The idea is to continue refining

---

[*] Work partially supported by the Spanish-British Acción Integrada HB 1999-0102 and Spanish project TIC 2000-0738.

T. Arts and M. Mohnen (Eds.): IFL 2001, LNCS 2312, pp. 88–104, 2002.
© Springer-Verlag Berlin Heidelberg 2002

one of these machines in order to arrive to the STG. First, to have a common language, we define a language similar to that of STG which can be considered a subset of the language used by Sestoft's machines. Then, we define and prove a *bisimulation* between the Sestoft machine called *Mark-2* and the STG. The bisimulation holds for a single-stack STG machine. The one described in [6] and implemented in the first versions of the GHC compiler had three separate stacks. The recent version of GHC has moved towards a single-stack implementation [9]. Nevertheless, it does not exist yet an operational description for this machine in the sense of the one given in [6]. We show that the three stack machine is *not* sound w.r.t. to the semantics for some ill-typed programs.

Other contributions are: improvements to Sestoft's semantics in order to solve a small problem related to freshness of variables and to take into account garbage collection. Also, a property about Sestoft's machines environments is proved.

The plan of the paper is as follows: After this introduction, in Section 2 Launchbury's semantics is summarized. Then, Sestoft's and our improvements are presented. Section 3 introduces Sestoft's *Mark-2* machine and presents our proposition about its environments. Section 4 defines the STG-like language, the single-stack STG machine and proves the bisimulation with the *Mark-2* machine. Section 5 shows that the three-stack STG machine is complete but not sound w.r.t. the semantics. Finally, Section 6 mentions related work and draws some conclusions. Propositions proofs can be found at [1].

2 Natural Semantics

2.1 Launchbury's Original Proposal

A well-known work from Launchbury [4] defines a big-step operational semantics for lazy evaluation. The only machinery needed is an explicit heap where bindings are kept. A heap is considered to be a finite mapping from variables to expressions, i.e. duplicated bindings to the same variable are disallowed. The language used was a normalized λ-calculus, extended with recursive *let*, (saturated) constructor applications and *case* expressions. To ensure sharing, arguments of applications are forced to be variables. A grammar for this language is given in Figure 1 where the overline notation $\overline{A_i}$ denotes a vector $A_1, \ldots, A_n$ of subscripted entities.

To avoid variable capture, the normalized language has the additional restriction that all bound variables (either lambda, let or case bound) in the initial expression must be distinct. (Weak head) normal forms are either lambda abstractions or constructions. Throughout the paper, the symbol w will be used to denote normal forms. The semantic rules are reproduced in Figure 2. There, a judgement $\Gamma : e \Downarrow \Theta : w$ means that expression e, with free variables bound in heap Γ, reduces to normal form w and produces a final heap Θ. The notation $\hat{w}$ means expression w where all bound variables have been replaced by fresh names. We say that $\Gamma : e \Downarrow \Theta : w$ is a (successful) derivation if it can be proved by using the rules. A derivation can fail to be proved for instance because of entering in a *blackhole*. This would happen in rule *Var* when a reference to variable x appears while reducing expression e and before reaching a normal form.

$$e \rightarrow x \qquad\qquad\qquad \text{-- variable}$$

| $\lambda x.e$ -- lambda abstraction
| $e\ x$ -- application
| **letrec** $\overline{x_i = e_i}$ **in** e -- recursive let
| $C\ \overline{x_i}$ -- constructor application
| **case** e **of** $\overline{C_i\ \overline{x_{ij}} \rightarrow e_i}$ -- case expression

Fig. 1. Launchbury's normalized λ-calculus

$$\Gamma : \lambda x.e \Downarrow \Gamma : \lambda x.e \qquad\qquad\qquad Lam$$

$$\Gamma : C\,\overline{x_i} \Downarrow \Gamma : C\,\overline{x_i} \qquad\qquad\qquad Cons$$

$$\frac{\Gamma : e \Downarrow \Delta : \lambda y.e' \quad \Delta : e'[x/y] \Downarrow \Theta : w}{\Gamma : e\ x \Downarrow \Theta : w} \qquad App$$

$$\frac{\Gamma : e \Downarrow \Delta : w}{\Gamma \cup [x \mapsto e] : x \Downarrow \Delta \cup [x \mapsto w] : \hat{w}} \qquad Var$$

$$\frac{\Gamma \cup [\overline{x_i \mapsto e_i}] : e \Downarrow \Delta : w}{\Gamma : \mathbf{letrec}\ \overline{x_i = e_i}\ \mathbf{in}\ e \Downarrow \Delta : w} \qquad Letrec$$

$$\frac{\Gamma : e \Downarrow \Delta : C_k\,\overline{x_j} \quad \Delta : e_k[\overline{x_j/y_{kj}}] \Downarrow \Theta : w}{\Gamma : \mathbf{case}\ e\ \mathbf{of}\ \overline{C_i\,\overline{y_{ij}} \rightarrow e_i} \Downarrow \Theta : w} \qquad Case$$

Fig. 2. Launchbury's natural semantics

As this is done in a heap Γ not containing a binding for x, no rule can be applied and the derivation cannot be completed. Other forms of failure are those corresponding to ill-typed programs or infinite loops.

The main theorem in [4] is that the operational semantics is sound and complete with respect to a lazy denotational semantics for the language, i.e. if e is a closed expression, then $[\![e]\!]\,\rho_0 = v \neq \bot$ if and only if there exist Θ and w such that $\{\ \} : e \Downarrow \Theta : w$ and $[\![w]\!]\,\rho_\Theta = v$, being ρ_0 the empty environment and ρ_Θ an environment defining the free variables of w and obtained from heap Θ.

2.2 Sestoft's Improvements

Sestoft introduces in [10] two main changes to the operational semantics of Figure 2: (1) to move the renaming of variables from the *Var* rule to the *Letrec* one, and (2) to make in the *Letrec* rule the freshness condition locally checkable by extending judgements with a set A of *variables under evaluation*. The first modification aims at getting the semantics closer to an implementation in terms of abstract machines. In the usual implementations, fresh variables (i.e. pointers) are created when introducing new closures in the heap in the *Letrec* rule. This is also more economical than renaming all bound variables in a normal form. The second modification makes more precise the definition of *freshness*: a variable is fresh in a judgement $\Gamma\ : e \Downarrow_A \Theta : w$ if it does not belong to either *dom* Γ or A, and it is not bound either in *range* Γ or e. The modified rules can be seen in

$$\Gamma : \lambda x.e \Downarrow_A \Gamma : \lambda x.e \qquad\qquad Lam$$

$$\Gamma : C\,\overline{p_i} \Downarrow_A \Gamma : C\,\overline{p_i} \qquad\qquad Cons$$

$$\frac{\Gamma : e \Downarrow_A \Delta : \lambda x.e' \quad \Delta : e'[p/x] \Downarrow_A \Theta : w}{\Gamma : e\,p \Downarrow_A \Theta : w} \qquad App$$

$$\frac{\Gamma : e \Downarrow_{A\cup\{p\}} \Delta : w}{\Gamma \cup [p \mapsto e] : p \Downarrow_A \Delta \cup [p \mapsto w] : w} \qquad Var$$

$$\frac{\Gamma \cup \overline{[p_i \mapsto \hat{e}_i]} : \hat{e} \Downarrow_A \Delta : w}{\Gamma : \textbf{letrec } \overline{x_i = e_i} \textbf{ in } e \Downarrow_A \Delta : w} \; \text{where } \overline{p_i} \text{ fresh} \qquad Letrec$$

$$\frac{\Gamma : e \Downarrow_A \Delta : C_k\,\overline{p_j} \quad \Delta : e_k\overline{[p_j/x_{kj}]} \Downarrow_A \Theta : w}{\Gamma : \textbf{case } e \textbf{ of } \overline{C_i\,\overline{x_{ij}} \to e_i} \Downarrow_A \Theta : w} \qquad Case$$

Fig. 3. Sestoft's natural semantics

Figure 3. In the *Letrec* rule, the notation $\hat{e}$ means the renaming $e\overline{[p_i/x_i]}$ where $\overline{p_i}$ are fresh variables in the judgement $\Gamma : \textbf{letrec } \overline{x_i = e_i} \textbf{ in } e \Downarrow_A \Delta : w$. The difference between the new rules and the ones in Figure 2 is the place where renaming is done. So, the only thing needed to prove the equivalence between the two sets of rules is that there is neither name capture nor duplicated bindings to the same variable.

Proposition 1. *(Sestoft) Let e be a closed expression and $\{\} : e \Downarrow_{\{\}} \Theta : w$ a successful derivation. Then, in no instance of rule App there can be variable capture in $e'[p/x]$, and in no instance of rule Var is p already bound in Δ.*

Moreover, Sestoft proves that, in every derivation tree, there is a clean distinction between free variables and bound variables in expressions appearing in judgements and in heaps. The first ones are always pointers (in Figure 3 and in what follows, they are denoted by p), and they are either bound in the corresponding heap, or they are under evaluation and belong to A. The second ones are program variables belonging to the original expression (in Figure 3 and in what follows, they are denoted by x or y).

Unfortunately, the proof of the theorem was done before introducing **case** expressions and constructors and, when the latter were introduced, the theorem was not redone. With the current *Case* rule the freshness property is not locally checkable anymore. While reducing the discriminant in judgement $\Gamma : e \Downarrow_A \Delta : C_k\,\overline{p_j}$, fresh variables may be created with the same names as bound variables in the alternatives, without violating the freshness condition. Then, in the second part of the premise, name capture may occur in expression $e_k\overline{[p_j/x_{kj}]}$.

In the next section we introduce a modification to the rules in order to keep the freshness locally checkable in presence of **case** expressions.

A problem not addressed by Sestoft is garbage collection. One invariant of the derivation of any expression is that heaps always grow with new bindings, i.e. in every judgement $\Gamma : e \Downarrow_A \Delta : w$, it turns out that $dom\ \Gamma \subseteq dom\ \Delta$. We are interested in having a semantics reflecting that garbage collection may happen at any time without altering the result of the evaluation. To this aim, we develop a set of rules in which all heaps are assumed to contain only live bindings. The rules express the exact points where the garbage collector would be mandatory in order to maintain minimal heaps along the computation. This forces us to maintain new sets during a derivation in order to keep all the roots of live bindings. This extension is also done in the next section.

2.3   A Modified Natural Semantics

To solve the first problem, i.e. having freshness locally checkable, we introduce a multiset C of *continuations* associated to every judgement. The alternatives of a **case** are stored in this multiset during the evaluation of the discriminant. We say then that a variable is fresh in a judgement $\Gamma : e \Downarrow_{AC} \Delta : w$ if it does not belong either to *dom* Γ or to A, and it is not a bound variable either in e, or in *range* Γ, or in any continuation of C.

To provide for garbage collection, we must first decide which are the roots of live closures. Of course, free variables of the current expression belong to the set of roots. By observing the rules, it is clear that the continuations in set C should also provide additional roots. Otherwise, a minimal heap during the derivation of the discriminant might not include bindings for the free variables of the alternatives. Symmetrically, during the derivation of the normal form of function e in rule *App*, we should include the argument p of an application in the set of roots. So, we introduce an additional multiset B in judgements standing for *arguments of pending applications*. A judgement will have the following form: $\Gamma : e \Downarrow_{ABC} \Delta : w$ where the intention is that Γ be minimal w.r.t. e, B and C, and Δ be minimal w.r.t. w, B and C. They are multisets because identical arguments or case alternatives may be stored in them several times and it seems clearer to maintain several copies instead of just one.

As the knowledgeable reader may have already noticed, set A is *not* an additional source of roots. This set represents bindings currently under evaluation or, in more operational terms, *pending updates*. If the only reference to a pending update is that of set A, this means that the value of the corresponding free variable will not be used anymore in the future. So, the variable can be safely deleted from A, and the corresponding update avoided[1]. Moreover, we want to have also *minimal* sets of pending updates in our derivations. This means that the set A associated to the initial expression of a given judgement need not be the same anymore than the set A' associated to the final expression. To take this into account, a last modification of judgements is needed. Their final form is the following one:

$$\Gamma A : e \Downarrow_{BC} \Delta A' : w$$

where Γ and A are minimal w.r.t. e, B and C, and Δ and A' are minimal w.r.t. w, B and C. Its meaning is that expression e reduces to normal form w starting with heap Γ and set A, and ending with heap Δ and set A'.

That heaps and sets of pending updates are minimal is just a property that must be proved. To preserve this property in derivations, garbage collections and

---

[1]   This *trimming* of the set of pending updates is done in the STG machine after each garbage collection. See [6, Section 10.7].

trimming of pending updates must be activated at certain points. The semantic rules exactly clarify which these points are.

Definition 2. *Given a heap Γ, an expression e, a multiset B of variables, and a multiset C of continuations, we define the set of live variables of Γ w.r.t. B, C and e, denoted $live_\Gamma^{BCe}$:*

$$live_\Gamma^{BCe} = \text{fix } (\lambda L \,.\, L \cup fv\ e \cup B \cup fv\ C \cup \bigcup_{p \in L} \{fv\ e' \mid (p \mapsto e') \in \Gamma\})$$

where $fv\ e$ denotes the set of free variables of expression e, $fv\ C$ is the obvious extension to a continuation and *fix* denotes the least fixed-point.

Definition 3. *Given a heap Γ, a set of pending updates A, an expression e, a multiset B of variables, and a multiset C of continuations, we define the live heap of Γ w.r.t. B, C and e, denoted Γ_{gc}^{BCe}, and the subset of live updates of A w.r.t. Γ, B, C and e, denoted $A_{gc}^{\Gamma BCe}$:*

$$\Gamma_{gc}^{BCe} = \{p \mapsto e \mid (p \mapsto e) \in \Gamma \wedge p \in live_\Gamma^{BCe}\}$$
$$A_{gc}^{\Gamma BCe} = A \cap live_\Gamma^{BCe}$$

In a judgement $\Gamma A : e \Downarrow_{BC} \Delta A' : w$, if a minimal heap and update set should be ensured before the derivation starts, we will write $\Gamma_{gc} A_{gc} : e \Downarrow_{BC} \Delta A' : w$, meaning that the initial heap and update set should respectively be Γ_{gc}^{BCe} and $A_{gc}^{\Gamma BCe}$. These gc annotations exactly mark the points in a derivation where a garbage collection or/and a trimming of the update set may be needed.

The new set of rules is shown in Figure 4. Some explanations follow:

Maintaining the correct set of roots. When evaluating the discriminant of a **case** (see rule *Case*), the pending alternatives must be included in set C in order to avoid losing bindings for the free variables of the alternatives. Also, when evaluating the function of an application (see rules *AppA* and *AppB*), the argument must be included in set B in order to avoid losing the binding for it.

Activating garbage collection in the appropriate points. The gc annotation, meaning the trimming of a heap or of an update set, must be written in those points where there may be the danger of dead bindings. These are:

- in rule *AppB*, when the parameter of the function does not appear in the body. There is a danger that the binding for p in Δ becomes dead.
- in rules *VarA* and *VarB*, when the reference to p disappears from the current expression. There may be no other reference to p either in e, B or C.
- in rule *Case*, when a particular alternative is chosen. The discarded alternatives may have free variables that now are dead.

Avoiding unnecessary updates. This is reflected in rule *VarB*. Assuming that the pair (Δ, A') is minimal w.r.t. w, B and C, and knowing that $p \notin A'$, then the update for variable p may be safely discarded (compare with rule *VarA*).

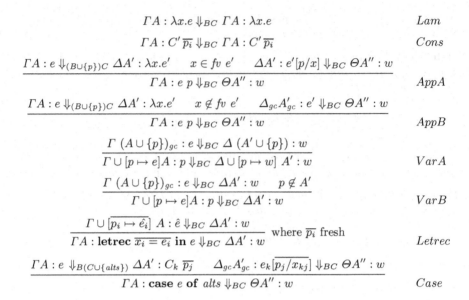

$$\Gamma A : \lambda x.e \Downarrow_{BC} \Gamma A : \lambda x.e \qquad\qquad Lam$$

$$\Gamma A : C' \, \overline{p_i} \Downarrow_{BC} \Gamma A : C' \overline{p_i} \qquad\qquad Cons$$

$$\frac{\Gamma A : e \Downarrow_{(B \cup \{p\})C} \Delta A' : \lambda x.e' \quad x \in fv \ e' \quad \Delta A' : e'[p/x] \Downarrow_{BC} \Theta A'' : w}{\Gamma A : e \ p \Downarrow_{BC} \Theta A'' : w} \qquad AppA$$

$$\frac{\Gamma A : e \Downarrow_{(B \cup \{p\})C} \Delta A' : \lambda x.e' \quad x \notin fv \ e' \quad \Delta_{gc} A'_{gc} : e' \Downarrow_{BC} \Theta A'' : w}{\Gamma A : e \ p \Downarrow_{BC} \Theta A'' : w} \qquad AppB$$

$$\frac{\Gamma \ (A \cup \{p\})_{gc} : e \Downarrow_{BC} \Delta \ (A' \cup \{p\}) : w}{\Gamma \cup [p \mapsto e] A : p \Downarrow_{BC} \Delta \cup [p \mapsto w] \ A' : w} \qquad VarA$$

$$\frac{\Gamma \ (A \cup \{p\})_{gc} : e \Downarrow_{BC} \Delta A' : w \quad p \notin A'}{\Gamma \cup [p \mapsto e] A : p \Downarrow_{BC} \Delta A' : w} \qquad VarB$$

$$\frac{\Gamma \cup \overline{[p_i \mapsto \hat{e_i}]} \ A : \hat{e} \Downarrow_{BC} \Delta A' : w}{\Gamma A : \mathbf{letrec} \ \overline{x_i = e_i} \ \text{in} \ e \Downarrow_{BC} \Delta A' : w} \ \text{where} \ \overline{p_i} \ \text{fresh} \qquad Letrec$$

$$\frac{\Gamma A : e \Downarrow_{B(C \cup \{alts\})} \Delta A' : C_k \, \overline{p_j} \quad \Delta_{gc} A'_{gc} : e_k[\overline{p_j/x_{kj}}] \Downarrow_{BC} \Theta A'' : w}{\Gamma A : \mathbf{case} \ e \ \text{of} \ alts \Downarrow_{BC} \Theta A'' : w} \qquad Case$$

Fig. 4. A natural semantics with minimal heaps and minimal update sets

Assuming no dead code in *letrec*. Notice in the antecedent of rule *Letrec* that no garbage collection is launched. So, we are assuming that all the new bindings are live. This is not true if there exists dead code in the **letrec** expression. It is easy for a compiler to eliminate unreachable bindings in a **letrec**. In what follows we will assume that dead code has been eliminated in our programs.

New definition of freshness. In the consequent of rule *Letrec* a set $\overline{p_i}$ of fresh variables is created. A variable is *fresh* in judgement $\Gamma A : e \Downarrow_{BC} \Delta A' : w$ if it does not belong to either *dom* Γ or A, and it is not bound either in *range* Γ, e or C.

We will see now that the properties desired for our semantics in fact hold.

Definition 4. *Given a judgement* $\Gamma A : e \Downarrow_{BC} \Delta A' : w$, *we say that the configuration* $\Gamma : e$ *is ABC-good, if*

1. $A \cap dom \ \Gamma = \emptyset$
2. $live_{\Gamma}^{BCe} = A \cup dom \ \Gamma$
3. $(bv \ \Gamma \cup bv \ e \cup bv \ C) \cap (A \cup dom \ \Gamma) = \emptyset$

where $bv \ e$ denotes the bound variables of expression e, $bv \ \Gamma$ its extension to all expressions in *range* Γ, and $bv \ C$ its extension to a continuation.

The first property has a similar counterpart in Sestoft's semantics and it asserts that variables under evaluation are not at the same time defined in the heap. The second one asserts that every free variable is either defined in the heap or is under evaluation and also that the pair (Γ, A) is minimal w.r.t. B, C and e. The third one asserts that free variables are different from bound ones.

Definition 5. *A judgement* $\Gamma A : e \Downarrow_{BC} \Delta A' : w$ *is* promising *if the configuration* $\Gamma : e$ *is ABC-good.*

This definition ensures that the starting point of a derivation already meets the requirements we want for the whole derivation. The following proposition and corollary establish that the desired properties in fact hold.

Proposition 6. *Let* $\Gamma A : e \Downarrow_{BC} \Delta A' : w$ *be a derivation using the rules of the semantics. If it is a promising judgement, then*

1. *The configuration* $\Delta : w$ *is* $A'BC$-*good*
2. $A' \subseteq A$
3. *Every judgement in the derivation is a promising one.*

Corollary 7. *Let* e *be a closed expression and* $\Gamma\{\} : e \Downarrow_{\{\}\{\}} \Delta A : w$ *be a derivation. Then,*

1. *In no instance of rules AppA and Case there can be variable capture in substitutions of the form* $e[p/x]$.
2. *In no instance of rule VarA is* p *already bound in* Δ.

The differences between our semantics and Sestoft's are two:

1. Sestoft's rules *App* and *Var* have been split into two in our semantics. In the first case, the distinction is due to the desire of not launching garbage collection when it is not needed, but in fact both rules could be combined in the following single one:

$$\frac{\Gamma A : e \Downarrow_{(B\cup\{p\})C} \Delta A' : \lambda x.e' \quad \Delta_{gc}A'_{gc} : e'[p/x] \Downarrow_{BC} \Theta A'' : w}{\Gamma A : e\,p \Downarrow_{BC} \Theta A'' : w}$$

   In the second case, our rule *VarB* does not add to the heap a binding $[p \mapsto w]$ that is known to be dead.
2. Our heaps and update sets are minimal in the corresponding judgements.

Otherwise, the semantic rules are the same. Once we have proved that free variables in judgements are either defined in the heap, or they belong to the pending updates set, both semantics produce exactly the same derivations.

3   Sestoft's Machine Mark-2

After revising Launchbury's semantics, Sestoft introduces in [10] several abstract machines in sequence, respectively called *Mark-1*, *Mark-2* and *Mark-3*. The one we will use for deriving an STG-like machine is *Mark-2*. There, a configuration consists of a heap Γ, a control expression e possibly having free variables, an environment E mapping free variables to pointers in the heap, and a stack S. The heap Γ is a function from pointers to closures, each one (e, E) consisting of an expression e and an environment E binding its free variables to pointers. The stack contains three kinds of objects: (1) arguments of pending applications,

Heap	Control	Environment	Stack	rule
Γ	$(e\ x)$	$E \cup [x \mapsto p]$	S	app1
$\Longrightarrow \Gamma$	e	$E \cup [x \mapsto p]$	$p : S$	
Γ	$\lambda y.e$	E	$p : S$	app2
$\Longrightarrow \Gamma$	e	$E \cup [y \mapsto p]$	S	
$\Gamma \cup [p \mapsto (e', E')]$	x	$E \cup [x \mapsto p]$	S	var1
$\Longrightarrow \Gamma$	e'	E'	$\#p : S$	
Γ	$\lambda y.e$	E	$\#p : S$	var2
$\Longrightarrow \Gamma \cup [p \mapsto (\lambda y.e, E)]$	$\lambda y.e$	E	S	
Γ	**letrec** $\{\overline{x_i = e_i}\}$ **in** e E		S	letrec $(*)$
$\Longrightarrow \Gamma \cup [\overline{p_i \mapsto (e_i, E')}]$	e	E'	S	
Γ	**case** e **of** $alts$	E	S	case1
$\Longrightarrow \Gamma$	e	E	$(alts, E) : S$	
Γ	$C_k\ \overline{x_i}$	$E \cup [\overline{x_i \mapsto p_i}]$	$(alts, E') : S$ case2 $(**)$	
$\Longrightarrow \Gamma$	e_k	$E' \cup [\overline{y_{ki} \mapsto p_i}]$	S	
Γ	$C_k\ \overline{x_i}$	E	$\#p : S$	var3
$\Longrightarrow \Gamma \cup [p \mapsto (C_k\ \overline{x_i}, E)]$	$C_k\ \overline{x_i}$	E	S	

$(*)$ $\overline{p_i}$ are distinct and fresh w.r.t. Γ, **letrec** $\{\overline{x_i = e_i}\}$ **in** e, and S. $E' = E \cup [\overline{x_i \mapsto p_i}]$
$(**)$ Expression e_k corresponds to alternative $C_k\ \overline{y_{ki}} \to e_k$ in $alts$

Fig. 5. Abstract machine *Mark-2*

represented by pointers; (2) continuations of pending pattern matchings, each one consisting of a pair $(alts, E)$ where $alts$ is a vector of **case** alternatives and E is an environment binding its free variables; and (3) update markers of the form $\#p$, where p is a pointer.

The reader may have already recognized that stack S represents in fact the union of sets B, C and A we introduced in the revised semantics of Section 2.3. The main difference now is that these entities form a list instead of a set or a multiset, and that they appear ordered from more recent to older ones. In Figure 5 the operational rules of *Mark-2* machine are shown.

We have followed Sestoft's convention that program variables are denoted by x or y, and pointers by p. The machine never makes explicit substitutions of pointers for program (free) variables as the semantics does. Instead, it maintains environments mapping program variables to pointers. Environments can be seen as delayed substitutions. To maintain them is much more efficient than doing substitutions. If e is a closed expression, the initial configuration is $(\{\}, e, \{\}, [\,])$. The machine stops when no rule can be applied. If the final configuration has the form $(\Gamma, w, E, [\,])$, then w has been successfully derived from e and we write $(\{\}, e, \{\}, [\,]) \Rightarrow^* (\Gamma, w, E, [\,])$.

The main theorem proved by Sestoft, is that successful derivations of the machine are exactly the same as those of the semantics.

Proposition 8. *(Sestoft) For any closed expression e, then*

$$(\{\}, e, \{\}, [\,]) \Rightarrow^* (\Gamma, w, E, [\,]) \text{ if and only if } \{\}\ e : \Downarrow_{\{\}} \Gamma : w$$

It is worth to note that the soundness and completeness of machine *Mark-2* w.r.t. the operational semantics (by transitivity, w.r.t. the denotational semantics), does not rely on programs being well typed. All ill-typed programs in a certain type system will be treated in the same way by both the semantics and the machine. For instance, a case with a lambda in the discriminant will make both the semantics and the machine to get blocked and not to reach a normal form.

3.1 Some Properties of Environments

Mark-2 environments have a complex evolution: they grow with lambda applications, pattern matching and **letrec** execution; they are stored either in closures or in the stack in some transitions, and they are retrieved from there in some other transitions. It is natural to wonder about how much can they grow.

Definition 9. *A closure* (e, E), *is consistent if*

1. $fv\ e \cap bv\ e = \emptyset$ *and all variables in* $bv\ e$ *are distinct.*
2. $fv\ e \subseteq dom\ E$.
3. $bv\ e \cap dom\ E = \emptyset$

This definition can be easily extended to a continuation of the form $(alts, E)$ and to a heap Γ consisting of a set of closures.

Definition 10. *A configuration* (Γ, e, E, S) *of machine Mark-2 is consistent if*

1. Γ *is consistent.*
2. *The pair* (e, E) *is consistent.*
3. *All continuations* $(alts, E) \in S$ *are consistent.*

These definitions only take care of program variables being well defined in environments. That pointers are well defined in the heap (or they belong to stack S as update markers) was already proved by Sestoft for all his machines.

Proposition 11. *Let* e *be a closed expression in which all bound variables are distinct, and* $(\{\}, e, \{\}, [\,]) \Rightarrow^* (\Gamma, e', E, S)$ *any (possibly partial) derivation of machine Mark-2. Then,*

1. (Γ, e', E, S) *is consistent.*
2. E *exactly binds all variables in scope in expression* e'.
3. *In any closure* $(e_i, E_i) \in \Gamma$, E_i *exactly binds all variables in scope in* e_i.
4. *In any pair* $(alts, E) \in S$, E *exactly binds all variables in scope in alts.*

4 The Abstract Machine STG-1S

4.1 The Common Language

In order to get closer to the STG machine, firstly we define a common λ-calculus for both machines, *Mark-2* and STG. This is presented in Figure 6 and we call it FUN. It is equivalent to the STG language (STGL) but expressed in a more traditional λ-calculus syntax. The differences with STGL are:

- In FUN there are no unboxed values, primitive operators or primitive **case** expressions. These have been excluded from our study.

$$
\begin{aligned}
e \quad &\rightarrow x \ \overline{x_i}^n \qquad\qquad\quad \text{-- } n \geq 0, \text{ application/variable} \\
&\mid \textbf{letrec } \overline{bind_i} \textbf{ in } e \text{ -- recursive let} \\
&\mid C \ \overline{x_i} \qquad\qquad\quad \text{-- constructor application} \\
&\mid \textbf{case } e \textbf{ of } \overline{alt_i} \mid^t \text{ -- case expression} \\
bind \quad &\rightarrow x = \mathit{lf} \mid^t \\
\mathit{lf} \quad &\rightarrow \lambda \ \overline{x_i}^n.e \qquad\qquad \text{-- } n \geq 0, \text{ lambda form} \\
alt \quad &\rightarrow C \ \overline{x_j} \rightarrow e
\end{aligned}
$$

Fig. 6. Definition of FUN

- In FUN the default alternative in **case** is missing. This could be added without effort.
- In STGL there is a flag $\backslash\pi$ in lambda forms to indicate that some updates can be safely avoided. This is an efficiency issue. Nevertheless, we modify the *Mark-2* to suppress updates in the obvious cases of bindings to normal forms.
- In STGL there is a non-recursive **let**. This can obviously be simulated by FUN's **letrec**.
- In STGL a program is a list of bindings with a distinguished variable *main* where evaluation starts. This can be simulated by **letrec** $\overline{bind_i}$ **in** *main*.

Compared to the original *Mark-2* λ-calculus (see Figure 1), it is clear that FUN is just a subset of it, having the following restrictions: that lambda abstractions may only appear in bindings and that applications have the form $x \ \overline{x_i}^n$ understood by *Mark-2* as $(\ldots (x \ x_1) \ldots) \ x_n$.

The notation $\lambda \ \overline{x_i}^n.e$ is an abbreviation of $\lambda x_n. \cdots .\lambda x_1.e$, where the arguments have been numbered downwards for convenience. In this way, $\lambda \ \overline{x_i}^{n-1}.e$ means $\lambda x_{n-1}. \cdots .\lambda x_1.e$ and $x \ \overline{x_i}^{n-1}$ means $x \ x_1 \ \ldots \ x_{n-1}$. When $n = 0$ we will simply write e instead of $\lambda \ \overline{x_i}^n.e$ and x instead of $x \ \overline{x_i}^n$.

A last feature added to FUN is *trimmers*. The notation $\mathit{lf} \mid^t$ means that a lambda form is annotated at compile time with the set t of its free variables. This set t was called a trimmer in [10]. It will be used when constructing a closure in the heap for the lambda form. The environment stored in the closure will only bind the variables contained in the trimmer. This implies a small penalty in terms of execution time but a lot of space saving. Analogously, $\overline{alt_i} \mid^t$ means the annotation of a set of **case** alternatives with the trimmer t of its free variables. When $\overline{alt_i}$ is pushed into the stack, its associated environment will be trimmed according to t. Both optimizations are done in the STG machine, even though the second one is not reflected in the rules given in [6].

4.2　Mark-2 Machine for Language FUN

In Figure 7, the transition rules of *Mark-2* for language FUN are shown. Let us note that the control expression is in general a lambda form lf. In particular, it can also be an expression e, if $\mathit{lf} = \lambda \overline{x_i}^0.e$. Also, all occurrences of superscripts n are assumed to be $n > 0$. Note that, this is not a different machine, but just the same machine *Mark-2* executed with a restricted input language. Additionally, there are some optimizations which do not essentially affect the original behavior:

Heap	Control	Environment	Stack	Last	rule
Γ	$x\ \overline{x_i}^n$	$E \cup [x_n \mapsto p]$	S	1	app1
$\Longrightarrow \Gamma$	$x\ \overline{x_i}^{n-1}$	$E \cup [x_n \mapsto p]$	$p : S$	app1	
Γ	$\lambda \overline{x_i}^n.e$	E	$p : S$	1	app2
$\Longrightarrow \Gamma$	$\lambda \overline{x_i}^{n-1}.e$	$E \cup [x_n \mapsto p]$	S	app2	
$\Gamma \cup [p \mapsto (\lambda \overline{x_i}^n.e', E')]$	x	$E \cup [x \mapsto p]$	S	1	var1a
$\Longrightarrow \Gamma \cup [p \mapsto (\lambda \overline{x_i}^n.e', E')]$	$\lambda \overline{x_i}^n.e'$	E'	S	var1a	
$\Gamma \cup [p \mapsto (C\ \overline{x_i}, E')]$	x	$E \cup [x \mapsto p]$	S	1	var1b
$\Longrightarrow \Gamma \cup [p \mapsto (C\ \overline{x_i}, E')]$	$C\ \overline{x_i}$	E'	S	var1b	
$\Gamma \cup [p \mapsto (e', E')]$	x	$E \cup [x \mapsto p]$	S	1	var1c $(*)$
$\Longrightarrow \Gamma$	e'	E'	$\#p : S$	var1c	
Γ	$\lambda \overline{x_i}^n.e$	E	$\#p : S$	1	var2
$\Longrightarrow \Gamma \cup [p \mapsto (\lambda \overline{x_i}^n.e, E)]$	$\lambda \overline{x_i}^n.e$	E	S	var2	
Γ	$\mathbf{letrec}\ \overline{x_i = lf_i}\ {|}^{t_i}\ \mathbf{in}\ e$	E	S	1	letrec $(**)$
$\Longrightarrow \Gamma \cup [\overline{p_i \mapsto (lf_i, E'}\ {|}^{t_i})]$	e	E'	S	letrec	
Γ	$\mathbf{case}\ e\ \mathbf{of}\ alts\ {|}^t$	E	S	1	case1
$\Longrightarrow \Gamma$	e	E	$(alts, E\ {|}^t) : S$	case1	
Γ	$C_k\ \overline{x_i}$	$E \cup [\overline{x_i \mapsto p_i}]$	$(alts, E') : S$	1	case2 $(***)$
$\Longrightarrow \Gamma$	e_k	$E' \cup [\overline{y_{ki} \mapsto p_i}]$	S	case2	
Γ	$C_k\ \overline{x_i}$	E	$\#p : S$	1	var3
$\Longrightarrow \Gamma \cup [p \mapsto (C_k\ \overline{x_i}, E\ {|}^{\{\overline{x_i}\}})]$	$C_k\ \overline{x_i}$	E	S	var3	

$(*)$ $e' \neq C\ \overline{x_i}$ and $e' \neq \lambda \overline{x_i}^n.e$.

$(**)$ Variables $\overline{p_i}$ are distinct and fresh w.r.t. Γ, $\mathbf{letrec}\ \overline{x_i = lf_i}\ {|}^{t_i}\ \mathbf{in}\ e$, and S, $E' = E \cup [\overline{x_i \mapsto p_i}]$

$(***)$ Expression e_k corresponds to alternative $C_k\ \overline{y_{ki}} \rightarrow e_k$ in $alts$

Fig. 7. Abstract machine *Mark-2* for FUN

- Original rule *var1* has been split into three: the one corresponding to the original *var1* is now called *var1c*; the two other rules are just special cases in which the expression referenced by pointer p is a normal form. The original *Mark-2* machine will execute in sequence either rule *var1* followed by rule *var2*, or rule *var1* followed by rule *var3*. These sequences have been respectively subsumed in the new rules *var1a* and *var1b*.
- Trimmer sets have been added to lambda forms and to continuations. Environments are trimmed to the set of free variables when new closures are created in the heap in rules *letrec* and *var3*, and also when continuations are stored in the stack in rule *case1*. This modification only affects to the set of live closures in the heap which now is smaller. Otherwise, the machine behavior is the same.

In Figure 7, a new column *Last* has been added recording the last rule executed by the machine. This field is important to define *stable* configurations, which will be used to compare the evolution of *Mark-2* and STG-1S (see Section 4.3).

Definition 12. *A configuration* (Γ, lf, E, S, l) *of machine Mark-2 is* stable *if one of these two conditions hold:*

1. $lf = e \wedge l \notin \{app1, var3\}$, *or*
2. $S = [\,] \wedge ((lf = \lambda \overline{x_i}^n.e \wedge n > 0) \vee lf = C\ \overline{x_i})$

In the STG machine, lambda abstractions never appear in the control expression, so it seems natural to exclude lambda abstractions from stable configurations.

If the last rule executed is *app1*, then *Mark-2* is still pushing arguments in the stack and it has not yet evaluated the variable x corresponding to the function to be applied. In the STG all these intermediate states do not exist. If the last rule applied is *var3*, then the STG is probably still doing updates and, in any case, pattern matching has not been done yet. As we want to compare configurations in which a FUN expression appears in the control, all these states must be regarded as 'internal'. The second possibility is just a termination state.

Definition 13. *Let us assume that m and m' are stable configurations of Mark-2 machine, and $m \Rightarrow^+ m'$, (i.e. there must be at least one transition) and there is no other stable configuration between m and m'. We will say that m evolves to m' and will denote it by $m \Rightarrow_s^+ m'$.*

4.3   The Machine STG-1S

In this section we define an abstract machine very close to the STG [6] and show that it is sound and complete w.r.t. *Mark-2* of Figure 7. We call it STG-1S because the main difference with the actual STG is that it has one stack instead of three. The single stack of STG-1S, contains the three usual kind of objects: arguments of applications, continuations and update markers. Being faithful to STGL, the control expression of STG-1S may have three different forms:

- *Eval e E*, where e is a FUN expression (we recall that this excludes lambda forms) and E is an environment mapping e's free variables to heap pointers.
- *Enter p*, where p is a heap pointer. Notice that there is no environment.
- *ReturnCon C $\overline{p_i}$*, where C is a data constructor and $\overline{p_i}$ are its arguments given as a vector of heap pointers. Also, there is no environment here.

We will call each of these expressions an *instruction*, and use the symbol i to denote them. In order to better compare it with the *Mark-2* machine, we will consider a configuration of the STG-1S to be a 4-tuple (Γ, i, E, S), where Γ is a heap mapping pointers to closures, i is the control instruction, E is the environment associated to instruction i in case the instruction is of the form *Eval e*, and the empty environment $\{\}$ otherwise, and S is the stack. In Figure 8, the transition rules of STG-1S are shown.

We have numbered the rules with the same numbers used in [6] for easy reference. As there is no explicit flag $\backslash\pi$ in FUN lambda forms in order to avoid unnecessary updates, rules 2 and 2' reflect that no update frame is pushed in the stack when explicit normal forms in the heap are referenced. Rule 2' does not appear in [6], but it is implicit in rule 2.

Now we proceed with the comparison. As in *Mark-2*, we first define *stable* configurations in STG-1S. A stable configuration corresponds either to the evaluation of a FUN expression or to a termination state.

Definition 14. *A configuration $s = (\Gamma, i, E, S)$ of machine STG-1S is stable if*

1. $i = $ *Eval e for some e, or*
2. $s = (\Gamma, ReturnCon\ C\ \overline{p_i}, \{\}, [\,])$, *or*
3. $s = (\Gamma \cup [p \mapsto (\lambda\overline{x_i}^n.e, E')], Enter\ p, \{\}, [p_1, \ldots, p_k]) \wedge n > k \geq 0$.

Heap	Control	Environment	S	rule
Γ	$Eval\ (x\ \overline{x_i}^n)$	$E \cup [x \mapsto p, \overline{x_i \mapsto p_i}]$	S	1
$\Longrightarrow \Gamma$	$Enter\ p$	$\{\}$	$\overline{p_i} : S$	
$\Gamma \cup [p \mapsto (\lambda\overline{x_i}^n.e, E)]$	$Enter\ p$	$\{\}$	$\overline{p_i}^n : S$	2
$\Longrightarrow \Gamma \cup [p \mapsto (\lambda\overline{x_i}^n.e, E)]$	$Eval\ e$	$E \cup [\overline{x_i \mapsto p_i}]$	S	
$\Gamma \cup [p \mapsto (C\ \overline{x_i}, E)]$	$Enter\ p$	$\{\}$	S	2'
$\Longrightarrow \Gamma \cup [p \mapsto (C\ \overline{x_i}, E)]$	$Eval\ (C\ \overline{x_i})$	E	S	
Γ	$Eval\ (\textbf{letrec}\ \{\overline{x_i = lf_i\ |^{t_i}}\}\ \textbf{in}\ e)$	E	S	3 [1]
$\Longrightarrow \Gamma \cup [\overline{p_i \mapsto (lf_i, E'\ |^{t_i})}]$	$Eval\ e$	E'	S	
Γ	$Eval\ (\textbf{case}\ e\ \textbf{of}\ alts\ |^t)$	E	S	4
$\Longrightarrow \Gamma$	$Eval\ e$	E	$(alts, E\ |^t) : S$	
Γ	$Eval\ (C\ \overline{x_i})$	$E \cup [\overline{x_i \mapsto p_i}]$	S	5
$\Longrightarrow \Gamma$	$ReturnCon\ C\ \overline{p_i}$	$\{\}$	S	
Γ	$ReturnCon\ C_k\ \overline{p_i}$	$\{\}$	$(alts, E) : S$	6 [2]
$\Longrightarrow \Gamma$	$Eval\ e_k$	$E \cup [\overline{y_{ki} \mapsto p_i}]$	S	
$\Gamma \cup [p \mapsto (e, E)]$	$Enter\ p$	$\{\}$	S	15 [3]
$\Longrightarrow \Gamma$	$Eval\ e$	E	$\#p : S$	
Γ	$ReturnCon\ C\ \overline{p_i}$	$\{\}$	$\#p : S$	16 [4]
$\Longrightarrow \Gamma \cup [p \mapsto (C\ \overline{x_i}, [\overline{x_i \mapsto p_i}])]$	$ReturnCon\ C\ \overline{p_i}$	$\{\}$	S	
$\Gamma \cup [p \mapsto (\lambda^n\overline{x_i}.e, E)]$	$Enter\ p$	$\{\}$	$\overline{p_i}^k : \#p' : S$	17 [5]
$\Longrightarrow \Gamma'$	$Enter\ p$	$\{\}$	$\overline{p_i}^k : S$	

[1] Variables $\overline{p_i}$ are distinct and fresh w.r.t. Γ, **letrec** $\overline{x_i = lf_i\ |^{t_i}}$ in e, and S, $E' = E \cup [\overline{x_i \mapsto p_i}]$
[2] Expression e_k corresponds to alternative $C_k\ \overline{y_{ki}} \to e_k$ in $alts$
[3] Expression $e \neq C\ \overline{x_i}$ and $e \neq \lambda\overline{x_i}^n.e'$
[4] In rule 16, $\overline{x_i}$ are arbitrary distinct variables.
[5] $k < n$ and $\Gamma' = \Gamma \cup [p \mapsto (\lambda^n\overline{x_i}.e, E), p' \mapsto (\lambda^{n-k}\overline{x_i}.e, E \cup [\overline{x_i \mapsto p_i}^k])]$

Fig. 8. Abstract machine $STG\text{-}1S$

Configurations 2 and 3 correspond to termination states. Notice in 3 that the STG-1S may successfully stop with a non-empty stack. This would happen when the initial expression evaluates to a lambda abstraction. As in *Mark-2* machine, we will use $s \Rightarrow_s^+ s'$ to denote the evolution between two stable configurations in STG-1S with no intermediate stable ones, and say that s *evolves* to s'. The notion of *consistent* configuration for the STG-1S machine is the same given in Definition 10 for machine *Mark-2*.

We will now compare two evolutions, one in each machine starting from equivalent states, and show that they exactly pass through the same number of stable configurations and that the corresponding configurations are equivalent. This amounts to saying that there exists a *bisimulation* between the machines. To simplify to notion of configuration equivalence, we will assume that both machines use exactly the same fresh name generator in rule *letrec*. So, if the generator is given the same inputs (i.e. the same control expression, heap and stack), it will generate the same set of fresh variables.

Definition 15. *A configuration* $m = (\Gamma, lf, E, S, l)$ *in a stable state of machine Mark-2 and a configuration* $s = (\Gamma', i, E', S')$ *in a stable state of machine STG-1S are said to be* equivalent, *written* $m \equiv s$, *if*

- $\Gamma = \Gamma'$, *and*
- *one of the following possibilities holds:*

1. $i = Eval\ e \wedge \mathit{lf} = e \wedge E = E' \wedge S = S'$
2. $i = ReturnCon\ C\ \overline{p_i} \wedge \mathit{lf} = C\ \overline{x_i} \wedge \overline{p_i} = E\ \overline{x_i} \wedge S = S' = [\,]$
3. $i = Enter\ p \wedge \Gamma'\ p = (\lambda\overline{x_i}^{n}.e, E'') \wedge S' = [p_1, \ldots, p_k] \wedge n > k \geq 0 \wedge \mathit{lf} = \lambda\overline{x_i}^{n-k}.e \wedge E\ [x_n, \ldots, x_{n-k+1}] = [p_1, \ldots, p_k] \wedge S = [\,]$

The following proposition and corollary establish that STG-1S and *Mark-2* machines bisimulate each other. By transitivity this shows that STG-1S is sound and complete w.r.t. Launchbury's natural semantics.

Proposition 16. *Given two stable and consistent configurations m and s in respectively Mark-2 and STG-1S machines such that $m \equiv s$,*

1. *If $m \Rightarrow_s^+ m'$, then there exists a stable and consistent configuration s' such that $s \Rightarrow_s^+ s'$ and $m' \equiv s'$.*
2. *If $s \Rightarrow_s^+ s'$, then there exists a stable and consistent configuration m' such that $m \Rightarrow_s^+ m'$ and $m' \equiv s'$.*

Corollary 17. *If e is a closed FUN expression, then $(\{\}, e, \{\}, [\,], \perp) \Rightarrow^* m_f$ in Mark-2 machine with $m_f = (\Delta, w, E, [\,])$ if and only if there exists a stable configuration s_f such that $(\{\}, Eval\ e, \{\}, [\,]) \Rightarrow^* s_f$ in STG-1S and $m_f \equiv s_f$.*

5   The Abstract Machine STG

It has three stacks: the *argument* stack as containing arguments for pending applications; the *return* stack rs containing pairs $(alts, E)$; and the *update* stack us containing update frames. An update frame is a triple (as, rs, p) consisting of an argument stack, a return stack and a pointer p to the closure to be updated. We do not show the STG rules as they can be easily derived from those of STG-1S. A configuration will be a 6-tuple $(\Gamma, i, E, as, rs, us)$.

The two differences with the STG-1S machine of previous section are:

- Pushing and popping is done in the appropriate stack according to the rule.
- Instead of pushing update markers, the STG machine pushes update frames and leaves empty argument and return stacks in the configuration. When a normal form is reached with empty stacks, or in the case of a lambda with less actual arguments than formal ones, an update is triggered.

Apparently, these differences are not essential and one may think that the behaviours of both machines are the same. This is not the case as we will see in a moment. The splitting of the single stack into three has the unfortunate consequence of losing the temporal order of events between stacks as and rs. Then, a continuation pushed into rs *before* an argument is pushed into as can be retrieved also *before* the argument is retrieved from as instead of *after*, as it would be the case in the STG-1S machine. Consider the following ill-typed program:

$$e = \mathbf{letrec} \quad y_1 = Nil$$
$$id = \lambda x.x$$
$$\mathbf{in\ case}\ y_1\ y_1\ \mathbf{of}$$
$$Nil \rightarrow id$$

which has no semantics. The STG machine reduces it as follows:

$$(\{\}, e, \{\}, [], [], [])$$
$$\Rightarrow (\Gamma_1, Eval\ (\textbf{case}\ y_1\ y_1\ \textbf{of}\ Nil \rightarrow id), E_1, [], [], [])$$
$$\Rightarrow (\Gamma_1, Eval\ (y_1\ y_1), E_1, [], [(Nil \rightarrow id, E_1)], [])$$
$$\Rightarrow (\Gamma_1, Enter\ p_1, \{\}, [p_1], [(Nil \rightarrow id, E_1)], [])$$
$$\Rightarrow (\Gamma_1, Eval\ Nil, \{\}, [p_1], [(Nil \rightarrow id, E_1)], [])$$
$$\Rightarrow (\Gamma_1, ReturnCon\ Nil\ \{\}, [p_1], [(Nil \rightarrow id, E_1)], [])$$
$$\Rightarrow (\Gamma_1, Eval\ id, E_1, [p_1], [], [])$$
$$\Rightarrow (\Gamma_1, Enter\ p_2, \{\}, [p_1], [], [])$$
$$\Rightarrow (\Gamma_1, Eval\ x, [x \mapsto p_1], [], [], [])$$
$$\Rightarrow (\Gamma_1, Eval\ Nil, \{\}, [], [], [])$$
$$\Rightarrow (\Gamma_1, ReturnCon\ Nil\ \{\}, [], [], [])$$

where $\Gamma_1 = [p_1 \mapsto (Nil, \{\}), p_2 \mapsto (\lambda x.x, \{\})]$ and $E_1 = [y_1 \mapsto p_1, id \mapsto p_2]$.

So, the soundness of the STG machine with three stacks relies on programs being well-typed. This was not the case with the STG-1S machine: if a program is ill-typed, both Launchbury's semantics and STG-1S will be unable to derive a normal form for it.

However, the STG is complete in the sense that every successful derivation done by the STG-1S can obviously be done by the STG. For every configuration of the STG-1S we can exactly compute a single equivalent configuration in the STG machine. The opposite is not true, i.e. given the three stacks as, rs and us of STG, many different stacks for the STG-1S can be constructed by interleaving the contents of the corresponding sections of stacks as and rs.

6   Related Work and Conclusions

There are some differences between this work and that of Mountjoy [5]:

1. Mountjoy refines Launchbury's semantics into two more elaborated ones. The first one excludes lambda abstractions from the control expressions and considers variables pointing to lambda abstractions as normal forms. The second one generalizes applications to n arguments at once.
2. From these semantics he 'derives' two STG-like abstract machines, the latter being very close to our STG-1S machine.

The first semantics is proven equivalent to Launchbury's (Proposition 4, [5]) but there is no such proof for the second one. In fact, there are some mistakes in this semantics. For instance, rule App_M (Figure 5, [5]) contains a λ-abstraction in the control expression and this was previously forbidden. Normal forms in this setting should be variables pointing to a lambda or a constructor. So that the semantics get blocked at this point and no normal form can be reached. The abstract machines are derived from the semantics but not formally proven sound and complete w.r.t. them. The machines introduce enough concepts not appearing in the semantics, such as environments and update marks, that the equivalence in not self-evident.

Our proof has followed all the way from an abstract operational semantics for lazy evaluation such as Launchbury's, to a very concrete and efficient abstract machine such as the STG. Part of that way had already been followed by Sestoft in [10]. We have started at one of his machines, the *Mark-2*, and have shown that a STG machine with one stack can be derived from it, and that a bisimulation can be defined between both.

We have solved a small problem of Sestoft's semantics regarding freshness of variables and also added some garbage collection considerations to his semantics. As a result, the stack of Sestoft's machines appears very naturally as a transformation of some sets *A*, *B* and *C* needed by the semantics in order to have a complete control over freshness and over live closures. It is interesting to note that the optimization of not using the set of update markers as roots for the garbage collector can be easily understood at the semantic level.

We have also shown that the soundness of the three stacks STG machine as described in [6] relies on program being well-typed. This was an underlying assumption which was not explicitly stated in that description.

The obvious solution to this 'problem' is to come back to a single stack machine, and this seems to be the option recently chosen by GHC's implementors (although probably due to different reasons) [9]. Having only one stack complicates the garbage collector task because pointers and non-pointers must be clearly distinguished. The presence of unboxed primitive values in the stack makes the problem even worse. In compensation, update markers are smaller than update frames and, most important of all, the temporal order of events is preserved.

References

1. A. de la Encina and R. Peña. A Proof of Correctness for the STG Machine. Technical Report 120-01, Dept. SIP, Universidad Complutense de Madrid, Spain, http://dalila.sip.ucm.es/ albertoe/publications.html, 2001.
2. J. Fairbairn and S. C. Wray. TIM: A Simple, Lazy Abstract Machine to Execute Supercombinators. In *Proc. of the 1987 Conference on Functional Programming Languages and Computer Architecture*, Portland, Oregon, September 1987.
3. T. Johnsson. Efficient Compilation of Lazy Evaluation. *ACM SIGPLAN Notices*, 19(6):58–69, June 1984.
4. J. Launchbury. A Natural Semantics for Lazy Evaluation. In *Proc. Conference on Principles of Programming Languages, POPL'93*. ACM, 1993.
5. J. Mountjoy. The Spineless Tagless G-machine, Naturally. In *Third International Conference on Functional Programming, ICFP'98, Baltimore*. ACM Press, 1998.
6. S. L. Peyton Jones. Implementing Lazy Functional Languages on Stock Hardware: the Spineless Tagless G-machine, Version 2.5. *Journal of Functional Programming*, 2(2):127–202, April 1992.
7. S. L. Peyton Jones, C. V. Hall, K. Hammond, W. D. Partain, and P. L. Wadler. The Glasgow Haskell Compiler: A Technical Overview. In *Joint Framework for Inf. Technology, Keele*, pages 249–257, 1993.
8. S. L. Peyton Jones and J. Hughes, editors. *Report on the Programming Language Haskell 98*. URL http://www.haskell.org, February 1999.
9. S. L. Peyton Jones, S. Marlow, and A. Reid. The STG Runtime System (revised). http://www.haskell.org/ghc/docs, 1999.
10. P. Sestoft. Deriving a Lazy Abstract Machine. *Journal of Functional Programming*, 7(3):231–264, May 1997.

Dynamic Cheap Eagerness

Karl-Filip Faxén

Dept. of Microelectronics and Information Technology,
Royal Institute of Technology,
Electrum 229, S-164 40 Kista, tel: +46 8 790 41 20
`kff@it.kth.se`

Abstract. Dynamic cheap eagerness extends cheap eagerness by allowing the decision of whether to build a thunk or speculatively evaluate its body to be deferred until run time. We have implemented this optimisation in a compiler for a simple functional language and measured its effect on a few benchmarks. It turns out that a large part of the overhead of graph reduction can be eliminated, but that run-times and instruction counts are not affected in the same degree.

1   Introduction

Cheap eagerness is an optimization, applicable to nonstrict functional languages, where expressions are evaluated before it is known that their values will actually be used. For instance, an argument in a function application may be evaluated before the call, even if it is not known that the function always uses that argument. This improves performance by eliminating a lot of book-keeping necessary for delaying and (often) later resuming the evaluation of expressions.

In order to preserve the meaning of the program, only expressions which terminate without yielding run-time errors can be evaluated speculatively. In general, global analysis must be used to find such expressions.

We have previously studied this problem in [Fax00], where we give an algorithm for detecting safe expressions for speculative evaluation. In that paper we also present experimental results showing that cheap eagerness does indeed yield a significant performance improvement, decreasing execution time by 12–58% over a range of benchmark programs. Given these numbers, and the fact that most thunks that are built are also evaluated sooner or later, we have been interested in extending cheap eagerness by speculatively evaluating even more expressions.

The technique used in our earlier work is *static* in the sense that it makes a single decision for each candidate expression in the program. An expression is speculated only if it is known that it is safe every time it is evaluated in any execution of the program. In this paper we generalize this condition to *dynamic cheap eagerness* where we may postpone the final decision to run-time by inserting a run-time test to control whether the expression is speculated or delayed. This has the consequence that, in a single execution of the program,

T. Arts and M. Mohnen (Eds.): IFL 2001, LNCS 2312, pp. 105–120, 2002.

the same expression may be speculated some of the times it is reached but not all of them.

We use such tests in two situations. First, we allow producers of lazy data structures to produce more than one element of the structure at a time. Typically, such functions contain a recursive call inside a thunk. If the thunk would be speculated, the entire, possibly infinite, structure would be produced at once, which is unacceptable. Instead we maintain a *speculation level* as part of the abstract machine state, and only speculate a thunk containing a recursive call if the speculation level is positive. The speculation level is decremented during the evaluation of the speculated thunk body. In this way, the depth of speculation can be controlled.

Second, some expressions can be statically speculated except that they evaluate some free variables which cannot be statically proved to be bound to WHNFs (weak head normal forms) at run-time. In this case, the variables in question can be tested and the expression speculated when none of them is bound to a thunk. Of course the two can be combined; an expression can be speculated if the speculation level is positive *and* some variables are not bound to thunks.

Note that we still use the full static analysis machinery from [Fax00], which is based on flow analysis, and we use an almost identical intermediate language where delayed evaluation is explicitly indicated by expressions of the form **thunk** e (where e is the delayed expression). The analysis then finds some **thunk** e expressions which can be replaced by e alone (static speculation), or annotated by a condition s giving **thunk** $s\,e$ (dynamic speculation).

2   The Language Fleet

Figure 1 gives the syntax of Fleet. It is a simple functional language containing the constructs of the lambda calculus as well as constructors, case expressions, built-in operators and recursive and nonrecursive let. Graph reduction is handled by explicit **eval** and **thunk** constructs; the rest of the language has a call-by-value semantics. Replacing call-by-need with call-by-value is the source-to-source transformation $\mathbf{thunk}^l\,e \Longrightarrow e$.

$$e \in \text{Expr} \;\rightarrow\; x \mid x_1\,x_2 \mid b \mid op^l\,x_1 \ldots x_k \qquad\qquad s \in \text{SCond} \rightarrow \mathsf{E} \mid \mathsf{R} \mid \varepsilon$$

$\qquad\qquad\mid$ case x of $alt_1; \ldots;\ alt_n$ end

$\qquad\qquad\mid$ let $x = e'$ in e $\qquad\qquad\qquad\qquad x \in \text{Var}$

$\qquad\qquad\mid$ letrec $x_1 = b_1; \ldots; x_n = b_n$ in e $\qquad\quad l \in \text{Label} \;\rightarrow\; \underline{1}, \underline{2}, \ldots$

$\qquad\qquad\mid$ thunk$^l\,s\,e \mid$ eval x $\qquad\qquad\qquad\qquad C \in \text{DataCon} \cup \text{IntLit}$

$b \in \text{Build} \;\rightarrow\; \lambda^l x.\,e \mid C^l\,x_1 \ldots x_k \mid$ thunk$^l\,e$

$alt \in \text{Alt} \;\rightarrow\; C\,x_1 \ldots x_k$ -> e

Fig. 1. The syntax of Fleet

```
letrec from = λ¹n.let r = thunk² let n1 = thunk³
                                          let n'= eval n
                                          in inc⁴ n'
                                in from n1
                    in Cons⁵ n r
in let z = 0⁶
   in from z
```

Fig. 2. The from program

Lambda abstractions, constructors and (unconditional) thunks are referred to as *buildable expressions*. These are the only kind of expressions allowed as right-hand-sides in letrec bindings.

In order to generalize static cheap eagerness to the dynamic version, we give thunk expressions a *speculation condition s* which is either

- empty, for a thunk that is never speculated,
- E for a thunk that is speculated if no free variable x which is an argument of an eval occurring in the thunk body (but not nested inside another thunk or abstraction) is bound to a thunk, or
- R for a thunk that is speculated if the E condition is true and the speculation level is positive.

The speculation conditions are chosen to be testable with just a few machine instructions; hence the restriction to eval arguments that are free variables of the thunk body (and thus available in registers for the purpose of building the thunk). Starting with a positive speculation level which is decremented similarly allows a simple test for a negative value for the R condition.

We expect the front end to produce thunks with empty speculation conditions with the analysis trying to either eliminate the thunks or replace the speculation conditions with E or R.

Buildable expressions and operator applications are labeled. These labels identify particular expressions and are used to convey flow information. They are also used by the cheapness analysis; its result records the labels of thunks that may be statically or dynamically speculated. Figure 2 gives an example Fleet program computing the list of all natural numbers.

We give Fleet a big step operational semantics in Fig. 3. The inference rules allow us to prove statements of the form

$$\rho, \sigma \vdash e \Downarrow v$$

where ρ is an environment mapping variables to values, σ is the speculation level, e is an expression, and v a value. A value is a *closure*; a pair of an environment and a buildable expression. Note that (unconditional) thunks are also values in this semantics since they are an explicit construct in the language. We refer to closures where the expression part is an abstraction or a constructor application as *weak head normal form (WHNF) closures*.

$$\rho, \sigma \vdash x \Downarrow \rho(x) \qquad\qquad\qquad\text{var}$$

$$\frac{\rho(x_1) = (\rho', \lambda^l x.\, e) \qquad \rho'[x \mapsto \rho(x_2)], \sigma \vdash e \Downarrow v}{\rho, \sigma \vdash x_1\, x_2 \Downarrow v} \qquad\qquad \text{app}$$

$$\rho, \sigma \vdash b \Downarrow (\rho, b) \qquad\qquad\qquad \text{build}$$

$$\frac{[\![op]\!]\, \rho(x_1) \,\ldots\, \rho(x_k) = C}{\rho, \sigma \vdash op^l\, x_1 \ldots x_k \Downarrow ([\,], C^l)} \qquad\qquad \text{op}$$

$$\frac{\rho(x) = (\rho', C^l\, x'_1 \ldots x'_k) \qquad \rho[\ldots, x_i \mapsto \rho'(x'_i), \ldots], \sigma \vdash e \Downarrow v}{\rho, \sigma \vdash \texttt{case } x \texttt{ of } \ldots; C\, x_1 \ldots x_k \texttt{ -> } e; \ldots \texttt{ end} \Downarrow v} \qquad \text{case}$$

$$\frac{\rho, \sigma \vdash e' \Downarrow v' \qquad \rho[x \mapsto v'], \sigma \vdash e \Downarrow v}{\rho, \sigma \vdash \texttt{let } x = e' \texttt{ in } e \Downarrow v} \qquad\qquad \text{let}$$

$$\frac{\rho' = \rho[\ldots, x_i \mapsto (\rho', b_i), \ldots] \qquad \rho', \sigma \vdash e \Downarrow v}{\rho, \sigma \vdash \texttt{letrec } x_1 = b_1; \ldots; x_n = b_n \texttt{ in } e \Downarrow v} \qquad \text{letrec}$$

$$\frac{x \in evars(e) \Rightarrow \rho(x) \text{ is WHNF closure} \qquad \rho, \sigma \vdash e \Downarrow v}{\rho, \sigma \vdash \texttt{thunk}^l\, \mathsf{E}\, e \Downarrow v} \qquad \text{thunk E}$$

$$\frac{x \in evars(e) \Rightarrow \rho(x) \text{ is WHNF closure} \qquad \sigma > 0 \qquad \rho, \sigma - 1 \vdash e \Downarrow v}{\rho, \sigma \vdash \texttt{thunk}^l\, \mathsf{R}\, e \Downarrow v} \qquad \text{thunk R}$$

$$\frac{\text{speculation condition } s \text{ not satisfied}}{\rho, \sigma \vdash \texttt{thunk}^l\, s\, e \Downarrow (\rho, \texttt{thunk}^l\, e)} \qquad \text{thunk}$$

$$\frac{\rho(x) = (\rho', \texttt{thunk}^l\, e) \qquad \rho', \sigma \vdash e \Downarrow v}{\rho, \sigma \vdash \texttt{eval } x \Downarrow v} \;\; \text{eval-i} \qquad \frac{\rho(x) \text{ is a WHNF closure}}{\rho, \sigma \vdash \texttt{eval } x \Downarrow \rho(x)} \;\; \text{eval-ii}$$

$$evars(\texttt{case } x \texttt{ of } alt_1; \ldots; alt_n \texttt{ end}) = evars_{alt}(alt_1) \cup \ldots \cup evars_{alt}(alt_n)$$
$$evars(\texttt{let } x = e' \texttt{ in } e) = evars(e') \cup (evars(e) \setminus \{x\})$$
$$evars(\texttt{letrec } x_1 = b_1; \ldots; x_n = b_n \texttt{ in } e) = evars(e) \setminus \{x_1, \ldots, x_n\}$$
$$evars(\texttt{eval } x) = \{x\}$$
$$evars(e) = \emptyset \text{ (for } e \text{ other than above)}$$
$$evars_{alt}(C\, x_1 \ldots x_r \texttt{ -> } e) = evars(e) \setminus \{x_1, \ldots, x_r\}$$

Fig. 3. Operational semantics of Fleet

Infinite values (rational trees where each variable binding in an environment is seen as a branch) arise in the [letrec] rule in the semantics and correspond to the cyclic structures built by an implementation.

The cheap eagerness analysis uses the results of a previous *flow analysis*. A flow analysis finds information about the data and control flow in a program [Fax95,Shi91,JW95,Ses91]. In our case, flow information takes the form of a *flow assignment* φ mapping variables (the flat syntax of Fleet ensures that every interesting expression is associated with a variable) to sets of expressions. These expressions are all *producers* of values and include buildable expressions and operator applications. Since all producers are labeled, flow information could record labels rather than expressions. We have chosen to record expressions in order to simplify the definition of the cheap eagerness analysis.

Figure 4 gives a flow assignment for the `from` program. Note that the flow information for the variable `n1`, bound to the `thunk` containing the increment, also includes the flow information for the `thunk` body. Including the flow information for the thunk body in the flow information for the thunk is necessary since the cheap eagerness transformation may replace the `thunk` with its body, and the flow information must not be invalidated by that transformation.

`from` : $\{\lambda^1 \mathtt{n}.E_1\}$ Abbreviations:

    `n` : $\{\mathtt{thunk}^3 E_3, \ \mathtt{inc}^4\, \mathtt{n}', \ \mathtt{0}^6\}$ $E_1 \ \equiv \ \mathtt{let\ r = thunk}^2\, E_2 \ \mathtt{in\ Cons}^5\, \mathtt{n\ r}$

    `r` : $\{\mathtt{thunk}^2 E_2, \ \mathtt{Cons}^5\, \mathtt{n\ r}\}$ $E_2 \ \equiv \ \mathtt{let\ n1 = thunk}^3\, E_3 \ \mathtt{in\ from\ n1}$

    `n1` : $\{\mathtt{thunk}^3 E_3, \ \mathtt{inc}^4\, \mathtt{n}'\}$ $E_3 \ \equiv \ \mathtt{let\ n}' = \mathtt{eval\ n\ in\ inc}^4\, \mathtt{n}'$

    `n'` : $\{\mathtt{inc}^4\, \mathtt{n}', \ \mathtt{0}^6\}$

    `z` : $\{\mathtt{0}^6\}$

Fig. 4. Flow information for `from`

3   The Analysis

The task of the analysis is to find out which expressions are *cheap*, that is, guaranteed to terminate without run-time error. In a denotational framework, this corresponds to having a semantics which is not $\bot$.

3.1   Cheap Expressions

We follow [Fax00] in considering most builtin operators cheap, with division and modulus being exceptions unless the divisor is a nonzero constant. Case expressions are cheap if all of their branches are. Pattern matching failure is encoded by speciall error operators in the offending branches; flow information has been used to prune these where possible. We also do not speculate **thunks** in the right-hand-sides of **letrec** bindings since buildable expressions are required there. The differences between our previous work and the present paper lies in the treatment of recursive functions and **eval** operators.

We refer to functions where the recursive calls only occur in the bodies of **thunk** expressions, as in the **from** function above where the recursive call is in the body of the **thunk**[2], as *lazily recursive*. Calling a lazily recursive function does not lead to any recursive calls, only to the building of thunks which may perform recursive calls if and when they are evaluated (typically, lazily recursive functions produce lazy data structures). In an *eagerly recursive* function such as **length** the recursive call is not nested inside a **thunk**.

We have previously speculated calls to lazily recursive functions, but we have not speculated the **thunks** containing the recursive calls themselves since that would make the recursion eager. We now relax that constraint by allowing such **thunks**, which we call *cycle breakers*, to be conditionally speculated based on the speculation level.

Previously, we did not speculate **thunks** containing **evals** whose arguments might be thunks since these thunks would in general have been expensive (inexpensive **thunks** are always eliminated). We now relax this constraint as well, by emitting run-time tests so that such a **thunk** may be speculated whenever the arguments to any residual **evals** in its body are actually WHNFs. For such a test to be efficient, the tested argument must be a free variable of the **thunk**.

We note that, as in our previous work, the legality of speculating a **thunk** may in general depend on the elimination of other **thunks**. In fact, if the body of a **thunk** contains an **eval** which might evaluate that **thunk** itself, we may have circular dependencies. These do not invalidate speculation since the elimination of the **thunk** makes the **eval** cheap in the transformed program.

3.2   Formalization

We formalize the cheapness analysis using an inference system, shown in Figs. 5 and 6, which allows us to prove judgements of the form

$$S, V \vdash^{\varphi} e : l$$

where S is a set of constraints, V is a set of thunk-local variables, φ a flow assignment, e is an expression and l is a label (in an implementation, S is the output while the other are inputs). If e occurs in the body of a **thunk**, V contains the variables that are in scope but not available for speculation tests since they are not free variables of the enclosing **thunk**. There are also auxilliary judgements of the form $S, V \vdash^{\varphi}_{R} b : l$ which express the restriction that **thunks** in **letrec** bindings cannot be eliminated.

Judgements of the form $S \vdash^{\varphi}_{l} E$, where E is an error check, ensure that expressions which may cause a run-time error are considered expensive.

There are four main forms of constraints: $l \leadsto_{c} l'$, $l \leadsto_{e} l'$, $l \leadsto_{x} l'$ and $l \leadsto_{t} l'$. The labels are labels of **thunk** expressions and lambda abstractions and the constraints relate the costs of evaluating the corresponding thunk or function bodies. A fifth form of constraint is $l \leadsto_c \Omega$, which is used to indicate that the body of the thunk or function labeled with l is expensive or unsafe to evaluate.

$$\boxed{S, V \vdash^\varphi e : l}$$

$$\{\}, V \vdash^\varphi x : l \qquad \text{VAR}$$

$$\frac{S, V \cup \{x\} \vdash^\varphi e : l'}{S, V \vdash^\varphi \lambda^{l'} x.e : l} \qquad \text{ABS}$$

$$\frac{S \vdash^\varphi_l \mathsf{IsAbs}(x_1)}{S \cup \{l \leadsto_c l' \mid \lambda^{l'} x.e \in \varphi(x_1)\}, V \vdash^\varphi x_1\, x_2 : l} \qquad \text{APP}$$

$$\frac{S \vdash^\varphi_l \mathsf{NoErr}(op\, x_1 \ldots x_r)}{S, V \vdash^\varphi op^{l'}\, x_1 \ldots x_r : l} \qquad \text{OP}$$

$$\{\}, V \vdash^\varphi C^{l'}\, x_1 \ldots x_r : l \qquad \text{CON}$$

$$\frac{S \vdash^\varphi_l \mathsf{OneOf}(x, C_1, \ldots, C_n) \quad S_1, V \cup \bar{x}_1 \vdash^\varphi e_1 : l \ \ldots \ S_n, V \cup \bar{x}_n \vdash^\varphi e_n : l}{S \cup S_1 \cup \ldots \cup S_n, V \vdash^\varphi \texttt{case } x \texttt{ of } \ldots; C_i\, \bar{x}_i \ \texttt{->} \ e_i; \ldots \texttt{ end} : l} \qquad \text{CASE}$$

$$\frac{S, V \vdash^\varphi e : l \qquad S', V \cup \{x\} \vdash^\varphi e' : l}{S \cup S', V \vdash^\varphi \texttt{let } x = e \texttt{ in } e' : l} \qquad \text{LET}$$

$$\frac{V' = V \cup \{x_1, \ldots, x_n\} \quad S_1, V' \vdash^\varphi_R b_1 : l \ \ldots \ S_n, V' \vdash^\varphi_R b_n : l \quad S, V' \vdash^\varphi e : l}{S \cup S_1 \cup \ldots \cup S_n, V \vdash^\varphi \texttt{letrec } x_1 = b_1; \ldots; x_n = b_n \texttt{ in } e : l} \qquad \text{LETREC}$$

$$\frac{S, \emptyset \vdash^\varphi e : l'}{S \cup \{l \leadsto_t l'\}, V \vdash^\varphi \texttt{thunk}^{l'}\, e : l} \qquad \text{THUNK}$$

$$\frac{x \in V}{\{l \leadsto_e l' \mid \texttt{thunk}^{l'}\, e \in \varphi(x)\}, V \vdash^\varphi \texttt{eval } x : l} \qquad \text{EVAL-I}$$

$$\frac{x \notin V}{\{l \leadsto_x l' \mid \texttt{thunk}^{l'}\, e \in \varphi(x)\}, V \vdash^\varphi \texttt{eval } x : l} \qquad \text{EVAL-II}$$

Fig. 5. Constraint derivation rules, part 1

$$\boxed{S, V \vdash^\varphi_R b : l}$$

$$\frac{b \text{ is not a } \texttt{thunk} \qquad S, V \vdash^\varphi b : l}{S, V \vdash^\varphi_R b \ : \ l} \qquad \text{R-WHNF}$$

$$\frac{S, \emptyset \vdash^\varphi e : l'}{S \cup \{l' \leadsto_c \Omega\}, V \vdash^\varphi_R \texttt{thunk}^{l'} e \ : \ l} \qquad \text{R-THUNK}$$

$$\boxed{S \vdash^\varphi_l E}$$

$$\frac{\forall e \in \varphi(x) \,.\, e \text{ is an abstraction}}{\{\} \vdash^\varphi_l \mathsf{IsAbs}(x)} \qquad \text{IS ABS}$$

$$\frac{\forall e \in \varphi(x) \,.\, e \text{ is built with one of the } C_i}{\{\} \vdash^\varphi_l \mathsf{OneOf}(x, C_1, \ldots, C_n)} \qquad \text{ONE OF}$$

$$\frac{op\, x_1 \ldots x_r \text{ is defined if the } x_i \text{ are described by } \varphi}{\{\} \vdash^\varphi_l \mathsf{NoErr}(op\, x_1 \ldots x_r)} \qquad \text{NO ERR}$$

$$\frac{\text{none of the above applies}}{\{l \leadsto_c \Omega\} \vdash^\varphi_l E} \qquad \text{ERROR}$$

Fig. 6. Constraint derivation rules, part 2

Figure 7 shows the constraints S derived from the `from` program in Fig. 2 using the flow assignment φ in Fig. 4 ($\underline{42}$ is an arbitrary label representing the top level context). Thus we have $S, \emptyset \vdash^\varphi P : \underline{42}$ where P is the `from` program.

We will solve constraints by assigning *costs* to labels in such a way that the constraints are satisfied.

$$\underline{2} \leadsto_c \underline{1}, \ \underline{42} \leadsto_c \underline{1}, \ \underline{1} \leadsto_t \underline{2}, \ \underline{2} \leadsto_t \underline{3}, \ \underline{3} \leadsto_x \underline{3}$$

$$\delta(\underline{1}) = 1, \quad \delta(\underline{2}) = \mathsf{R}, \quad \delta(\underline{3}) = 1, \quad \delta(\underline{42}) = 2$$

Fig. 7. The constraints derived from the `from` program and their least model

Definition 1 (Costs) *A cost Δ is of one of the forms below. Costs are ordered by $<$.*

- *A natural number n is called a* finite cost; *the costs defined below are called* infinite costs. *Finite costs are ordered numerically.*
- *If n is a finite cost, then E^n is a cost. If $n < m$ then $n < \mathsf{E}^m$ and $\mathsf{E}^n < \mathsf{E}^m$.*
- *R is a cost and for all n, $\mathsf{E}^n < \mathsf{R}$.*
- *Ω is the greatest cost; for all Δ, $\Delta < \Omega$.*

We will write $\leq$ for the reflexive closure of $<$ and $\Delta \vee \Delta'$ for the least upper bound of Δ and Δ'.

Costs of the form n represent safe computations which can be statically speculated (the n is related to the height of the derivation of the evaluation relation for the computation). The costs E^n and R stand for costs which, if they are assigned to a thunk label, implies that the thunk may be dynamically speculated. Essentially, E^n means that the thunk body may be speculated when all variables which are arguments to the remaining `eval`s are bound to WHNFs, and R adds the further restriction that the speculation level must be positive (the n in E^n is analogous to the finite cost n of evaluating the thunk body if the conditions for speculation are satisfied).

Definition 2 *A cost assignment δ is a function from labels to costs. Further, δ is a* model *of a constraint set S, written $\delta \models S$ iff all of the following holds:*

- *For every constraint $l \rightsquigarrow_c l' \in S$, $\delta(l) > \delta(l')$ and $\delta(l) \neq \mathsf{E}^n, \mathsf{R}$. For every constraint $l \rightsquigarrow_c \Omega \in S$, $\delta(l) = \Omega$.*
- *For every constraint $l \rightsquigarrow_e l' \in S$, either $\delta(l) = \Omega$ or $\delta(l')$ is finite.*
- *For every constraint $l \rightsquigarrow_x l' \in S$, either $\delta(l) \geq \mathsf{E}^0$ or $\delta(l')$ is finite.*
- *For every constraint $l \rightsquigarrow_t l' \in S$, either $\delta(l) > \delta(l')$ or $\delta(l') \geq \mathsf{R}$.*

A model δ of a constraint set S is minimal *iff for every δ' such that $\delta' \models S$ the following holds for all l*

- *$\delta(l)$ infinite implies $\delta'(l)$ infinite*
- *$\delta(l) = \Omega$ implies $\delta'(l) = \Omega$.*

The constraint set derived from the `from` program has a minimal model, which is shown in Fig. 7.

Looking at the inference rules in Figs. 5 and 6, we can see that constraints of the form $l \rightsquigarrow_c l'$ correspond to function calls, where l is the label of the caller (the innermost lambda abstraction or `thunk`) and l' is the label of the callee (a lambda abstraction). If the callee (l') is associated with an infinite cost, the caller (l) must have cost Ω since the caller cannot determine if the callee is actually going to do whatever possibly expensive thing its infinite costs warns of. Constraints of the form $l \rightsquigarrow_c \Omega$ indicate that the evaluation of the thunk or function body l might cause a run-time error. Such constraints are generated by the error checking judgements $S \vdash_l^\varphi E$.

Similarly, $l \leadsto_e l'$ and $l \leadsto_x l'$ correspond to an `eval`, occurring in the thunk or function body l, which may evaluate a thunk labeled l'. If l' is assigned a finite cost, the thunk will be eliminated. Thus there will be no such thunk for the `eval` to find, so the cost of the thunk body does not affect the cost of the `eval`. If, on the other hand, a thunk might occur at an `eval` inside a `thunk` body, there is a difference between the case where the argument to the `eval` is available for testing outside the body ($l \leadsto_x l'$) or not ($l \leadsto_e l'$). In the first case, dynamic speculation is possible (the thunk label l is assigned a cost of the form E^n), otherwise it is not (l must be assigned Ω).

The fourth kind of constraint, $l \leadsto_t l'$, corresponds to a `thunk` labeled with l' nested inside a thunk or function labeled with l. The other constraints are monotonic, in the sense that the more expensive the label on the right is, the more expensive is the label on the left. This nesting constraint is different; if l' is assigned R or Ω, l can be assigned any cost.

The motivation for this rule is as follows: Recall that the cost assigned to l' (the label of the `thunk`) is the cost associated with the thunk body; if that cost is Ω, the `thunk` is left as a thunk rather than being eliminated, and `thunk` expressions are always safe and cheap (that is their raison d'être, after all). A thunk that is assigned a finite cost, however, is replaced by the thunk body, making the enclosing expression more expensive than the body. The cost R represents bounded depth speculation; the speculation counter ensures that the cost of evaluating the `thunk` body is finite. In the case of a cost of the form E^n, the speculation counter is not consulted, so the n is used to guarantee terminating evaluation statically. This form of constraint is used to ensure that the transformation does not turn lazy recursion into eager recursion.

The nonmonotonicity of nesting constraints implies that not all constraint sets have minimal models. This happens when there is a lazily recursive cycle of otherwise safe thunks and any one could be chosen to break the cycle (by mapping it to R). In that case we will have a cycle of $\leadsto_t$ and $\leadsto_c$ constraints which cannot all be legally assigned finite costs.

We have designed an algorithm which computes a model of any constraint set, finding a minimal model if one exists. The algorithm is derived from the one in [Fax00] but is omitted from this paper for space reasons.

4   Experimental Results

We have implemented dynamic cheap eagerness in an experimental compiler for a simple lazy higher order functional language called Plain. The compiler has a (rather primitive) strictness analyzer based on demand propagation and a (rather sophisticated) flow analyzer based on polymorphic subtype inference [Fax95]. Except being used for cheap eagerness, the flow information is exploited by update avoidance and representation analysis [Fax99]. The compiler also uses *cloning* to be able to generate tailor made code for different uses of the same function [Fax01]. Since several optimizations are program-wide, separate compilation is not supported. The compiler is described more fully in the author's PhD thesis [Fax97, chapter 3].

The compiler can be instructed to generate code counting various events, including the construction and evaluation of thunks. We have measured user level (machine) instruction counts using the `icount` analyzer included in the Shade distribution. The execution times measured are the sum of user and system times, as reported by the `clock()` function, and is the average of four runs. Both times and instruction counts include garbage collection. All measurements were performed on a lightly loaded Sun Ultra 5 workstation with 128MB of memory and a 270MHz UltraIIi processor.

We have made preliminary measurements of the effectiveness of dynamic cheap eagerness using a set of small test programs (the largest is ≈ 700 lines of code). The small size of the programs makes any claims based on these experiments very tentative. With this caveat, we present the programs:

nqh The N-Queens program written with higher order functions wherever possible (`append` is defined in terms of `foldr` etc), run with input 11.

q1 Same as **nqh**, but with all higher order functions manually removed by specialization, run with input 11.

nrev Naive reverse, a *very* silly program, but it shows a case where dynamic cheap eagerness really pays off, run on a list of length 4141 elements.

event A small event driven simulator from Hartel and Langendoen's benchmark suite [HL93], run with input 400000.

sched A job scheduler, also from that benchmark suite, run with input 14.

infer A simple polymorphic type checker from [HL93][1], run with input 600.

4.1 Strategies

We have measured several strategies which differ in which `thunks` they are willing to dynamically speculate.

s: Only static cheap eagerness, corresponding to the most aggressive strategy in [Fax00].

e: Thunks with `evals` of free variables (speculation condition E) are speculated, but not cycle breakers. The speculation depth is not used.

c: Cycle breakers with no `evals` are speculated (speculation condition R with an empty *evars* set), but no thunks with `evals` are speculated. Run with speculation depth 1, 2 and 9.

ce+c: Cycle breakers and thunks with conservative `evals` are speculated. A conservative `eval` is an `eval` which is guaranteed never to evaluate a `thunk` with an empty speculation condition. Effectively, we add the condition that if $l \leadsto_x l'$ and $\delta(l') = \Omega$ then $\delta(l) = \Omega$. Speculation conditions of both E and R are used. Run with speculation depth 1, 2 and 9.

e+c: Cycle breakers and `thunks` with `evals` of free variables are speculated, as described in Sec. 3. Run with speculation level 1, 2 and 9.

---

[1] It is called `typecheck` there.

The motivation of the **ce+c** strategy is to decrease the number of failed speculation tests. Typically, such a test costs 7–8 instructions, including branches and two **nops** in delay slots (we statically predict that the speculation will be done).

Since dynamic cheap eagerness duplicates the bodies of conditionally speculated **thunks**, code growth is potentially an issue. Since **thunks** may be nested inside **thunk** bodies, there is in principle a risk of exponential code growth. In our measurements, however, we have not seen code growth above 10%, with 1–2% being more common.

4.2   Execution Times and Operation Counts

Looking at the results in Table 1, we immediately see that for most programs, and in particular for the somewhat larger programs **event**, **sched** and **typecheck**, dynamic cheap eagerness has very little to offer beyond its static version in terms of reductions of execution time and instruction count. No optimization strategy is even able to consistently improve performance, although for all of the programs there is some startegy that can reduce instruction counts, albeit often only a by tiny amount.

In **nrev**, we see an example where dynamic cheap eagerness works as intended. This program is dominated by calls to **append** with large left arguments which themselves are results from **append**.

On the other hand, dynamic cheap eagerness is successful in reducing the number of thunks built and evaluated, which are the operations targeted by speculative evaluation. Again, **nrev** stands out with up to 90% of these operations eliminated with the **ce+c** and **e+c** strategies and a speculation depth of 9. The larger programs also get some reductions, ranging from 4% of thunks built and 5% of thunks evaluated for **sched** (the **c**, **ce+c** and **e+c** strategies with depth 9) to 15% and 27%, respectively, for **infer** (the **e+c** strategy with depth 9).

One of the causes of these results is apparent if we study Table 2 which gives the average number of thunks built and thunks evaluated for every 1000 instructions executed. Given that building or evaluating a thunk yields an overhead of very roughly ten instructions, the numbers can be interpreted as percentages of the executed instructions that are spent on these operations. It is then clear that the larger programs spend at most some 13–15% of their instructions on the operations which are targeted by this optimization. The program with the best speedup, **nrev**, spends the largest amount of instructions, some 36%, on the targeted operations.

4.3   Speculation Statistics

To further understand the results, we can study Table 3 which give other statistics relevant to speculative evaluation. For **nqh**, we see that all of the strategies which speculate cycle breakers yield the same results, with deeper speculation yielding improved speedup. This is not surprising since effectively all thunks built are also evaluated. The same behaviour is shown by **q1**.

Table 1. Execution times and operation counts.

		s	e	c			ce+c			e+c		
				1	2	9	1	2	9	1	2	9
nqh	t	1.60	1.60	1.60	1.60	1.50	1.60	1.60	1.50	1.60	1.60	1.50
	I	418.0	418.0	420.3	412.9	405.8	420.3	412.9	405.8	420.3	412.9	405.8
	%I	100	100	101	99	97	101	99	97	101	99	97
	T	3979	3979	2994	2665	2337	2994	2665	2337	2994	2665	2337
	%T	100	100	75	67	59	75	67	59	75	67	59
	E	3979	3979	2994	2665	2337	2994	2665	2337	2994	2665	2337
	%E	100	100	75	67	59	75	67	59	75	67	59
q1	t	1.20	1.20	1.17	1.10	1.00	1.13	1.10	1.00	1.13	1.10	1.00
	I	314.3	314.3	316.7	309.4	302.1	316.7	309.4	302.1	316.7	309.4	302.1
	%I	100	100	101	98	96	101	98	96	101	98	96
	T	2170	2170	1185	856	528	1185	856	528	1185	856	528
	%T	100	100	55	39	24	55	39	24	55	39	24
	E	2170	2170	1185	856	528	1185	856	528	1185	856	528
	%E	100	100	55	39	24	55	39	24	55	39	24
nrev	t	3.60	3.63	3.60	3.63	3.67	2.90	2.50	1.93	2.87	2.50	1.93
	I	472.1	472.1	472.1	472.1	472.1	465.9	422.5	363.2	465.9	422.5	363.2
	%I	100	100	100	100	100	99	89	77	99	89	77
	T	8576	8576	8576	8576	8576	4289	2860	859	4289	2860	859
	%T	100	100	100	100	100	50	33	10	50	33	10
	E	8576	8576	8576	8576	8576	4289	2860	859	4289	2860	859
	%E	100	100	100	100	100	50	33	10	50	33	10
event	t	2.20	2.20	2.20	2.20	2.20	2.20	2.23	2.23	2.20	2.30	2.23
	I	315.6	316.1	315.5	315.4	315.4	314.0	317.0	316.1	330.5	333.8	331.8
	%I	100	100	100	100	100	99	100	100	105	106	105
	T	2222	2222	2219	2218	2217	2122	2091	2078	1946	1929	1902
	%T	100	100	100	100	100	95	94	94	88	87	86
	E	2096	2096	2093	2092	2091	1996	1965	1952	1820	1803	1776
	%E	100	100	100	100	100	95	94	93	87	86	85
sched	t	27.13	26.77	26.70	26.50	26.53	26.67	26.50	26.50	26.37	26.13	26.20
	I	5120.8	5151.1	5115.4	5100.7	5089.0	5115.4	5100.7	5089.0	5145.7	5131.0	5119.2
	%I	100	101	100	100	99	100	100	99	100	100	100
	T	42293	42293	41204	40881	40650	41204	40881	40650	41204	40881	40650
	%T	100	100	97	97	96	97	97	96	97	97	96
	E	35619	35619	34531	34207	33977	34531	34207	33977	34531	34207	33977
	%E	100	100	97	96	95	97	96	95	97	96	95
infer	t	4.00	3.97	3.93	4.00	4.00	4.00	4.00	4.07	4.03	3.90	4.07
	I	710.3	710.1	711.8	712.5	725.3	712.0	705.4	727.5	713.9	707.2	728.8
	%I	100	100	100	100	102	100	99	102	101	100	103
	T	4727	4643	4588	4569	4729	4157	3926	4142	4052	3815	4023
	%T	100	98	97	97	100	88	83	88	86	81	85
	E	4241	4149	4071	4021	3942	3609	3337	3204	3522	3245	3104
	%E	100	98	96	95	93	85	79	76	83	77	73

Legend: t is CPU time, I is millions of instructions, T is thousands of thunks built, E is thousands of thunks evaluated, %I,%T,%E are percentages relative to the s column (100 means no change).

Table 2. Average number of thunks built or evaluated per 1000 instructions executed.

Program	thunks built	thunks evaluated
nqh	9.5	9.5
q1	6.9	6.9
nrev	18.2	18.2
event	7.0	6.6
sched	8.3	7.0
infer	6.7	6.0

For nrev we see that cycle breaking must be combined with speculation of evaluation since the cycle-breaking thunk in append also contains an eval. Otherwise no speculation is performed.

As for sched, there are few of the thunks built that are candidates for speculative evaluation at all, and combined with the small amount of instructions spent on building and evaluating thunks, it is unsurprising that the effects, positive or negative, are small. The conservative evaluation speculation strategy ce+c is clearly beneficial, as the strategies with aggressive speculation of evaluation gets the worst slowdowns.

Finally, infer is the only program where speculation regularly creates more work by speculating thunks which would otherwise not have been evaluated, leading to slowdown for deep speculation of cycle breakers. It is interresting to note that in this case both the number of thunks built and speculation conditions evaluated increase, which is possible if the speculation of one thunk body leads to other thunks being built or more speculation conditions being evaluated.

5   Conclusions and Further Work

We have implemented a generalization of the static cheap eagerness optimization discussed in [Fax00] and measured its effectiveness. The good news is that speculative evaluation can further reduce the number of thunks built and evaluated by between 5 and 90%. The bad news is that this hardly improves run-times and instructions counts at all for most programs since the gains are offset by losses in terms of the costs of the dynamic tests and wasted work due to speculation.

Another reason why going from no speculation to static speculation gave better speedup than going from static to dynamic speculation is that static speculation enables other optimizations such as unboxing and removal of redundant eval operations. This is not the case for dynamic speculation since other passes must still assume that conditionally speculated thunks might occur, only less often.

We believe that other techniques can be used to exploit dynamic cheap eagerness. Specifically, partial unrolling of recursion can eliminate the need for maintaining the speculation counter at run-time and it also opens up possibilities for e.g. sharing heap checks between several allocations. Eventually, list unrolling [SRA94,CV94] can be used to replace several cells in a data structure with a single larger cell so that a data structure is in effect produced a few items at a time. This optimisation is correct in the same cases that dynamic cheap

Table 3. Speculative evaluation statistics.

		s	e	c			ce+c			e+c		
				1	2	9	1	2	9	1	2	9
nqh	%I	100	100	101	99	97	101	99	97	101	99	97
	T	3979	3979	2994	2665	2337	2994	2665	2337	2994	2665	2337
	%TE	100	100	100	100	100	100	100	100	100	100	100
	C	0	0	1807	1807	1807	1807	1807	1807	1807	1807	1807
	%CS	0	0	55	73	91	55	73	91	55	73	91
	%SE	-	-	99	100	100	99	100	100	99	100	100
q1	%I	100	100	101	98	96	101	98	96	101	98	96
	T	2170	2170	1185	856	528	1185	856	528	1185	856	528
	%TE	100	100	100	100	100	100	100	100	100	100	100
	C	0	0	1807	1807	1807	1807	1807	1807	1807	1807	1807
	%CS	0	0	55	73	91	55	73	91	55	73	91
	%SE	-	-	99	100	100	99	100	100	99	100	100
nrev	%I	100	100	100	100	100	99	89	77	99	89	77
	T	8576	8576	8576	8576	8576	4289	2860	859	4289	2860	859
	%TE	100	100	100	100	100	100	100	100	100	100	100
	C	0	0	0	0	0	8572	8572	8572	8572	8572	8572
	%CS	0	0	0	0	0	50	67	90	50	67	90
	%SE	-	-	-	-	-	100	100	100	100	100	100
event	%I	100	100	100	100	100	99	100	100	105	106	105
	T	2222	2222	2219	2218	2217	2122	2091	2078	1946	1929	1902
	%TE	94	94	94	94	94	94	94	94	94	93	93
	C	0	92	6	6	6	146	146	146	1598	1598	1598
	%CS	0	0	50	67	90	68	90	99	17	18	20
	%SE	-	-	99	99	92	100	100	100	100	100	100
sched	%I	100	101	100	100	99	100	100	99	100	100	100
	T	42293	42293	41204	40881	40650	41204	40881	40650	41204	40881	40650
	%TE	84	84	84	84	84	84	84	84	84	84	84
	C	0	4017	1642	1642	1642	1642	1642	1642	5660	5660	5660
	%CS	0	0	66	86	100	66	86	100	19	25	29
	%SE	-	-	100	100	100	100	100	100	100	100	100
infer	%I	100	100	100	100	102	100	99	102	101	100	103
	T	4727	4643	4588	4569	4729	4157	3926	4142	4052	3815	4023
	%TE	90	89	89	88	83	87	85	77	87	85	77
	C	0	206	374	406	646	1315	1368	1732	1715	1769	2133
	%CS	0	67	54	71	94	57	79	92	50	68	81
	%SE	-	67	84	76	49	84	84	65	84	83	66

Legend: %I is relative instruction count as percentage (100 means same as with the **s** strategy), T is thousands of thunks built, %TE is the percentage of thunks built that are also evaluated, C is thousands of speculation conditions evaluated, %CS is percentage of conditions that selected speculation, %SE is percentage of speculated thunks which would have been evaluated (- means no thunks were speculated).

eagerness is correct, that is, when each item of the structure, but not necessarily the entire structure, can be computed in advance. Thus our results indicate that list unrolling is often valid in a lazy functional language. It would be interesting to explore these possibilities in the future.

References

CV94.   Hall Cordelia V. Using Hindley-Milner type inference to optimise list representation. In *Lisp and Functional Programming*, June 1994.

Fax95.   Karl-Filip Faxén. Optimizing lazy functional programs using flow inference. In Allan Mycroft, editor, *Proceedings of the Second International Symposium on Static Analysis*, pages 136–153, Glasgow, UK, September 1995. Springer-Verlag.

Fax97.   Karl-Filip Faxén. *Analysing, Transforming and Compiling Lazy Functional Programs*. PhD thesis, Department of Teleinformatics, Royal Institute of Technology, June 1997.

Fax99.   Karl-Filip Faxén. Representation analysis for coercion placement. In Konstantinos Sagonas and Paul Tarau, editors, *Proceedings of the International Workshop on Implementation of Declarative Languages*, September 1999.

Fax00.   Karl-Filip Faxén. Cheap eagerness: Speculative evaluation in a lazy functional language. In Philip Wadler, editor, *Proceedings of the 2000 International Conference on Functional Programming*, September 2000.

Fax01.   Karl-Filip Faxén. The costs and benefits of cloning in a lazy functional language. In Stephen Gilmore, editor, *Trends in Functional Programming, volume 2*, pages 1–12. Intellect, 2001. Proc. of Scottish Functional Programming Workshop, 2000.

HL93.   Pieter Hartel and Koen Langendoen. Benchmarking implementations of lazy functional languages. In *Functional Programming & Computer Architecture*, pages 341–349, Copenhagen, June 93.

JW95.   Suresh Jagannathan and Stephen Weeks. A unified treatment of flow analysis in higher-order languages. In *Principles of Programming Languages*, 1995.

Ses91.   Peter Sestoft. *Analysis and efficient implementation of functional programs*. PhD thesis, DIKU, University of Copenhagen, Denmark, October 1991.

Shi91.   O. Shivers. The semantics of Scheme control-flow analysis. In *Proceedings of the Symposium on Partial Evaluation and Semantics-Based Program Manipulation*, volume 26, pages 190–198, New Haven, CN, June 1991.

SRA94.   Zhong Shao, John H. Reppy, and Andrew W. Appel. Unrolling lists. In *Lisp and Functional Programming*, June 1994.

A Polynomial-Cost Non-determinism Analysis[*]

Ricardo Peña and Clara Segura

Departamento de Sistemas Informáticos y Programación
Universidad Complutense de Madrid, Spain
{ricardo,csegura}@sip.ucm.es

Abstract. This paper is an extension of a previous work where two non-determinism analyses were presented. One of them was efficient but not very powerful and the other one was more powerful but very expensive. Here, we develop an intermediate analysis in both aspects, efficiency and power. The improvement in efficiency is obtained by speeding up the fixpoint calculation by means of a widening operator, and the representation of functions through easily comparable signatures. Also details about the implementation and its cost are given.

1 Introduction

The parallel-functional language Eden [2] extends the lazy functional language Haskell by constructs to explicitly define and communicate processes. It is implemented by modifying the *Glasgow Haskell Compiler* (GHC) [13]. The three main new concepts are *process abstractions*, *process instantiations* and the non-deterministic process abstraction `merge`. Process abstractions of type `Process a b` can be compared to functions of type `a -> b`, and process instantiations can be compared to function applications. An instantiation is achieved by using the predefined infix operator `(#)` :: `Process a b -> a -> b`. Each time an expression `e1 # e2` is evaluated, a new parallel process is created to evaluate (`e1 e2`). Non-determinism is introduced in Eden by means of a predefined process abstraction `merge` :: `Process [[a]] [a]` which *fairly* interleaves a set of input lists, to produce a single non-deterministic list.

The presence of non-determinism creates some problems in Eden: It affects the referential transparency [8,17] of programs and invalidates some optimizations done in the GHC [16]. Such problems were precisely described in [11]. In [11] a solution was proposed to solve this problem: To develop a static analysis to determine when an Eden expression is sure to be deterministic and when it may be non-deterministic. Two different abstract interpretation based analyses were presented and compared with respect to expresiveness and efficiency. The first one $[\![\cdot]\!]_1$ was efficient (linear) but not very powerful, and the second one $[\![\cdot]\!]_2$ was powerful but less efficient (exponential). This paper presents an intermediate analysis $[\![\cdot]\!]_3$ that tries to be a compromise between power and efficiency

---

[*] Work partially supported by the Spanish-British Acción Integrada HB 1999-0102 and Spanish project TIC 2000-0738.

T. Arts and M. Mohnen (Eds.): IFL 2001, LNCS 2312, pp. 121–137, 2002.

and describes its implementation. Its definition is based on the second analysis $[\![\cdot]\!]_2$. The improvement in efficiency is obtained by speeding up the fixpoint calculation by means of a widening operator wop, and by using an easily comparable representation of functions. By choosing different operators we obtain different variants of the analysis $[\![\cdot]\!]_3^{wop}$. The paper describes the analysis and one particular variant $[\![\cdot]\!]_3^w$ in detail. It also describes an algorithm, written in Haskell, that implements the analysis and annotates the program expressions with non-determinism information, so that it can be used to avoid the harmful transformations.

The plan of the paper is as follows: In Section 2 the language and the analysis $[\![\cdot]\!]_2$ are briefly summarised (full details in [11,10]). In Section 3 the new analysis $[\![\cdot]\!]_3^w$ is described. First, some theoretical results that help in the implementation of the analysis are presented, and then its relation with $[\![\cdot]\!]_2$ is studied. We mention other variants of the analysis and their mutual relations. In Section 4 we describe the annotation algorithm and its cost. In Section 5 some conclusions are drawn. The proofs of all the propositions and examples of the output produced by the algorithm can be found in [10].

2   A Non-determinism Analysis

2.1   The Language

The language being analysed is an extension of Core-Haskell [13], i.e. a simple functional language with second-order polymorphism, so it includes type abstraction and type application. A program is a list of possibly recursive bindings from variables to expressions. Such expressions include variables, lambda abstractions, applications of a functional expression to an atom, constructor applications $C_j \; \overline{x_j}$, primitive operators applications, and also **case** and **let** expressions. We will use v to denote a variable, k to denote a literal, and x to denote an atom (a variable or a literal). Constructor and primitive operators applications are saturated. In **case** expressions there may be a default alternative, denoted as $[v \rightarrow e]$ to indicate it is optional.

The variables contain type information, so we will not write it explicitly in the expressions. When necessary, we will write $e :: t$ to make explicit the type of an expression. A type may be a basic type K, a type variable β, a tuple type $(t_1, \ldots, t_m)$, an algebraic (sum) type $T \; t_1 \ldots t_m$, a functional type $t_1 \rightarrow t_2$ or a polymorphic type $\forall \beta.t$. The new Eden expressions are a process abstraction **process** $v \rightarrow e$, and a process instantiation $v \; \# \; x$. There is also a new type $Process \; t_1 \; t_2$ representing the type of a process abstraction **process** $v \rightarrow e$ where v has type t_1 and e has type t_2. Frequently t_1 and t_2 are tuple types and each tuple element represents an input or an output channel of the process.

2.2   The Analysis

In Figure 1 the abstract domains for $[\![\cdot]\!]_2$ are shown. There is a domain *Basic* with two values: d represents *determinism* and n *possible non-determinism*, with

$$Basic = \{d, n\} \text{ where } d \sqsubseteq n$$
$$D_{2K} = D_{2T \ t_1 \ldots t_m} = D_{2\beta} = Basic$$
$$D_{2(t_1, \ldots, t_m)} = D_{2t_1} \times \ldots \times D_{2t_m}$$
$$D_{2t_1 \to t_2} = D_{2 Process \ t_1 \ t_2} = [D_{2t_1} \to D_{2t_2}]$$
$$D_{2\forall \beta.t} = D_{2t}$$

Fig. 1. Abstract domains for the analysis

$\alpha_t : D_{2t} \to Basic$

$\alpha_K = \alpha_{T \ t_1 \ldots t_m} = \alpha_\beta = id_{Basic}$

$\alpha_{(t_1, \ldots, t_m)}(e_1, \ldots, e_m) = \bigsqcup_i \alpha_{t_i}(e_i)$

$\alpha_{Process \ t_1 \ t_2}(f) = \alpha_{t_1 \to t_2}(f)$

$\alpha_{t_1 \to t_2}(f) = \alpha_{t_2}(f(\gamma_{t_1}(d)))$

$\alpha_{\forall \beta.t} = \alpha_t$

$\gamma_t : Basic \to D_{2t}$

$\gamma_K = \gamma_{T \ t_1 \ldots t_m} = \gamma_\beta = id_{Basic}$

$\gamma_{(t_1, \ldots, t_m)}(b) = (\gamma_{t_1}(b), \ldots, \gamma_{t_m}(b))$

$\gamma_{Process \ t_1 \ t_2}(b) = \gamma_{t_1 \to t_2}(b)$

$\gamma_{t_1 \to t_2}(b) = \begin{cases} \lambda z \in D_{2t_1}.\gamma_{t_2}(n) \text{ if } b = n \\ \lambda z \in D_{2t_1}.\gamma_{t_2}(\alpha_{t_1}(z)) \text{ if } b = d \end{cases}$

$\gamma_{\forall \beta.t} = \gamma_t$

Fig. 2. Abstraction and concretisation functions, α_t and γ_t

the ordering $d \sqsubseteq n$. This is the abstract domain corresponding to basic types and algebraic types. The abstract domains corresponding to a tuple type and a function/process type are respectively the cartesian product of the components' domains and the domain of continuous functions between the domains of the argument and the result. Polymorphism is studied below.

In Figure 3 the abstract interpretation for this analysis is shown. It is an abstract interpretation based analysis in the style of [3]. We outline here only some cases. The interpretation of a tuple is the tuple of the abstract values of the components. Functions and processes are interpreted as abstract functions. So, application and process instantiation are interpreted as abstract functions applications. The interpretation of a constructor belongs to $Basic$, obtained as the least upper bound (lub) of the component's abstract values. But each component $x_i :: t_i$ has an abstract value belonging to D_{2t_i}, that must be first *flattened* to a basic abstract value. This is done by a function called *abstraction function* $\alpha_t : D_{2t} \to Basic$, defined in Figure 2. The idea is to flatten the tuples (by applying the lub operator) and to apply the functions to deterministic arguments.

In a recursive **let** expression the fixpoint can be calculated by using Kleene's ascending chain. We have three different kinds of *case* expressions (for tuple, algebraic types and primitive types). The more complex one is the algebraic *case*. Its abstract value is non-deterministic if either the discriminant or any of the expressions in the alternatives is non-deterministic. Note that the abstract value of the discriminant e, let us call it b, belongs to $Basic$. That is, when it was interpreted, the information about the components was lost. We want now to interpret each alternative's right hand side in an extended environment with abstract values for the variables $v_{ij} :: t_{ij}$ in the left hand side of the alternative. We do not have such information, but we can safely approximate it by using the *concretisation function* $\gamma_t : Basic \to D_{2t}$ defined in Figure 2. Given a type t, it *unflattens* a basic abstract value and produces an abstract value in D_{2t}. The idea is to obtain the best safe approximation both to d and n in a given

$$\llbracket v \rrbracket_2 \, \rho_2 = \rho_2(v)$$
$$\llbracket k \rrbracket_2 \, \rho_2 = d$$
$$\llbracket (x_1, \ldots, x_m) \rrbracket_2 \, \rho_2 = (\llbracket x_1 \rrbracket_2 \, \rho_2, \ldots, \llbracket x_m \rrbracket_2 \, \rho_2)$$
$$\llbracket C \, x_1 \ldots x_m \rrbracket_2 \, \rho_2 = \bigsqcup_i \alpha_{t_i}(\llbracket x_i \rrbracket_2 \, \rho_2) \text{ where } x_i :: t_i$$

$$\llbracket e \, x \rrbracket_2 \, \rho_2 = (\llbracket e \rrbracket_2 \, \rho_2) \, (\llbracket x \rrbracket_2 \, \rho_2)$$
$$\llbracket op \, x_1 \ldots x_m \rrbracket_2 \, \rho_2 = (\gamma_{t_{op}}(d)) \, (\llbracket x_1 \rrbracket_2 \, \rho_2) \ldots (\llbracket x_m \rrbracket_2 \, \rho_2) \text{ where } op :: t_{op}$$
$$\llbracket p \# x \rrbracket_2 \, \rho_2 = (\llbracket p \rrbracket_2 \, \rho_2) \, (\llbracket x \rrbracket_2 \, \rho_2)$$
$$\llbracket \lambda v.e \rrbracket_2 \, \rho_2 = \lambda z \in D_{2t_v}.\llbracket e \rrbracket_2 \, \rho_2 \, [v \mapsto z] \text{ where } v :: t_v$$
$$\llbracket \mathbf{process} \, v \rightarrow e \rrbracket_2 \, \rho_2 = \lambda z \in D_{2t_v}.\llbracket e \rrbracket_2 \, \rho_2 \, [v \mapsto z]$$
$$\llbracket merge \rrbracket_2 \, \rho_2 = \lambda z \in Basic.n$$
$$\llbracket \mathbf{let} \, v = e \, \mathbf{in} \, e' \rrbracket_2 \, \rho_2 = \llbracket e' \rrbracket_2 \, \rho_2 \, [v \mapsto \llbracket e \rrbracket_2 \, \rho_2]$$
$$\llbracket \mathbf{let \, rec} \, \overline{\{v_i = e_i\}} \, \mathbf{in} \, e' \rrbracket_2 \, \rho_2 = \llbracket e' \rrbracket_2 \, (\mathit{fix} \, (\lambda \rho_2'.\rho_2 \, \overline{[v_i \mapsto \llbracket e_i \rrbracket_2 \, \rho_2']}))$$
$$\llbracket \mathbf{case} \, e \, \mathbf{of} \, (v_1, \ldots, v_m) \rightarrow e' \rrbracket_2 \, \rho_2 = \llbracket e' \rrbracket_2 \, \rho_2 \, \overline{[v_i \mapsto \pi_i(\llbracket e \rrbracket_2 \, \rho_2)]}$$

$$\llbracket \mathbf{case} \, e \, \mathbf{of} \, \overline{C_i \, \overline{v_{ij}} \rightarrow e_i}; \, [v \rightarrow e'] \rrbracket_2 \, \rho_2 = \begin{cases} \gamma_t(n) & \text{if } \llbracket e \rrbracket_2 \, \rho_2 = n \\ \bigsqcup_i \llbracket e_i \rrbracket_2 \, \rho_{2i} \, [\, \sqcup \, \llbracket e' \rrbracket_2 \, \rho_2' \,] & \text{otherwise} \end{cases}$$
$$\text{where } \rho_{2i} = \rho_2 \, \overline{[v_{ij} \mapsto \gamma_{t_{ij}}(d)]}, v_{ij} :: t_{ij}, e_i :: t$$
$$\rho_2' = \rho_2 \, [v \mapsto d]$$

$$\llbracket \mathbf{case} \, e \, \mathbf{of} \, \overline{k_i \rightarrow e_i}; \, [v \rightarrow e'] \rrbracket_2 \, \rho_2 = \begin{cases} \gamma_t(n) & \text{if } \llbracket e \rrbracket_2 \, \rho_2 = n \\ \bigsqcup_i \llbracket e_i \rrbracket_2 \, \rho_2 \, [\, \sqcup \, \llbracket e' \rrbracket_2 \, \rho_2' \,] & \text{otherwise} \end{cases}$$
$$\text{where } e_i :: t, \rho_2' = \rho_2 \, [v \mapsto d]$$

$$\llbracket \Lambda \beta.e \rrbracket_2 \, \rho_2 = \llbracket e \rrbracket_2 \, \rho_2$$
$$\llbracket e \, t \rrbracket_2 \, \rho_2 = \gamma_{t' tinst}(\llbracket e \rrbracket_2 \, \rho_2) \text{ where } e :: \forall \beta.t', tinst = t'[\beta := t]$$

Fig. 3. Abstract interpretation $\llbracket \cdot \rrbracket_2$

domain. The abstraction and concretisation functions are mutually recursive. In [11] they were explained in detail and an example was given to illustrate their definitions. They have some interesting properties (e.g. they are a Galois insertion pair [5]), studied in [10,9]. In abstract interpretation, abstraction and concretisation functions usually relate the standard and abstract semantics. We use here the same names for a different purpose because they are similar in spirit.

The abstract interpretation of a polymorphic expression is the abstract interpretation of its 'smallest instance' [1], i.e. that instance where K (the basic type) is substituted for the type variables. This is the reason why the abstract domain corresponding to a type variable β is $Basic$, and the abstract domain corresponding to a polymorphic type is that of the type without qualifier.

When an application to a type t is done, the abstract value of the appropriate instance must be obtained. Such abstract value is in fact obtained as an approximation constructed from the abstract value of the smallest instance. From now on, the instantiated type $t'[\beta := t]$ will be denoted as $tinst$. The approximation to the instance abstract value is obtained by using a *polymorphic concretisation function* $\gamma_{t' tinst} : D_{2t'} \rightarrow D_{2tinst}$, which is defined in Figure 4 (where $tinst_i$ represents $t_i[\beta := t]$). This function *adapts* an abstract value in $D_{2t'}$ to one in D_{2tinst}. Another function, $\alpha_{tinst t'} : D_{2tinst} \rightarrow D_{2t'}$, which we will call the *polymorphic abstraction function*, is also defined in Figure 4. They are a generalisation of α_t and γ_t. These operated with values in $Basic$ and D_{2t}. Now we operate with values in the domains $D_{2t'}$ and D_{2tinst}, that is, between

$$t' = K, T\ t_1 \ldots t_m\quad (\gamma_{t'\,tinst}, \alpha_{tinst\,t'}) = (id_{Basic}, id_{Basic})$$
$$t' = (t_1, \ldots, t_m)\quad (\gamma_{t'\,tinst}, \alpha_{tinst\,t'}) = \times^m((\gamma_{t_1\,tinst_1}, \alpha_{tinst_1\,t_1}), \ldots, (\gamma_{t_m\,tinst_m}, \alpha_{tinst_m\,t_m}))$$
$$t' = t_1 \rightarrow t_2\quad (\gamma_{t'\,tinst}, \alpha_{tinst\,t'}) = \ \rightarrow ((\gamma_{t_1\,tinst_1}, \alpha_{tinst_1\,t_1}), (\gamma_{t_2\,tinst_2}, \alpha_{tinst_2\,t_2}))$$
$$t' = Process\ t_1\ t_2\quad (\gamma_{t'\,tinst}, \alpha_{tinst\,t'}) = \ \rightarrow ((\gamma_{t_1\,tinst_1}, \alpha_{tinst_1\,t_1}), (\gamma_{t_2\,tinst_2}, \alpha_{tinst_2\,t_2}))$$
$$t' = \beta\quad (\gamma_{t'\,tinst}, \alpha_{tinst\,t'}) = (\gamma_t, \alpha_t)$$
$$t' = \beta'\ (\neq \beta)\quad (\gamma_{t'\,tinst}, \alpha_{tinst\,t'}) = (id_{Basic}, id_{Basic})$$
$$t' = \forall \beta'.t_1\quad (\gamma_{t'\,tinst}, \alpha_{tinst\,t'}) = (\gamma_{t_1\,tinst_1}, \alpha_{tinst_1\,t_1})$$

$$\times((f^e, f^c), (g^e, g^c)) = (f^e \times g^e, f^c \times g^c)$$
$$\rightarrow ((f^e, f^c), (g^e, g^c)) = (\lambda h.g^e \cdot h \cdot f^c, \lambda h'.g^c \cdot h' \cdot f^e)$$

Fig. 4. Polymorphic abstraction and concretisation functions

the domains corresponding to the polymorphic type and each of its concrete instances. So in case $t' = \beta$ they will coincide with α_t and γ_t. These functions and their properties are described in detail in [10,9].

3 The Intermediate Analysis

3.1 Introduction

The high cost of $[\![\cdot]\!]_2$ is due to the fixpoint calculation. At each iteration a comparison between abstract values is done. Such comparison is exponential in case functional domains are involved. So, a good way of speeding up the calculation of the fixpoint is finding a quickly comparable representation of functions. Some different techniques have been developed in this direction, such as frontiers algorithms [12] and widening/narrowing operators [4,6,14]. Here, we will represent functions by *signatures* in a way similar to [14]. A signature for a function is obtained by *probing* such function with some explicitly chosen combinations of arguments. For example, in the strictness analysis of [14], a function f with m arguments was probed with m combination of arguments, those where $\perp$ occupies each argument position and the rest of arguments are given a $\top$ value: $\perp, \top, \ldots, \top$; $\top, \perp, \top, \ldots, \top$; $\ldots$; $\top, \top, \ldots, \perp$. So, for example, the function $f = \lambda x :: Int.\lambda y :: Int.y$ has a signature $\top\ \perp$.

If we probe only with some arguments, different functions may have the same signature and consequently some information is lost. Then the fixpoint calculation is not exact, but just approximate. A compromise must be found between the amount of information the signature keeps and the cost of signatures comparison. Several probings can be proposed. Here we concentrate on the one we have implemented, and just mention other possibilities. We probe a function of m arguments with $m+1$ combinations of arguments. In the first m combinations, a non-deterministic abstract value (of the corresponding type) $\gamma_{t_i}(n)$ occupies each argument position while a deterministic abstract value $\gamma_{t_i}(d)$ is given to the rest of the arguments: $\gamma_{t_1}(n), \gamma_{t_2}(d), \ldots, \gamma_{t_m}(d)$; $\gamma_{t_1}(d), \gamma_{t_2}(n), \ldots, \gamma_{t_m}(d)$; $\ldots$; $\gamma_{t_1}(d), \gamma_{t_2}(d), \ldots, \gamma_{t_m}(n)$. In the $m + 1$-th combination, all the arguments are given a deterministic value: $\gamma_{t_1}(d), \gamma_{t_2}(d), \ldots, \gamma_{t_m}(d)$. This additional com-

$$S_K = S_T \ _{t_1 \ldots t_m} = S_\beta = \{D, N\} \text{where } D \preceq N$$
$$S_{(t_1,\ldots,t_m)} = S_{t_1} \times \ldots \times S_{t_m}$$
$$S_{\forall \beta.t} = S_t$$
$$S_t = \{s_1 \ s_2 \ \ldots \ s_m \ s_{m+1} \ |$$
$$\forall \ i \in \{1..(m+1)\}.s_i \in S_{t_r} \wedge s_{m+1} \preceq s_i\}$$
$$\text{where} \quad t = t_1 \to t_2, Process \ t_1 \ t_2$$
$$m = nArgs(t), t_r = rType(t)$$

$$\mathcal{H}_K = \mathcal{H}_T \ _{t_1 \ldots t_m} = \mathcal{H}_\beta = 1$$
$$\mathcal{H}_{(t_1,\ldots,t_m)} = \sum_{i=1}^{m} \mathcal{H}_{t_i}$$
$$\mathcal{H}_{\forall \beta.t} = \mathcal{H}_t$$
$$\mathcal{H}_t = (m+1) \ \mathcal{H}_{t_r}$$
$$\text{where}$$
$$t = t_1 \to t_2, Process \ t_1 \ t_2$$
$$m = nArgs(t), t_r = rType(t)$$

Fig. 5. The domain of signatures and its height $\mathcal{H}_t$

bination is very important for us, as we want the analysis to be more powerful than $[\![\cdot]\!]_1$, where the functions were probed with only this combination.

3.2   The Domain of Signatures

In Figure 5 the domains S_t of signatures are formally defined. The domain corresponding to a basic or an algebraic type is a two-point domain, very similar to the *Basic* domain. However we will use uppercase letters D and N when talking about signatures. The domain corresponding to a tuple type is a tuple of signatures of the corresponding types, for example we could have (D, N) for the type (Int, Int). The ordering between tuples is the usual componentwise one. The domain corresponding to a polymorphic type is the domain corresponding to the smallest instance. With respect to the functions some intuition must be given. First of all, we will say that a type t is functional if $t = t_1 \to t_2$, $t = Process \ t_1 \ t_2$ or $t = \forall \beta.t'$ where t' is functional. If a type t is functional we will write $fun(t)$; otherwise we will write $nonfun(t)$. If a function has m arguments then its signature is composed by $m+1$ signatures, each one corresponding to the (non-functional) type of the result. By m arguments, we mean that taking out all the polymorphism qualifiers, and transforming the process types into functional types, the type is $t_1 \to \ldots \to t_m \to t_r$, where t_r is not functional. We will call this type the *unrolled* version of the functional type. As an example, the unrolled version of $Int \to (\forall \beta.Process \ \beta \ (\beta, Int))$ is $Int \to \beta \to (\beta, Int)$. Three useful functions, *nArgs*, *rType* and *aTypes*, can be easily defined (for lack of space they do not appear here). Given a type t, the first one returns the number of arguments of t; the second one returns the (non-functional) type of its result (it is the identity in the rest of cases); and the third one returns the list (of length $nArgs(t)$) of the types of the arguments. Then the unrolled version of a type t has $nArgs(t)$ arguments of types $aTypes(t)$, and $rType(t)$ as result type. In order to make the signatures for a function type readable, in the examples the last component is separated with a + symbol. So, an example of signature for the type $Int \to (Int, Int)$ could be $(N, D) + (D, D)$. But not every sequence of signatures is a valid signature. As we have previously said, the last component is obtained by probing the function with all the arguments set to a deterministic value, while the rest of them are obtained by probing the function with one non-deterministic value. As the functions are monotone, this means that the last component must always be less than or equal to all the other components. The

$$\wp_t :: D_{2t} \to S_t$$
$$\wp_K(b) = \wp_{T \ t_1 \dots t_m}(b) = \wp_\beta(b) = B$$
$$\wp_{(t_1, \dots, t_m)}(e_1, \dots, e_m) = (\wp_{t_1}(e_1), \dots, \wp_{t_m}(e_m))$$
$$\wp_{\forall \beta . t} = \wp_t$$
$$\wp_t(f) = \wp_{t_r}(f \ \gamma_{t_1}(n) \ \gamma_{t_2}(d) \dots \gamma_{t_m}(d)) \ \wp_{t_r}(f \ \gamma_{t_1}(d) \ \gamma_{t_2}(n) \dots \gamma_{t_m}(d)) \dots$$
$$\wp_{t_r}(f \ \gamma_{t_1}(d) \ \gamma_{t_2}(d) \dots \gamma_{t_m}(n)) \ \wp_{t_r}(f \ \gamma_{t_1}(d) \ \gamma_{t_2}(d) \dots \gamma_{t_m}(d))$$
$$\text{where} \quad t = t_1' \to t_2', Process \ t_1' \ t_2', \quad t_r = rType(t), \quad [t_1, \dots, t_m] = aTypes(t)$$

Fig. 6. The probing function

ordering between the signatures ($\preceq$) is componentwise, so least upper bound and greatest lower bound can also be obtained in the same way. It is easy to see that with this ordering, the domain of signatures S_t for a given type t is a complete lattice of height $\mathcal{H}_t$, see Figure 5.

3.3   The Probing

In this section we define the probing function $\wp_t :: D_{2t} \to S_t$, that given an abstract value in D_{2t}, obtains the corresponding signature in S_t. In Figure 6 the formal definition is shown. The signature of a basic value b is the corresponding basic signature B, that is, if $b = d$ then $B = D$ and if $b = n$ then $B = N$. The signature of a tuple is the tuple of signatures of the components. And finally, the signature for a function or a process $f :: t$ is a sequence of $m + 1$ signatures, where $m = nArgs(t)$, that are obtained by probing f with the combinations of arguments we have previously mentioned.

We have already said that in the probing process some information is lost. This means that a signature represents several abstract values. When we want to recover the original value, we can only return an approximation. This is what the *signatures concretisation function* $\Re_t :: S_t \to D_{2t}$ does. This function is defined in Figure 7. All the cases but the functional one are simple. Given a signature $s = s_1 \dots s_m \ s_{m+1}$, where $s \in S_t$, $\Re_t(s)$ is a function of m arguments $z_i \in D_{2t_i}$. We know that the last element s_{m+1} was obtained by probing the original function with $\gamma_{t_i}(d)$, $i \in \{1..m\}$. So, if all the arguments are less than or equal to the corresponding $\gamma_{t_i}(d)$, then the concretisation of s_{m+1} can be safely returned. The original function might have more precise information for some of the arguments combinations below $\gamma_{t_i}(d)$, but now it is lost. We already know that s_i was obtained by probing the original function with $\gamma_{t_i}(n)$ value for the ith argument and $\gamma_{t_j}(d)$ for the rest of them ($j \in \{1..m\}$, $j \neq i$). So, if all the arguments but the ith one are less than or equal to the corresponding $\gamma_{t_j}(d)$, then we can safely return the concretisation of s_i. Again we are losing information. If there is more than one value that is not less than or equal to the corresponding $\gamma_{t_j}(d)$, we can only return the pessimistic value $\gamma_{t_r}(n)$, as we do not have information for these combinations of arguments in the signature.

We have said that we will use a widening operator to speed up the fixpoint calculation. This is defined as $\mathcal{W}_t = \Re_t \cdot \wp_t$. In fact we will prove that $\mathcal{W}_t$ is an upper closure operator ($\mathcal{W}_t \sqsupseteq id_{D_{2t}}$). The definition of a widening operator is more general [4], but given an upper closure operator $\mathcal{W}_t$, we can define a

$$\Re_t :: S_t \to D_{2t}$$
$$\Re_K(B) = \Re_{T\ t_1...t_m}(B) = \Re_\beta(B) = b$$
$$\Re_{(t_1,...,t_m)}(s_1,...,s_m) = (\Re_{t_1}(s_1),...,\Re_{t_m}(s_m))$$
$$\Re_{\forall \beta.t} = \Re_t$$

$$\Re_t(\overline{s_j}) = \lambda z_j \in D_{2t_j}.\begin{cases} \Re_{t_r}(s_{m+1}) \text{ if } \bigwedge_{j=1}^{m} z_j \sqsubseteq \gamma_{t_j}(d) \\ \Re_{t_r}(s_i) \text{ if } \bigwedge_{j=1,j\neq i}^{m} z_j \sqsubseteq \gamma_{t_j}(d) \wedge z_i \not\sqsubseteq \gamma_{t_i}(d) \quad \forall i \in \{1..m\} \\ \gamma_{t_r}(n) \text{ otherwise } (m > 1) \end{cases}$$

$$\text{where } \overline{s_j} = s_1...s_m\ s_{m+1}, \quad t = t'_1 \to t'_2, Process\ t'_1\ t'_2$$
$$m = nArgs(t), \quad t_r = rType(t), \quad [t_1,...,t_m] = aTypes(t)$$

Fig. 7. The concretisation function corresponding to the probing

corresponding widening operator $\nabla_t = \lambda(x,y).x \sqcup \mathcal{W}_t(y)$, as done in [6]. So we will use the word widening operator instead, as in [14].

The analysis The analysis is very similar to the second analysis, presented in Section 2. We will use a 3 underscript to identify it. The only expression where there are differences is the recursive **let** expression where a fixpoint must be calculated: $[\![\textbf{let rec } \{v_i = e_i\} \textbf{ in } e']\!]_3\ \rho_3 = [\![e']\!]_3\ (fix\ (\lambda\rho'_3.\rho_3\ \overline{[v_i \mapsto \mathcal{W}_{t_i}([\![e_i]\!]_3\ \rho'_3)]}))$, where $e_i :: t_i$. Notice that by modifying the widening operator we can have several different variants of the analysis. We can express them parameterised by the (collection of) widening operator wop_t, $[\![\cdot]\!]_3^{wop}$.

3.4   Some Theoretical Results

In this section we will prove some properties of the functions defined in the previous section and some others that will help in the implementation of the analysis. Proposition 1 tells us that $\wp_t$ and $\Re_t$ are a Galois insertion pair, which means that $\Re_t$ recovers as much information as possible, considering how the signature was built. As a consequence, $\mathcal{W}_t$ is a widening operator. Proposition 2 tells us that $\gamma_t(d)$ and $\gamma_t(n)$ can be represented by their corresponding signatures without losing any information, which will be very useful in the implementation of the analysis. Finally, Proposition 3 tells us that the comparison between an abstract value and $\gamma_t(d)$ can be done by comparing their corresponding signatures, which is much less expensive. This will be very useful in the implementation, as such comparison is done very often. In the worst case it is made in $\mathcal{H}_t$ steps.

Proposition 1 *For each type t,*

(a) *The functions $\wp_t$, $\Re_t$, and $\mathcal{W}_t$ are monotone and continuous.*
(b) $\mathcal{W}_t \sqsupseteq id_{D_{2t}}.$
(c) $\wp_t \cdot \Re_t = id_{S_t}.$

Proposition 2 *For each type t, $\mathcal{W}_t \cdot \gamma_t = \gamma_t$.*

Proposition 3 *For each type t, $\forall z \in D_{2t}.z \sqsubseteq \gamma_t(d) \Leftrightarrow \wp_t(z) \preceq \wp_t(\gamma_t(d))$.*

3.5 Polymorphism

We would like to have a property similar to Proposition 2, $\mathcal{W}_{tinst} \cdot \gamma_{t'tinst} = \gamma_{t'tinst}$ so that we could represent the instantiations' abstract value by its signature, but this is not true. We show a counterexample. Let the polymorphic type $\forall \beta.t'$, where $t' = (\beta, \beta) \to \beta$, be instantiated with the type $t = Int \to Int$. Then $tinst = t'[t/\beta] = (Int \to Int, Int \to Int) \to Int \to Int$. To abbreviate, we will call E_p to $Basic \times Basic$ and F_p to $[Basic \to Basic] \times [Basic \to Basic]$. Let $f \in D_{2t'}$ be $f = \lambda p \in E_p.\pi_1(p)$. By definition we have that $\gamma_{t'tinst}(f) = \lambda p \in F_p.\gamma_{t_2 tinst_2}(f\ (\alpha_{tinst_1 t_1}(p)))$. Also by definition we have that

$$\mathcal{W}_{tinst}(\gamma_{t'tinst}(f)) = \lambda p \in F_p. \begin{cases} \lambda u \in Basic.u \text{ if } p \sqsubseteq (\lambda z \in Basic.z, \lambda z \in Basic.z) \\ \lambda u \in Basic.n \text{ otherwise} \end{cases}$$

Let $q = (\lambda z \in Basic.z, \lambda z \in Basic.n)$. Then

$$\gamma_{t'tinst}(f)\ q = \lambda u \in Basic.u \sqsubset \lambda u \in Basic.n = (\mathcal{W}_{tinst}(\gamma_{t'tinst}(f)))\ q$$

3.6 A Hierarchy of Analyses

This analysis was intended to be an intermediate one between the two analyses presented in [11]. In this section we study its relation with $[\![\cdot]\!]_2$. It can also be proved that some of its variants are better than $[\![\cdot]\!]_1$, see [10,9]. First, Proposition 4 tells us that the third analysis is less precise than the second one. This is true for any variant of the third analysis, and in particular for the one we have described. Also, Proposition 5 tells us that given two comparable widening operators, the corresponding variants of the third analysis are also comparable. In [10] other variants ($\mathcal{W}_b$, $\mathcal{W}_c$ and $\mathcal{W}_d$) of the third analysis were presented. The relations between them and with $[\![\cdot]\!]_1$ and $[\![\cdot]\!]_2$ are shown in Figure 8. The main difference between them lies in their treatment of tuples, in the argument and/or in the result of the functions, either as indivisible entities or as componentwise ones.

Proposition 4 *Let $\mathcal{W}'_t : D_{2t} \to D_{2t}$ be a widening operator for each type t. Let ρ_2 and ρ_3 be such that for each variable $v :: t_v$ $\rho_2(v) \sqsubseteq \rho_3(v)$. Then for each expression $e :: t_e$, $[\![e]\!]_2\ \rho_2 \sqsubseteq [\![e]\!]_3^{\mathcal{W}'}\ \rho_3$*

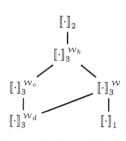

Fig. 8. A hierarchy of analyses

```
e = let rec
      f = λp.λx.case p of
        (p₁, p₂) → case p₂ of
          0 → (p₁, x)
          z → (f (p₁ * p₁, p₂ − 1)) (x * p₂)
    in let
      f₁ = (f (q, 3)) 4
      f₂ = (f (1, 2)) q
      x₁ = case f₁ of (f₁₁, f₁₂) → f₁₂
      x₂ = case f₂ of (f₂₁, f₂₂) → f₂₁
    in (x₁, x₂)
```

Fig. 9. An example expression e

Proposition 5 *Let $\mathcal{W}'_t$, $\mathcal{W}''_t$ be two widening operators for each type t. Let ρ_3, ρ'_3 such that for each variable $v :: t_v$, $\rho_3(v) \sqsubseteq \rho'_3(v)$. If for each type t, $\mathcal{W}'_t \sqsubseteq \mathcal{W}''_t$, then for each expression $e :: t_e$, $\llbracket e \rrbracket_3^{\mathcal{W}'} \rho_3 \sqsubseteq \llbracket e \rrbracket_3^{\mathcal{W}''} \rho'_3$*

An example In Figure 9 an example expression $e :: (Int, Int)$ shows the difference in power between $\llbracket \cdot \rrbracket_1$, $\llbracket \cdot \rrbracket_3^w$ and $\llbracket \cdot \rrbracket_2$. In order to save some space, the syntax is sugared. Given a pair of integers (p_1, p_2) and another integer x, the function $f :: t$, where $t = (Int, Int) \to Int \to (Int, Int)$, calculates the pair $(p_1{}^{2*p_2}, x * p_2!)$. q is a free variable in e. Let us assume that in our abstract environment it has an abstract value n, that is, $\rho = [q \mapsto n]$. Then, by applying the analyses definitions (see [11] for the details of $\llbracket \cdot \rrbracket_1$) we obtain that $\llbracket e \rrbracket_1 \rho = (n, n) \sqsupset \llbracket e \rrbracket_3^w \rho = (n, d) \sqsupset \llbracket e \rrbracket_2 \rho = (d, d)$.

4   Implementation of the Analysis

4.1   Introduction

In this section we describe the main aspects of the analysis implementation. The algorithm we describe here not only obtains the abstract values of the expressions, but it also annotates each expression (and its subexpressions) with its corresponding signature. A full version of this algorithm has been implemented in Haskell. The implementation of the analysis includes also a little parser and a pretty printing [7]. It is important to annotate the subexpressions, even inside the body of a lambda-abstraction. In [11] we explained that the full laziness transformation [15] may change the semantics of a program when non-deterministic expressions are involved. Given an expression $f = \lambda y.\mathbf{let}\ x = e_1\ \mathbf{in}\ x + y$, where e_1 does not depend on y, the full laziness transformation would produce $f' = \mathbf{let}\ x = e_1\ \mathbf{in}\ \lambda y.x + y$. It was shown that the problem appears when e_1 is non-deterministic. So the annotation of expressions inside functions is necessary.

$av \to$	b	$b \to$	$\mid d$
	$\mid (av_1, \ldots, av_m)$		$\mid n$
	$\mid \lambda v.(e, \rho)$	$aw \to$	$\mid b$
	$\mid G\ t'\ t'[t/\beta]\ av$		$\mid (aw_1, \ldots, aw_m)$
	$\mid A\ t'[t/\beta]\ t'\ av$		$\mid <t,\ aw_1 \ldots aw_m + aw>$
	$\mid \boxed{F}[av_1, \ldots, av_m]$		$\mid <t,\ +aw>$
	$\mid aw$		

Fig. 10. Abstract values definition

In the algorithm we make use of the fact that it is implemented in a lazy functional language. The interpretation of a lambda $\lambda v.e$ in an environment ρ is an abstract function. We will use a suspension $\lambda v.(e, \rho)$ to represent the abstract value of $\lambda v.e$. Only when the function is applied to an argument, the body e of the function will be interpreted in the proper environment, emulating

$$\gamma'_t :: Basic \rightarrow S_t$$

$$\gamma'_t(b) = \begin{cases} B \text{ if } t = K, t = T\,t_1\ldots t_m, t = \beta \\ (\gamma'_{t_1}(b),\ldots,\gamma'_{t_m}(b)) \text{ if } t = (t_1,\ldots,t_m) \\ \gamma'_{t_1}(b) \text{ if } t = \forall t.t_1 \\ <t,\ \gamma'_{t_r}(n) \overset{(m)}{\cdots} \gamma'_{t_r}(n) + \gamma'_{t_r}(b)> \quad \text{if } t = t_1 \rightarrow t_2, Process\,t_1\,t_2 \\ \quad \text{where } m = nArgs(t),\ t_r = rType(t) \end{cases}$$

Fig. 11. The signatures corresponding to $\gamma_t(n)$ and $\gamma_t(d)$.

	$\gamma'_{t'\,tinst} : D_{2\,t'} \rightarrow D_{2\,tinst}$	$\alpha'_{tinst\,t'} : D_{2\,tinst} \rightarrow D_{2\,t'}$
$t' = K, T\,t_1\ldots t_m,$	$\gamma'_{t'\,tinst} = id_{Basic}$	$\alpha'_{tinst\,t'} = id_{Basic}$
$\beta'(\neq \beta)$		
$t' = (t_1,\ldots,t_m)$	$\gamma'_{t'\,tinst}(av_1,\ldots,av_m) =$	$\alpha'_{tinst\,t'}(av_1,\ldots,av_m) =$
	$(\gamma'_{t_1\,tinst_1}(av_1),\ldots,\gamma'_{t_m\,tinst_m}(av_m))$	$(\alpha'_{tinst_1\,t_1}(av_1),\ldots,\alpha'_{tinst_m\,t_m}(av_m))$
$t' = t_1 \rightarrow t_2,$	$\gamma'_{t'\,tinst}(av) = G\,t'\,t'[t/\beta]\,av$	$\alpha'_{tinst\,t'}(av) = A\,t'[t/\beta]\,t'\,av$
$Process\,t_1\,t_2$		
$t' = \beta$	$\gamma'_{t'\,tinst} = \gamma'_t$	$\alpha'_{tinst\,t'} = \alpha_t$
$t' = \forall\beta'.t_1$	$\gamma'_{t'\,tinst} = \gamma'_{t_1\,tinst_1}$	$\alpha'_{tinst\,t'} = \alpha'_{tinst_1\,t_1}$

Fig. 12. Implementation of functions $\alpha_{tinst\,t'}$ and $\gamma_{t'\,tinst}$

in this way the behaviour of the abstract function. So, we use the lazy evaluation of Haskell as our interpretation machinery. Otherwise, we should build a whole interpreter which would be less efficient. But this decision introduces some problems. Sometimes we need to build an abstract function that does not come from the interpretation of a lambda in the program. There are several situations where this happens. One of these is the application of $\gamma_t(b)$ when t is a function or a process type. By Proposition 2 we can use the corresponding signature to represent $\gamma_t(b)$ without losing information. So, in this case we do not need to build a function. Given a basic value b, function $\gamma'_t = \wp_t \cdot \gamma_t$, see Figure 11, returns the signature of $\gamma_t(b)$.

This also happens when computing $\alpha_{tinst\,t'}(av)$ and $\gamma_{t'\,tinst}(av)$ where t' is a function or a process type. But in this case, as we saw in Section 3.5, we cannot represent these values by their signatures without losing information. So we build two new suspensions $A\,t'[t/\beta]\,t'\,av$ and $G\,t'\,t'[t/\beta]\,av$ to represent them, see Figure 10. In Figure 12 the implementation of functions $\gamma_{t'\,tinst}$ and $\alpha_{tinst\,t'}$, respectively called $\gamma'_{t'\,tinst}$ and $\alpha'_{tinst\,t'}$ are shown. In the functional case they just return the suspension. Only when they are applied to an argument, their definitions are applied, see Figure 14.

We also need to build a function when computing a lub of functions. In this case, we also use a new suspension $\lfloor_{\mathrm{F}\rfloor}[av_1,\ldots,av_m]$, see Figure 10. When the function is applied, the lub will be computed, see Figure 14.

4.2   Abstract Values Definition

In the implementation of the analysis, signatures are considered also as abstract values, where a signature $s \in S_t$ is just a representation of the abstract value $\Re_t(s)$. In Figure 10 the abstract values are defined. They can be basic

$$n \sqcup b = n$$
$$d \sqcup b = b$$
$$(av_1, \ldots, av_m) \sqcup (av'_1, \ldots, av'_m) = (av_1 \sqcup av'_1, \ldots, av_m \sqcup av'_m)$$
$$<t, \; aw_1 \ldots aw_m + aw> \sqcup <t, \; aw'_1, \ldots, aw'_m + aw'> =$$
$$<t, \; (aw_1 \sqcup aw'_1) \ldots (aw_m \sqcup aw'_m) + (aw \sqcup aw')>$$
$$<t, \; +aw> \sqcup <t, \; +aw'> = <t, \; +(aw \sqcup aw')>$$
$$<t, \; aw_1 \ldots aw_m + aw> \sqcup <t, \; +aw'> = <t, \; +aw'> \sqcup <t, \; aw_1 \ldots aw_m + aw>$$
$$= <t, \; +(aw \sqcup aw')>$$
$$(\lfloor \text{F} \rfloor avs) \sqcup av = av \sqcup (\lfloor \text{F} \rfloor avs) = \lfloor \text{F} \rfloor av : avs$$
$$av \sqcup \lambda v.(e, \rho) = \lambda v.(e, \rho) \sqcup av = \lfloor \text{F} \rfloor [av, \lambda v.(e, \rho)]$$
$$(G \; t' \; t'[t/\beta] \; av) \sqcup av' = av' \sqcup (G \; t' \; t'[t/\beta] \; av) = \lfloor \text{F} \rfloor [av', G \; t' \; t'[t/\beta] \; av]$$
$$(A \; t'[t/\beta] \; t' \; av) \sqcup av' = av' \sqcup (A \; t'[t/\beta] \; t' \; av) = \lfloor \text{F} \rfloor [av', A \; t'[t/\beta] \; t' \; av]$$
$$\sqcup [av_1, \ldots, av_m] = av_1 \sqcup \ldots \sqcup av_m$$

Fig. 13. Lub operator definition

abstract values d or n, that represent both a true basic abstract value or a basic signature. Tuples of abstract values are also abstract values. A functional abstract value may have several different representations: It may be represented by a signature or as a *suspension*. In Figure 10 a functional signature is either $<t, aw_1 \ldots aw_m + aw>$ or $<t, +aw>$. The first one is a normal signature. The signature $<t, +aw>$ represents a function returning aw when all the arguments are deterministic (that is, less than or equal to $\gamma_{t_i}(d)$) and $\gamma_{t_r}(n)$ otherwise. So, it is just a particular case of $<t, aw_1 \ldots aw_m + aw>$ where $aw_i = \gamma_{t_r}(n)$ ($i \in \{1..m\}$). A function may also be represented as a suspension. As we have previously said, it can be a suspended lambda abstraction $\lambda v.(e, \rho)$, a suspended lub $\lfloor \text{F} \rfloor [av_1, \ldots, av_m]$ or a polymorphism suspension.

In Figure 13 the lub operator between abstract values is defined. For basic values/signatures and tuples it is simple. In the functional case, if both functions are represented by a signature then we just apply the lub operator componentwise. If one of the functions is a suspension, then the result is a lub suspension.

4.3 Abstract Application of a Function

In Figure 14 the definition of the application of an abstract function to an abstract argument is shown. In case the abstract function is a signature of the form $<t_1 \to \ldots \to t_m \to t_r, \; aw_1 \ldots aw_m + aw>$ we check if the argument av' is less than or equal to $\gamma_{t_1}(d)$. This is done by comparing their signatures, $\wp_{t_1}(av')$ and $\gamma'_{t_1}(d)$ (this can be done by Proposition 3). Should this happen, then we discard the first element aw_1 of the signature and return $<t_2 \to \ldots \to t_m \to t_r, aw_2 \ldots aw_m \; + \; aw>$, as these elements have been obtained by giving the first argument a value $\gamma_{t_1}(d)$. Otherwise, we can return aw_1 as result of the function, only if the rest of the arguments are deterministic, so a signature $<t_2 \to \ldots \to t_m \to t_r, +aw_1>$ is returned. If the abstract function is a signature $<t_1 \to \ldots \to t_m \to t_r, \; +aw>$, only if all the arguments are deterministic (that is, less than or equal to $\gamma_{t_i}(d)$) the value aw is returned. If any of them is not, a non-deterministic result is returned.

$$(\lambda v.(e, \rho))\ av = [\![e]\!]'\ \rho[v \mapsto (av, aw, b)] \text{ where } v :: t_v, \quad aw = \wp_{t_v}(av), \quad b = \alpha_{t_v}(av)$$
$$([\![\mathrm{F}]\!]\ [av_1, \ldots, av_m])\ av' = \bigsqcup\ [av_1\ av', \ldots, av_m\ av']$$
$$(G\ t'\ t'[t/\beta]\ av)\ av' = \gamma'_{t_2\ tinst_2}(av\ (\alpha'_{tinst_1\ t_1}(av')))$$
$$(A\ t'[t/\beta]\ t'\ av)\ av' = \alpha'_{tinst_2\ t_2}(av\ (\gamma'_{t_1\ tinst_1}(av')))$$
$$< t_1 \to \ldots \to t_m \to t_r,\ aw_1 \ldots aw_m + aw > av'\ (m > 1)$$
$$\quad |\ \wp_{t_1}(av') \preceq \gamma'_{t_1}(d) = < t_2 \to \ldots \to t_m \to t_r,\ aw_2 \ldots aw_m + aw >$$
$$\quad |\ \text{otherwise} = < t_2 \to \ldots \to t_m \to t_r,\ + aw_1 >$$
$$< t_1 \to t_r,\ aw_1 + aw > av'$$
$$\quad |\ \wp_{t_1}(av') \preceq \gamma'_{t_1}(d) = aw$$
$$\quad |\ \text{otherwise} = aw_1$$
$$< t_1 \to \ldots \to t_m \to t_r,\ + aw > av'\ (m > 1)$$
$$\quad |\ \wp_{t_1}(av') \preceq \gamma'_{t_1}(d) = < t_2 \to \ldots \to t_m \to t_r,\ + aw >$$
$$\quad |\ \text{otherwise} = \gamma'_{t_2 \to \ldots \to t_m \to t_r}(n)$$
$$< t_1 \to t_r,\ + aw > av'$$
$$\quad |\ \wp_{t_1}(av') \preceq \gamma'_{t_1}(d) = aw$$
$$\quad |\ \text{otherwise} = \gamma'_{t_r}(n)$$

Fig. 14. Application of abstract functions

The suspensions are just a way of delaying the evaluation until the arguments are known. The application of a suspended function to an argument evaluates the function as far as it is possible, until the result of the function or a new suspension is obtained. If it is a suspension $\lambda v.(e, \rho)$, we continue by evaluating the body e with the interpretation function $[\![\cdot]\!]'$, studied in the following section. The environment ρ keeps the abstract values of all the free variables but v in e. So we just have to add a mapping from v to the abstract value of the argument.

If it is a suspended lub, we apply each function to the argument and then try to calculate the lub of the results. If it is a polymorphism suspension then we continue by applying the (temporally suspended) definition of $\gamma_{t'\ tinst}$ and $\alpha_{tinst\ t'}$. The algorithm proceeds by suspending and evaluating once and again.

4.4   The Algorithm

In the algorithm there are two different interpretation functions $[\![\cdot]\!]'$ and $[\![\cdot]\!]$. Given a non-annotated expression e and an environment ρ, $[\![e]\!]\ \rho$ returns a pair $(av, e'@aw)$ where av is the abstract value of e, e' is e where all its subexpressions have been annotated, and aw is the external annotation of e. While annotations in the expressions are always signatures, the first component of the pair is intended to keep as much information as possible, except in the fixpoint calculation where it will be replaced by its corresponding signature. In Figure 15 the algorithm for $[\![\cdot]\!]$ is shown in pseudocode. The one for $[\![\cdot]\!]'$ is very similar: $[\![e]\!]'\ \rho$ returns just the abstract value of the expression. The rest of computations of $[\![e]\!]\ \rho$ are not done. In an environment ρ, there is a triple (av, aw, b) of abstract values associated to each program variable v. The first component av is the abstract value of the expression, aw is the corresponding signature $\wp_t(av)$, and b is the basic abstract value corresponding to $\alpha_t(av)$. As these three values may be used several times along the interpretation, they are calculated just once, when the variable is bound, and used wherever needed.

$[\![\cdot]\!]' :: Expr \to Env \to AbsVal$

$[\![e]\!]' \, \rho = \pi_1([\![e]\!] \, \rho)$

$[\![\cdot]\!] :: Expr(\,) \to Env \to (AbsVal, Expr \; AbsVal)$

$[\![v]\!] \, \rho = (av, v@aw)$
  where $(av, aw, \_) = \rho(v)$;

$[\![k]\!] \, \rho = (d, k@d)$

$[\![(x_1, \ldots, x_m)]\!] \, \rho = ((av_1, \ldots, av_m), (x'_1, \ldots, x'_m)@(aw_1, \ldots, aw_m))$
  where $(av_i, x'_i) = [\![x_i]\!] \, \rho; \quad x_i@aw_i = x'_i$

$[\![C \; x_1 \ldots x_m]\!] \, \rho = (aw, C \; x'_1 \ldots x'_m@aw) \qquad \{x_i :: t_i\}$
  where $(av_i, x'_i) = [\![x_i]\!] \, \rho; \quad aw = \sqcup_{i=1}^m b_i; \quad b_i = $ if $isvar(x_i)$ then $(\pi_3(\rho(x_i)))$ else d

$[\![op \; x_1, \ldots, x_m]\!] \, \rho = (aw, op \; x'_1 \ldots x'_m@aw) \qquad \{op :: top\}$
  where $(av_i, x'_i) = [\![x_i]\!] \, \rho; \quad aw = \gamma'_{top}(d) \; aw_1 \; \ldots \; aw_m; \quad aw_i = $ if $isvar(x_i)$ then $(\pi_2(\rho(x_i)))$ else d

$[\![\lambda v.e]\!] \, \rho = (a, (\lambda v@awv.e')@aw) \qquad \{v :: t_v, (\lambda v.e) :: t\}$
  where $a = \lambda v.(e, \rho); \quad aw = \wp_t(a); \quad awv = \gamma'_{t_v}(n); \quad (\_, e') = [\![e]\!] \, \rho[v \mapsto (awv, awv, n)]$

$[\![\textbf{process} \; v \to e]\!] \, \rho = (a, (\textbf{process} \; v@awv \to e')@aw) \qquad \{v :: t_v, (\textbf{process} \; v \to e) :: t\}$
  where $a = \lambda v.(e, \rho); \quad aw = \wp_t(a); \quad awv = \gamma'_{t_v}(n); \quad (\_, e') = [\![e]\!] \, \rho[v \mapsto (awv, awv, n)]$

$[\![e \; x]\!] \, \rho = (a, (e' \; x')@aw) \qquad \{(e \; x) :: t\}$
  where $(ae, e') = [\![e]\!] \, \rho; \quad (ax, x') = [\![x]\!] \, \rho; \quad a = ae \; ax; \quad aw = \wp_t(a)$

$[\![v\#x]\!] \, \rho = (a, (v'\#x')@aw) \qquad \{(v\#x) :: t\}$
  where $(av, v') = [\![v]\!] \, \rho; \quad (ax, x') = [\![x]\!] \, \rho; \quad a = av \; ax; \quad aw = \wp_t(a)$

$[\![merge]\!] \, \rho = (aw, merge@aw) \qquad \{merge :: t_{merge}\}$
  where $aw = \gamma'_{t_{merge}}(n)$

$[\![\textbf{let} \; bind \; \textbf{in} \; e]\!] \, \rho = (a, (\textbf{let} \; bind' \; \textbf{in} \; e')@aw) \qquad \{e :: t\}$
  where $(\rho', bind') = [\![bind]\!]_B \, \rho; \quad (a, e') = [\![e]\!] \, \rho' \quad e''@aw = e'$

$[\![\textbf{case} \; e \; \textbf{of} \; (v_1, \ldots, v_m) \to e']\!] \, \rho = (a, (\textbf{case} \; (e_1@awe) \; \textbf{of} \; (v'_1, \ldots, v'_m) \to (e'_1@aw))@aw) \qquad \{v_i :: t_i\}$
  where $(ae, e1@awe) = [\![e]\!] \, \rho; \quad aw_i = \pi_i(awe); \quad v'_i = v_i@aw_i; \quad av_i = \pi_i(ae);$
    $b_i = \alpha_{t_i}(av_i); \qquad\qquad (a, e'_1@aw) = [\![e']\!] \, \rho[v_i \mapsto (av_i, aw_i, b_i)]$;

$[\![\textbf{case} \; e \; \textbf{of} \; \overline{alt_i}]\!] \, \rho = (av, (\textbf{case} \; e' \; \textbf{of} \; \overline{alt'_i})@aw) \qquad \{\textbf{case} \; e \; \textbf{of} \; alt_i :: t\}$
  where $(ae, e') = [\![e]\!] \, \rho; \quad (av_i, alt'_i) = [\![alt_i]\!]_A \; ae \; \rho; \quad C_i \; v_{i1} \ldots v_{im_i} \to (e_i@wa_i) = alt'_i;$
    $aw = $ if $ae = n$ then $\gamma'_t(n)$ else $\sqcup_{i=1}^m aw_i; \quad av = $ if $ae = n$ then $\gamma'_t(n)$ else $\sqcup_{i=1}^m av_i$

$[\![\Lambda\beta.e]\!] \, \rho = (av, (\Lambda\beta.e')@awv)$
  where $(av, e') = [\![e]\!] \, \rho; \quad e''@awv = e'$

$[\![(e \; t)]\!] \, \rho = (av, e' \; t@aw) \qquad \{e :: (\forall\beta.t), tinst = t'[t/\beta]\}$
  where $(av', e') = [\![e]\!] \, \rho; \quad av = \gamma'_{t' \, tinst}(av'); \quad aw = \wp_{tinst}(av)$

$[\![v = e]\!]_B \, \rho = (\rho[v \mapsto (av, aw, b)], v@aw = e'@aw)$
  where $(av, e'@aw) = [\![e]\!] \, \rho; \quad b = \alpha_{t_v}(av)$

$[\![\textbf{rec} \; \overline{v_i = e_i}]\!]_B \, \rho = (\rho_{fix}, \textbf{rec} \; \overline{v'_i = e''_i}) \qquad \{v_i :: t_i\}$
  where $\rho_{fix} = fix \; f \; init; \quad init = \rho[v_i \mapsto (aw_i, aw_i, d)]; \qquad aw_i = \gamma'_{t_i}(d)$
    $f\rho' = \rho'[v_i \mapsto (aw'_i, aw'_i, b_i)] \quad$ where $av'_i = [\![e_i]\!]' \, \rho'; \qquad aw'_i = \wp_{t_i}(av'_i); \; b_i = \alpha_{t_i}(av'_i)$
    $(\_, e''_i) = [\![e_i]\!] \, \rho_{fix}; \quad (\_, aw_i, \_) = \rho_{fix}(v_i); \quad v'_i = v_i@aw_i$

$[\![C \; v_1 \ldots v_m \to e]\!]_A \; avd \; \rho = (av, C \; v'_1 \ldots v'_m \to e') \qquad \{v_i :: t_i\}$
  where $aw_i = \gamma'_{t_i}(avd); \quad (av, e') = [\![e]\!] \, \rho[v_i \mapsto (aw_i, aw_i, avd)]; \quad v'_i = v_i@aw_i$

$[\![v \to e]\!]_A \; avd \; \rho = (av, v' \to e')$
  where $(av, e') = [\![e]\!] \, \rho[v \mapsto (avd, avd, avd)]; \quad v' = v@avd$

Fig. 15. The expressions annotation algorithm

The computation of the first component of the result av follows the definition of $[\![\cdot]\!]_3^w$, so we just explain the annotation part. In general, to annotate the expression we first recursively annotate its subexpressions and then calculate the annotation for the whole expression by probing the resulting abstract value (the first component) of the expression. But, in many cases the annotations of the subexpressions are used to build the annotation of the whole expression, which is more efficient.

4.5   Cost of the Analysis

Analysing the cost of the interpretation algorithm has proved to be a hard task. This is due to the fact that many of the functions involved —in particular $[\![\cdot]\!]$, $[\![\cdot]\!]'$, abstract application, $\gamma'_{t\,tinst}$, $\wp_t$, $\alpha'_{tinst\,t'}$, and α'_t— are heavily mutually recursive. Fortunately, there are small functions whose cost can be directly computed. For instance, a comparison between two signatures in S_t, or computing their lub, can be done in $O(\mathcal{H}_t)$. So, the lub of m abstract values of type t is in $O((m-1)\,\mathcal{H}_t)$. The cost of $\gamma'_t(b)$ is in $O(m + \mathcal{H}_{t_r})$, being $m = nArgs(t)$ and $t_r = rType(t)$. To analyse the cost of the main interpretation functions we define in [10] two functions $s, s' : Expr \rightarrow Int$ respectively giving the 'size' of an expression e when interpreted by $[\![\cdot]\!]$ and by $[\![\cdot]\!]'$. Then $[\![e]\!]'\, \rho \in O(s'(e))$ and $[\![e]\!]\, \rho \in O(s(e))$. Most of the time, $s(e)$ and $s'(e)$ are linear with e using any intuitive notion of size of an expression and including in this notion the size of the types involved. There are three exceptions to this linearity: (1) **Applications**: Interpreting a lambda binding with $[\![\cdot]\!]'$ costs $O(1)$ because a suspension is immediately created. But the body of this lambda is interpreted as many times as the lambda appears applied in the text, each time with possibly different arguments. Being e_λ the body of a lambda, the algorithm costs $O(s'(e_\lambda))$ each time the lambda is applied. (2) **Probing a function**: It is heavily used by $[\![\cdot]\!]$ to annotate expressions with signatures and also by both $[\![\cdot]\!]$ and $[\![\cdot]\!]'$ in fixpoints. The cost of $\wp_t(e)$ involves $m + 1$ abstract applications, each one to m parameters, being $m = nArgs(t)$. Calling e_λ to e's body, the cost will be in $O((m + 1)\, s'(e_\lambda))$. (3) **Fixpoints** Assuming a recursive binding $v = e$ of functional type t, being $m = nArgs(t)$, $t_r = rType(t)$, and e_λ the body of e, algorithm $[\![\cdot]\!]'$ will compute a fixpoint in a maximum of $\mathcal{H}_t = (m + 1)\,\mathcal{H}_{t_r}$ iterations. At each iteration, the signature of e is obtained, so the cost of fixpoints is in $O(m^2\,\mathcal{H}_{t_r}\, s'(e_\lambda))$. The annotation algorithm $[\![\cdot]\!]$ will add to this cost that of completely annotating e, which involves m probings more, each one with one parameter less, i.e. in total $O(m^2\, s'(e_\lambda))$.

Summarizing, the complete interpretation/annotation algorithm is linear with e except in applications —where the interpretation of the body must be multiplied by the number of applications—, in the annotation of functions —where it is quadratic because of probing—, and in fixpoints where it can reach a cubic cost. We have tried the algorithm with actual definitions of typical Eden skeletons. For files of 3.000 net lines and 80 seconds of compilation time in a SUN 4 250 MHz Ultra Sparc-II, the analysis adds an overhead in the range of 0.5 to 1 second, i.e. less than 1 % overhead.

5   Conclusions

This paper has presented a non-determinism analysis, both from a theoretical and from a practical point of view. Although the main motivation for this work has been the correct compilation of our language Eden, most of the work presented here can be applied to any other non-deterministic polymorphic functional language. A possible application of the analysis could be to annotate a source text written in such a language with deterministic annotations, showing the programmer where equational reasoning would still be possible.

In [11] we presented two other analyses for this problem and related them to other abstract interpretation based analyses, such as strictness analysis. The first one had linear cost but it lost most of the information collected for a function when the function was applied. The second one has been summarized in Section 2. It is very powerful but has exponential cost. The one explained here represents a balance between power and cost: It needs polynomial time, and compared to the second analysis, it only loses information in the fixpoints. We have tried it with many example programs keeping a trace of the number of iterations at every fixpoint, and the results show that the upper bound $\mathcal{H}_t$ is almost never reached. So, for our purposes, this work closes the initial problem: We have achieved a powerful enough analysis with an acceptable cost. We have not found any previous analyses for this problem in the literature.

The implementation itself deserves a closing comment: Implementing the analysis in a lazy functional language such as Haskell has offered some advantages. The first one is that an abstract function can be represented by a suspended interpretation. Related to it, abstract interpretation can make use of abstract application and the other way around without any danger of non-termination, thanks to lazy evaluation. Also, $[\![\cdot]\!]$ and $[\![\cdot]\!]'$ have in fact been implemented by a single Haskell function. $[\![\cdot]\!]'$ is just a call to $[\![\cdot]\!]$ after which the second component is simply ignored. Lazy evaluation actually does not compute this component in these calls. All this would have not been so easy in an eager and/or imperative language. Other features such as higher-order, polymorphism and overloading has contributed to a compact algorithm: The whole interpretation fits in a dozen of pages including comments.

References

1. G. Baraki. *Abstract Interpretation of Polymorphic Higher-Order Functions*. PhD thesis, University of Glasgow, February 1993.
2. S. Breitinger, R. Loogen, Y. Ortega Mallén, and R. Peña. Eden: Language Definition and Operational Semantics. Technical Report, Bericht 96-10. Revised version 1.998, Philipps-Universität Marburg, Germany, 1998.
3. G. L. Burn, C. L. Hankin, and S. Abramsky. The Theory of Strictness Analysis for Higher Order Functions. In *Programs as Data Objects*, volume 217 of *LNCS*, pages 42–62. Springer-Verlag, October 1986.
4. P. Cousot and R. Cousot. Abstract interpretation: A unified lattice model for static analysis of programs by construction of approximation of fixed points. In

Proceedings of the 4th ACM Symposium on Principles of Programming Languages, pages 238–252. ACM, 1977.

5. P. Cousot and R. Cousot. Systematic design of program analysis frameworks. In *Conference Record of the 6th Annual ACM Symposium on Principles on Programming Languages*, pages 269–282. ACM, 1979.

6. C. Hankin and S. Hunt. Approximate fixed points in abstract interpretation. In B. Krieg-Brückner, editor, *ESOP '92, 4th European Symposium on Programming*, volume 582 of *LNCS*, pages 219–232. Springer, Berlin, 1992.

7. J. Hughes. The design of a pretty-printing library. In J. Jeuring and E. Meijer, editors, *Advanced Functional Programming*, volume 925 of *LNCS*, pages 53–96. Springer Verlag, 1995.

8. R. J. M. Hughes and J. O'Donnell. Expressing and Reasoning About Non-Deterministic Functional Programs. In *Functional Programming: Proceedings of the 1989 Glasgow Workshop*, pages 308–328. Springer-Verlag, 1990.

9. R. Peña and C. Segura. A Comparison between three Non-determinism Analyses in a Parallel-Functional Language. In *Selected papers in Primeras Jornadas sobre Programación y Lenguajes, PROLE'01*, 2001.

10. R. Peña and C. Segura. Three Non-determinism Analyses in a Parallel-Functional Language. Technical Report 117-01 (SIP). Universidad Complutense de Madrid, Spain, 2001. (http://dalila.sip.ucm.es/miembros/clara/publications.html).

11. R. Peña and C. Segura. Non-Determinism Analysis in a Parallel-Functional Language. In *12th International Workshop on Implementation of Functional Languages, IFL00*, volume 2011 of *LNCS*, pages 1–18. Springer-Verlag, 2001.

12. S. L. Peyton Jones and C. Clack. Finding fixpoints in abstract interpretation. In S. Abramsky and C. Hankin, editors, *Abstract Interpretation of Declarative Languages*, chapter 11, pages 246–265. Ellis-Horwood, 1987.

13. S. L. Peyton Jones, C. V. Hall, K. Hammond, W. D. Partain, and P. L. Wadler. The Glasgow Haskell Compiler: A Technical Overview. In *Joint Framework for Inf. Technology, Keele, DTI/SERC*, pages 249–257, 1993.

14. S. L. Peyton Jones and W. Partain. Measuring the effectiveness of a simple strictness analyser. In *Glasgow Workshop on Functional Programming 1993*, Workshops in Computing, pages 201–220. Springer-Verlag, 1993.

15. S. L. Peyton Jones, W. Partain, and A. L. M. Santos. Let-floating: Moving Bindings to give Faster Programs. *Proceedings of the 1996 ACM SIGPLAN International Conference on Functional Programming, ICFP'96*, pages 1–12, 24-26 May 1996.

16. S. L. Peyton Jones and A. L. M. Santos. A Transformation-based Optimiser for Haskell. *Science of Computer Programming 32(1-3):3-47*, September 1998.

17. H. Søndergaard and P. Sestoft. Referential Transparency, Definiteness and Unfoldability. *Acta Informatica*, 27(6):505–517, May 1990.

Comparative Cross-Platform Performance Results from a Parallelizing SML Compiler

Norman Scaife[1], Greg Michaelson[2], and Susumu Horiguchi[1]

[1] Japan Advanced Institute for Science and Technology,
1/8 Asahidai, Tatsunokuchi, Nomigun, Ishikawa, 923-1211
{norman,hori}@jaist.ac.jp
[2] Department of Computing and Electrical Engineering
Heriot-Watt University, Edinburgh EH14 4AS, Scotland
greg@cee.hw.ac.uk

Abstract. We have developed a parallelising compiler for Standard ML which allows instantiation of a fixed set of higher order functions with equivalent parallel algorithmic skeletons. The compiler is intended to be both portable and semi-automatic. Here we discuss the performance of the code generated by the compiler, for five exemplar programs on four MIMD parallel machines. Results show consistent cross-platform behaviour and good relative speedup for small numbers of processors but with limited scalability to larger numbers of processors.

1   Compiler Overview

We have developed a parallelising compiler [15] for a pure functional subset of Standard ML in which the sole source of parallelism is indicated by specific higher order functions (HOFs). These are translated into calls to parallel algorithmic skeletons[3] implemented either in C or Objective Caml linked with an MPI library [13].

The main objective of this work is to build a compiler for which all parallelism is *implicit*. Our use of algorithmic skeletons allows us to partially achieve this goal. On the one hand the selection and parallel implementation of the higher-order functions from the skeleton library is done automatically by the compiler, although we provide purely sequential equivalents for our HOFs to allow a reduction in the size of the search space by the forced sequential implementation of specious instances. On the other hand the programmer is constrained to use the particular set of HOFs provided by our compiler and is required to express an application using them, hence we term our compiler *semi-automatic*. A subsidiary objective is to allow implementation upon multiple architectures *without source modifications*. The main purpose of this paper is to assess the degree of architectural independence and automation of the current state of the compiler.

We have focused on two HOFs; *map* and *fold*:

```
fun map [] = []
  | map f (h::t) = f h::map f t
```

T. Arts and M. Mohnen (Eds.): IFL 2001, LNCS 2312, pp. 138–154, 2002.
© Springer-Verlag Berlin Heidelberg 2002

```
fun foldr b f [] = b
  | foldr b f (h::t) = f h (foldr b f t)
```

These functions capture paradigmatic programming patterns and prove to have wide applications in programming.

Each function may be realised through a parallel algorithmic skeleton, a template for a generic parallel computation pattern, which may be instantiated with particular argument function instances. Thus, *map* is implemented as a *process farm*, where a *farmer* process sends list elements to *worker* processes, each of which runs the mapped function f. The result from each worker is returned to the farmer for reassembly into the final result list. Similarly, *fold* with an associative and commutative function is realised as a process farm whereby each worker process applies the fold function f to its sub-list and returns the result to the farmer process. The farmer process successively farms out sections of the list until only one element remains. We have had considerable success with the farming paradigm in the past [19]. There are some problems with this method, however, in terms of scalability. The dependence upon a central *master* processor results in a bottleneck at that processor which limits the scalability of both the map and fold skeletons. Other models of parallelism are possible, however, but we use the simplest scheme possible by making use of the strict semantics of the language.

A novel feature of our compiler is the ability to *arbitrarily* nest these two skeletons to any depth. Nesting of HOFs is common in functional programs and a rich source of potential parallelism. However, exploiting nested parallelism is known to be a difficult problem involving many program analysis and resource allocation issues [15]. In particular there are heavy overheads to launching nested skeletons involving re-transmission of data and propagation of bottlenecks to lower nested levels. Our skeletons have a number of operating parameters such as granularity control and weighted processor allocation which allow a limited degree of "tuning" to a particular application. Moreover, we are sometimes able to mitigate re-transmission of data by direct transmission of data from outer to inner nested layers, omitting intermediate layers. This analysis is partial, however, and requires programmer intervention in the general case.

2 Compiler Structure

We use the ML Kit [2] as the host compiler for our system. This provides basic compilation support for SML and is well-suited to the type of analysis we wish to perform. The target compiler for our system is Objective Caml [5]. This was chosen because it is a relatively lightweight implementation of ML with low memory requirements and a bidirectional, untyped C language interface, enabling linkage with MPI libraries.

The structure of the compiler is shown in Figure 1 and is organised as a series of modules. They are controlled by an overarching executive which initialises data and calls the appropriate modules according to a set of control flags.

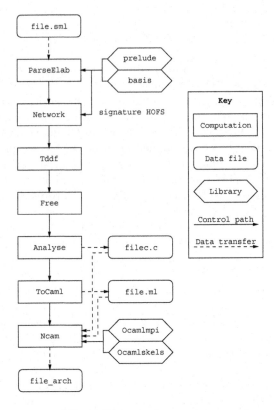

Fig. 1. The compiler modules

After *parsing* and *elaboration* [16] the `Network` module takes the elaborated syntax tree and extracts a description of the *topography* of recognised HOFs from the program. We define the topography to be the relationship between HOFs in the source code and between skeletons in the executing program.

Optionally, the program can be defunctionalized [1] by the `Tddf` module. Our runtime system does not have the ability to transmit functional values which prevents the use of some parallel structures without extensive restructuring of the program by hand. By applying the `Tddf` module, closures are represented by `datatype` values, at the source level, which allows us to transmit partially-applied functions at runtime. There is a serious performance penalty upon applying this transformation to the code so it is only used when necessary. The decision to apply it is made by the programmer. Unfortunately, we could find no simple metric to guide this decision; the effect of the transformation is rather subtle and the situations in which it becomes necessary are complex.

To ensure that free-variables are present at the point of calling a skeleton and are available for transmission at runtime, the `Free` module performs free-variable analysis and implements Johnsson's lambda-lifting algorithm [10]. An attempt is made to limit the transmission of such values to those which will actually be required for remote computation. Note that if defunctionalization is performed then free-variable analysis is not required since free values are bound up in the `datatype` representations.

HOFs nominated by the implementors of the skeleton library are transformed into skeleton calls and code is added to launch the skeletons at runtime by the `Analyse` module. This involves registering functions with the runtime system, passing free values to the runtime system and also reconstructing the types of skeleton results. If the skeletons are implemented in C then a C file is generated containing code to construct the network description at runtime. If the skeletons are implemented in Objective Caml then a description of the network is embedded in the program. In either case this data includes the names of the registered skeleton instantiation functions.

The program is translated from `Core` SML into Objective Caml by the `ToCaml` module. This is mostly a direct conversion between semantic entities but requires some compilation support to iron out minor differences, particularly between the two type systems. There are some inefficiencies introduced by this process which means that our code does not perform, in general, as well as native Objective Caml. The generated code is compiled by the `Ncam` compiler script.

The analysis performed by the compiler allows the replacement of HOFs with parallel skeletons arbitrarily situated within the code. The programmer does not have to consider issues such as free-value placement or the type-correctness of transmitted data. The compiler cannot, at present, make any decisions about which HOFs are viable for parallel implementation, the programmer has to manually prevent replacement of specious HOFs by using equivalent functions under alternative names. At runtime, the skeletal harnesses are able to use the network information in conjunction with the current number of processors to implement sequentially any skeletons for which there are insufficient processors. The programmer is able to partially control this process by a system of weights associated with individual skeletons. The weights will eventually be derived from the profiler information but are set by the programmer at present.

3   Parallel Machines

We have ported the compiler to an Intel Celeron Beowulf, an IBM SP2, a Fujitsu AP3000 and a Sun Enterprise 10000. System characteristics are:

Machine	Processor	Procs[a]	OS
Beowulf	Intel Celeron 533MHz	32	Linux 2.2.16
RS/6000 SP2	PowerPC 332MHz	68(32)	AIX 3.4
AP3000	UltraSPARC 300MHz	76(16)	Solaris 2.6
Enterprise 10000	UltraSPARC2 250MHz	32	Solaris 2.7

[a] Numbers in brackets are the available processors due to scheduling.

The communications setup for each machine is as follows:

Machine	Network	MPI
Beowulf	Ethernet	LAM 6.3.2
RS/6000 SP2	GigaSwitch 150MB/s	Native
AP3000	AP-Net 200Mb/s	Fujitsu MPIAP
Enterprise 10000	GigaPlane-XB[a]	MPICH 1.2.1

[a] Shared memory

Note that several implementations of MPI are available for each machine, for instance the SP2 can use LAM, MPICH or IBM's own implementation of MPI. This is also true for the AP3000. The native MPI libraries were preferred for each machine. MPICH has not been installed on the Beowulf so LAM was chosen for that machine. MPICH was used for the Sun Enterprise since it is implemented for shared memory using the *ch_shmem* driver.

4   Exemplar Programs

The following sections present results for five exemplars, on each ported archi-tecture. None of the exemplars requires defunctionalization so free-value analysis was used in all cases. The runtimes are the average of three executions of the program. Since we are using dedicated parallel machines there was very little variation in performance between runs. The only analysis presented is the run-time and the relative speedup over the available range of processors. This does not unconditionally support claims about the performance of the compiler in an arbitrary situation but enables discussion of portability and scalability. The exemplars themselves are not necessarily the most efficient methods but are the best which could be obtained using the limited number of skeletons available. The development of each exemplar is not discussed but the central code frag-ment illustrating how parallelism arises is shown. Note also that the program parameters are not fully tuned to give the most flattering profile; in general they were chosen to show limitations of the applications. Similarly there are param-eters to the parallel skeletons such as granularity control or weighted processor allocation which could be optimised for a particular application and number of processors. Defaults were used in all cases. Although this might create discrep-ancies between the different machines it was felt that this was more in keeping with testing the degree of automation of our compiler.

4.1   Sum of Euler Numbers

This is a simple program to sum the Euler numbers of a list of integers [8]. It is interesting, however, because several variants involving `map` and `fold` can be investigated. The naive approach can be expressed as:

```
fun gcd x 0 = x
  | gcd x y = gcd y (x mod y)
fun relprime x y = gcd x y = 1
fun euler n =
```

```
if n < 1
  then 0
  else length (filter (relprime n) (fromTo 1 (n-1)))
val result = fold (op +) 0 (map euler nList)
```

Here, `fromTo n m` generates a list of integers from n to m, inclusively. There is a complexity problem since the `fromTo` function is called for each number, a better solution is to generate the list of integers up to a number greater than the maximum in the list and perform a truncated filter over this list:

```
fun euler n = if n < 1 then 0 else zfilter (relprime n) n
```

where `zfilter p n` counts the number of elements for which the predicate p is true in the integer list `[1,...,n]`. The naive approach is therefore a sequence of a `map` followed by a `fold`. The `fold` is not suitable for parallelisation but the `map` should lead to respectable speedup. We can combine the two operations into a single `fold` by representing the integers in a datatype to indicate Euler computation:

```
datatype EI = E of int | I of int
fun eiplus (I i1,I i2) = E ((euler i1) + (euler i2))
  | eiplus (I i,E e) = E ((euler i) + e)
  | eiplus (E e,I i) = E (e + (euler i))
  | eiplus (E e1,E e2) = E (e1 + e2)
val (E result) = fold eiplus (E 0) (seqmap I nList)
```

The datatype is needed to ensure the `fold` function is of the required type. Here there is the disadvantage of having to transmit the datatypes with the integers but this is offset by the ability to combine the two HOFs into one. Note that `seqmap` is an implementation of `map` which is not parallelised by the compiler. A rather contrived nested implementation can be obtained by representing the integers as lists of the EI datatype:

```
fun eulerEI (I n) = E (euler n)
  | eulerEI (E n) = E n
fun sumeulerEI (eil1,eil2) =
  [seqfold eiplus (E L0) (map eulerEI (eil1 @ eil2))]
val [E result] = fold sumeulerEI [E L0] (split c (seqmap I nList))
```

In this case, `split c l` splits a list into c-sized sub-lists. Only the outer `fold` and the inner `map` are likely to lead to parallelism, resulting in a nested `map` within a `fold`. A comparison of the three methods for the SP2 is shown in Figure 2. There is very little difference either in runtime or relative speedup between the methods which is to be expected since the implementation is not dominated by communications times for a list of 300 integers. In practice the single `fold` version performs marginally better over a range of different parameters. The `fold` version is presented for each of the target architectures in Figure 3. The runtimes are very similar, given the different speeds of the processors and the relative speedups are identical apart from the Enterprise which tails off badly at higher numbers of processors.

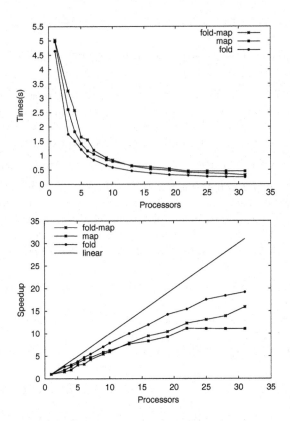

Fig. 2. Sum of Euler numbers on SP2

4.2   Matrix Multiplication

This program calculates the product of two arbitrary-length integer matrices [15]. It has also been used as an exemplar for Hamdan's EKTRAN skeleton-based system [7]. The structure is a nested `map` where the two skeletons are very closely coupled:

```
fun inner Arow Bcol = dotprod Arow Bcol
fun outer BT Arow = map (inner Arow) BT
fun mmult A B = map (outer (transpose B)) A
```

The `mmult` function multiplies two matrices by mapping the matrix-vector operation `outer` over the rows of matrix `A`. This function, in turn, maps the `dotprod` vector-vector operation over the columns of matrix `B`. Note that the entire matrix `B` is passed as an argument to the intermediate skeletons result-ing in transmission at runtime. There are methods which mitigate this such as Gentleman's algorithm [6] but these are not expressible using a functional `map`. We can, however, implement a block structured algorithm which does not need to transmit the entire `B` matrix to all the processors:

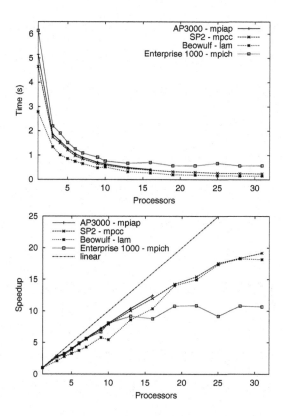

Fig. 3. Comparison of sum of Euler numbers

```
fun BMmult (A,B) =
  let
    val rows = length A
    val outerAB = outer_product (A,transpose B)
    val AB = map Mdotprod outerAB
  in
    split rows AB
  end
```

The outer_product function calculates the outer product of two lists. This method is slightly less communications-bound than the naive approach but is not a geometric decomposition since the same segment of the B matrix could be transmitted to different processors. There is also a sequential overhead where the result matrix is reconstructed from the result list.

A comparison of the row-structured versus block-structured algorithms is shown in Figure 4. This clearly illustrates that both algorithms are seriously communications-bound and that the block-structured method performs much better at larger processor counts. The performance of the block-structured ver-

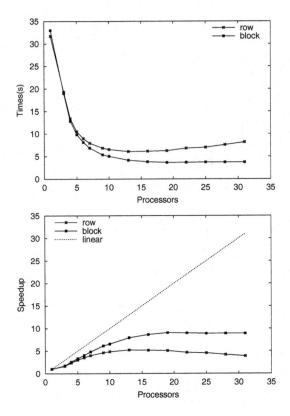

Fig. 4. Matrix multiplication on SP2

sion on the four architectures is presented in Figure 5. Again, there is a very similar runtime and relative speedup profile on all platforms.

4.3 Ray Tracer

This ray tracing algorithm for spheres is implemented as a nested `map` structure. The top level code is a map of the tracing function over the pixels of the image:

```
val ind = indxs 0 (winsize - 1) 0 (winsize - 1)
fun ff (x,y) =
  ((x,y),tracepixel spheres lights x y firstray scrnx scrny)
val image = map (seqmap ff) ind
```

The `indxs` function generates a list of `(x,y)` indices for the image. In practice, the two maps are so closely coupled and the decomposition domain (pixels) is too fine-grained to give speedup from the inner `map`. The results shown in Figure 6 are for a 350×350 image from a complex scene with the single outer `map` implemented in parallel. Close to linear speedup is achieved on all architectures.

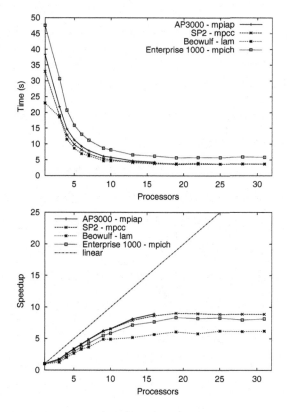

Fig. 5. Matrix multiplication comparison

4.4   Genetic Algorithm

We have implemented a subset of the libraries for RPL2 (Reproductive Plan Language) for developing parallel genetic algorithms. It is based around a simple flat imperative language with data-parallel iterators for manipulating genome pools. RPL2 was developed originally at the Edinburgh Parallel Computing Centre in a joint project with British Gas [17] investigating pipe-network optimisation problems. It is now maintained and distributed by Quadstone Ltd. In this subset we have implemented a linear equation solver applied to data generated by our profiler [14]. Here we have a triply-nested `map` structure: mapping over genome lists, mapping over genomes and calculating the fitness function itself. The innermost `map` is far too fine-grained for efficient parallel execution:

```
fun nextgeneration gsPop = map pfitness (breed gsPop)
fun run population =
  <until convergence> run (map nextgeneration population)
```

A bug in our current runtime system prevents nested structures from appearing within iterative constructs so the results are presented for a non-nested

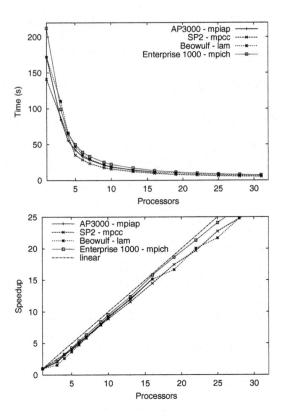

Fig. 6. Ray tracing

implementation. There is a lengthy sequential initialization cost which takes about 10 times as long as a single generation (iteration) but convergence takes about 50 to 100 generations so the iteration time dominates. The results presented in Figure 7 are for a single iteration with the initialization cost elided. Here we see a typical speedup profile for our **map** skeleton under significant communications loads. There is again a considerable agreement between the various architectures in terms of both runtimes and speedups but the speedup tails off at larger numbers of processors.

4.5   Linear Equation Solver

This algorithm finds an exact solution of a linear system of equations of the form $Ax = b$, where all values are in the integer domain, and is discussed in detail by Loidl [12]. The original algorithm was coded in Haskell and has been directly translated into SML. The method is to map the problem onto multiple *homomorphic images*, modulo a prime number, and solve in the homomorphic domain. The final solution is generated by applying the Chinese Remainder

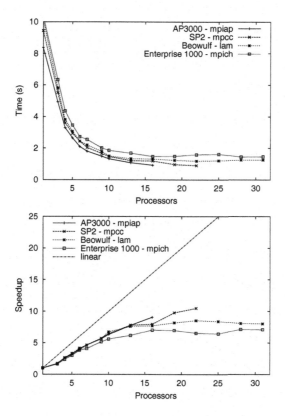

Fig. 7. Genetic algorithm

Algorithm to the homomorphic solutions. Parallelism is a single `map` over the images as nested parallelism within the image was found to be too fine-grained:

```
fun g_hS p = get_homSol aN bN p
val xList = map g_hS boundPrimes
```

The function `get_homSol` solves the equation (aN x = bN) modulo prime number `p`, the value `boundPrimes` is a list of prime numbers estimated to be the number of primes required for a solution. For this application there are significant differences between the runtimes but with almost identical speedup profiles (the Enterprise again tails off at higher processor numbers). The results generally tail off at large numbers of processors as the estimated number of primes is only about 38 for the matrix used in the test. The tail-off is due to residual computation. This is a general problem with our method where we are dealing with short lists, the degree of parallelism (number of primes) only grows very slowly with the problem size resulting in bounded parallelism.

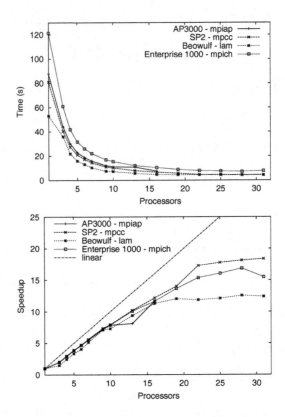

Fig. 8. Linear equation solver

5   Related Work

The HDC compiler project by Herrmann *et al.* [9] is a skeletons-based compiler founded on a strict subset of Haskell. A global heap is not provided so HDC cannot transmit function closures resulting in many similarities with our work. A transformational approach to compilation is used and compilation output is to C with MPI calls. Several skeletons are provided, including `map`, `red` (`fold`), `filter` and `scan` but special emphasis is given to *divide-and-conquer* skeletons. HDC uses the same lambda-lifting and defunctionalization methods as our compiler. HDC is slightly more expressive than our compiler, for instance list comprehensions are transformed into loops and filters which can be exploited by skeleton compilation. Nesting is not explicitly mentioned, however.

Serot *et al.* have developed the SKiPPER language in which skeletons are built using Objective Caml and MPI [4]. Here, co-ordination is carried out using a dataflow model and skeletons such as *task farm* and *data farm* are provided. Arbitrary nesting of skeletons is supported. This method is intended to allow irregular parallelism to be handled but one potential problem with the approach is that free-values have to be transmitted upon each instance.

Hamdan [7] presents a skeletal compiler based on a small functional language called Ektran. The `map` and `fold` skeletons are provided and arbitrary nesting is supported by exposing inner nested functions by inlining. This is translated into C for linkage with MPI libraries.

Skeletons have been implemented in Eden [11], a Haskell extension with primitives to allow the creation of processes and where co-ordination is expressed explicitly by the use of channels. Within this framework skeletons such as parallel `map` and `fold` can be defined but the application of such skeletons is controlled explicitly by the programmer.

Glasgow Parallel Haskell by Trinder *et al.* (GPH) [12] provides the primitives 'par' and 'seq' and uses a *thread-based* execution model. Co-ordination is expressed independently from the main algorithm using *evaluation strategies* [18]. GPH has the ability to transmit function closures by the expedient of providing a global heap and free-values are provided by the runtime system. Within this framework skeletons such as parallel `map` can easily be expressed but require explicit control of granularity and data locality using user-defined strategies.

6   Conclusions

The results indicate consistency in the behaviour of our exemplars across the platforms. This is to be expected for the three distributed-memory machines since they use broadly similar compilation, processor and interconnection technologies. Variations between the three MIMD machines were to be expected from variations in processor speed, interconnection speed and from the varying degrees of optimisation in the MPI implementations. The behaviour of the only shared-memory machine is subtly different and tends to perform worse than the distributed-memory machines at higher processor numbers. The exact reason for this is unclear but could be a property of the shared-memory architecture or the implementation of MPI on such architectures.

Differences in the sequential runtimes across all the platforms can be correlated directly with processor speed. The following table shows the sequential processing times for the exemplars, normalised with respect to the processor speed of the slowest machine (the Enterprise). This shows that the sequential runtimes are comparable apart from the Beowulf which has slower normalised times on the Raytracer and Gafit applications.

Machine	Sumeuler	Matrix	Raytracer	Gafit	Linsolv
Beowulf	6.11	49.03	366.9	21.55	113.2
RS/6000 SP2	6.16	43.82	187.1	12.53	107.5
AP3000	6.18	45.96	207.1	10.04	105.2
Enterprise 10000	6.13	47.6	212.2	10.36	121.3

Although the relative speedups are very good at low numbers of processors the performance at higher processor counts is unreliable. This is due to a number of factors. Firstly, we use the Objective Caml `Marshal` module for linearization of our data for communication via MPI. This library is intended for portability rather than compactness and as such results in unnecessarily large communications. For example, a 200 × 200 32-bit integer matrix uses 160000 bytes of raw data but is encoded in 200175 bytes by the `Marshal` module and takes 680421 bytes when using arbitrary-length integers. This means that our skeletons are communications-bound. Secondly, both of our skeletons use a *master-slave* model which tends to result in a bottleneck at the master processor. This is much worse for `fold` than for `map`, particularly when the size of the data is not reduced by applying the `fold` operator. Thirdly, as noted for the linear equation solver, we are dependent upon there being suitably-sized data within the program. With a regular application it is usually possible to *tune* the granularity to get good parallel performance, for example the ray tracer, but some applications do not exhibit such behaviour, for example the linear equation solver.

Initial investigations suggest that our overall results do not compare favourably with sequential, imperative implementations. For example, the sum of Euler numbers application can easily be implemented in C using the GNU gmp library. This program takes 0.116 seconds to process the same data as our functional implementation which takes 2.79 seconds on one processor and 0.153 seconds on 31 processors giving an absolute speedup of 0.76. This is not a representative application, however, since it is highly dependent upon the performance of the arbitrary-length integer library. The performance disadvantages of functional languages are often offset by other benefits.

The main contribution of this paper is in demonstrating consistency of cross-platform behaviour for a small set of significant exemplars on a range of MIMD machines. The software components that make up the compiler, and the tools used to realise it, contribute substantially to this consistency. In particular, these results suggest that the C compilers, which generate code for skeletons, and the OCaml back end, which generates code for sequential program constructs, offer excellent consistency of generated code behaviour across platforms. The different MPI implementations also display consistent cross-platform behaviours.

More generally, we have provided further evidence of the utility of the automatic extraction of parallelism from functional programs by realising higher order functions as algorithmic skeletons. Parallel programming is hard even with deep knowledge of underlying parallel software and hardware architectures. Algorithmic skeletons offer an appropriate level of granularity for exploring various forms of parallelism. The corresponding higher order functions offer a high degree of abstraction to programmers, minimising necessary awareness of low-level parallel implementation concerns. Finally, functional languages provide a succinct, expressive and formally based medium for writing parallel programs.

Work continues on refining the compiler. Our priorities are to:
- identify useful parallelism in higher order functions from profiling. We use sequential rule counts, from an interpreter based on the SML structural operational semantics, to instantiate linear equations relating counts to par-

allel times. We are currently exploring numerical and genetic approaches to finding stable solutions to the equations;
- add additional algorithmic skeletons to the compiler, in particular for function composition realised as a pipeline;
- benchmark the compiler on exemplars offering multiple sites of useful, deeply nested parallelism.

Acknowledgements

This work was supported by grant number GR/L42889 from the UK's Engineering and Physical Sciences Research Council (EPSRC) and Postdoctoral fellowship P00778 of the Japan Society for the Promotion of Science (JSPS). We would also like to thank the Imperial College Parallel Computing Centre for the use of the AP3000, Quadstone Ltd. for access to the RPL2 code and Hans-Wolfgang Loidl for the linear equation solver and the sum of Euler numbers applications.

References

1. J. M. Bell, F. Bellegarde, and J. Hook. Type-driven defunctionalization. In *Proceedings of the ACM SIGPLAN ICFP '97*, pages 25–37. ACM, Jun 1997.
2. L. Birkedal, N. Rothwell, M. Tofte, and D. N. Turner. The ML Kit (Version 1). Technical Report 93/14, Department of Computer Science, University of Copenhagen, 1993.
3. M. I. Cole. *Algorithmic Skeletons: Structured Management of Parallel Computation*. Pitman, 1989.
4. R. Coudarcher, J. Serot, and J.-P. Derutin. Implementation of a skeleton-based parallel programming environment supporting arbitrary nesting. In F. Meuller, editor, *High-Level Parallel Programming Models and Supportive Environments*, volume 2026 of *LNCS*. Springer-Verlag, Apr 2001.
5. G. Cousineau and M. Mauny. *The Functional Approach to Programming*. Cambridge University Press, Cambridge, 1998.
6. W. M. Gentleman. Some Complexity Results for Matrix Computations on Parallel Processors. *JACM*, 25:112–115, 1978.
7. M. Hamdan. *A Combinational Framework for Parallel Programming Using Algorithmic Skeletons*. PhD thesis, Department of Computing and Electrical Engineering, Heriot-Watt University, 2000.
8. K. Hammond and G. Michaelson. *Research Directions in Parallel Functional Programming*. Springer, 1999.
9. Christoph A. Herrmann and Christian Lengauer. The hdc compiler project. In Alain Darte, Georges-André Silber, and Yves Robert, editors, *Proc. Eighth Int. Workshop on Compilers for Parallel Computers (CPC 2000)*, pages 239–254. LIP, ENS Lyon, 2000.
10. T. Johnsson. *"Lambda Lifting: transforming programs to recursive equations"*, volume 201 of *LNCS*, pages 190–302. Springer-Verlag, 1985.
11. Ulrike Klusik, Rita Loogen, Steffen Priebe, and Fernando Rubio. Implementation skeletons in eden: Low-effort parallel programming. In *12th Int. Workshop on Implementation of Functional Languages (IFL 2000)*, LNCS. Springer, 2000. to appear.

12. H-W. Loidl, P.W. Trinder, K. Hammond, S.B. Junaidu, R.G. Morgan, and S.L. Peyton Jones. Engineering Parallel Symbolic Programs in GPH. *Concurrency — Practice and Experience*, 11:701–752, 1999.

13. Message Passing Interface Forum. MPI: A Message-Passing Interface Standard. *International Journal of Supercomputer Applications and High Performance Computing*, 8(3/4), 1994.

14. G. Michaelson and N.Scaife. "parallel functional island model genetic algorithms through nested skeletons". In M. Mohnen and P. Koopman, editors, *"Proceedings of 12th International Workshop on the Implementation of Functional Languages"*, pages 307–313, Aachen, September 2000. {ISSN 0935-3232}.

15. G. Michaelson, N. Scaife, P. Bristow, and P. King. Nested algorithmic skeletons from higher order functions. *Parallel Algorithms and Applications special issue on High Level Models and Languages for Parallel Processing*, 16(2-3), 2001.

16. R. Milner, M. Tofte, and R. Harper. *The Definition of Standard ML*. MIT Press, 1990.

17. P. Surry. RPL2 Functional Specification. Technical Report EPCC-PAP-RPL2-FS 1.0, University of Edinburgh/British Gas, 1993.

18. P. W. Trinder, K. Hammond, H-W. Loidl, and S. L. Peyton-Jones. Algorithm + strategy = parallelism. *Journal of Functional Programming*, 8(1):23–60, Jan 1998.

19. A. M. Wallace, G. J. Michaelson, N. Scaife, and W. J. Austin. A Dual Source, Parallel Architecture for Computer Vision. *The Journal of Supercomputing*, 12(1/2):37–56, Jan/Feb 1998.

Runtime Behavior of Conversion Interpretation of Subtyping

Yasuhiko Minamide

Institute of Information Sciences and Electronics
University of Tsukuba
and
PRESTO, JST
minamide@is.tsukuba.ac.jp

Abstract. A programming language with subtyping can be translated into a language without subtyping by inserting conversion functions. Previous studies of this interpretation showed only the extensional correctness of the translation. We study runtime behavior of translated programs and show that this translation preserves execution time and stack space within a factor determined by the types in a program. Both the proofs on execution time and stack space are based on the method of logical relations where relations are extended with the factor of slowdown or increase of stack space.

1 Introduction

A programming language with subtyping can be translated into a language without subtyping by inserting conversion functions. Previous studies of this interpretation showed only the extensional correctness of the translation [3,?]. In this paper, we study runtime behavior of the conversion interpretation of subtyping in call-by-value evaluation. We show that this translation preserves execution time and stack space within a factor determined by the types in a program, if subtyping relation is a partial order.

The translation of conversion interpretation changes the runtime behavior of programs in several respects. It inserts conversion functions and may increase the total number of closures allocated during execution. It translates tail-calls into non-tail-calls and, therefore, it may increase stack space usage. Although the translation causes these changes of runtime behavior, execution time and stack space usage are preserved asymptotically. This contrasts with type-directed unboxing of Leroy where both time and space complexity are not preserved [11].

Type systems with subtyping can be used to express information obtained by various program analyses such as control flow analyses [7]. One strategy of utilizing types obtained by program analysis is to adopt conversion interpretation of the subtyping. For example, it is possible to choose an optimized representation of values based on types and to insert conversion functions as type-directed unboxing of polymorphic languages [8]. In order to adopt this compilation method

T. Arts and M. Mohnen (Eds.): IFL 2001, LNCS 2312, pp. 155–167, 2002.

we need to show that the conversion interpretation is safe with respect to performance. The results in this paper ensure safety with respect to execution time and stack space.

Both the safety proofs on execution time and stack space are based on the method of logical relations. The method of logical relations has been used for correctness proofs of many type-directed program transformations [8,14,12] and was extended to prove time safety of unboxing by Minamide and Garrigue [11]. One motivation of this work is to show that the method of logical relations can be extended to prove safety with respect to stack space. The structure of the proof we obtained for stack space is almost the same as that for the execution time. This is because the operational semantics profiling stack space can be formalized in the same manner as the semantics profiling execution time. We believe this is the first proof concerning stack space based on the method of logical relations.

We believe that the conversion interpretation is also safe with respect to heap space. However, it seems that it is difficult to extend the method of logical relations for heap space. We would like to study safety with respect to heap space in future work.

This paper is organized as follows. We start with a review of conversion interpretation and runtime behavior of translated programs. In Section 3 we define the language we will use in the rest of the paper and formally introduce conversion interpretation. We prove that conversion interpretation preserves stack space and execution time in Section 4 and Section 5. Finally we review related work and presents the conclusions.

2 Review of Conversion Interpretation

We review conversion interpretation of subtyping and intuitively explain that the interpretation preserves stack space and execution time if the subtyping relation is a partial order. Since the subtyping relation is transitive and reflexive, the subtyping relation is a partial order if it contains no equivalent types.

The conversion interpretation is a translation from a language with subtyping into a simply typed language without subtyping. The idea is to insert a conversion function (or coercion) where the subsumption rule is used. If the following subsumption rule is used in the typing derivation,

$$\frac{\Gamma \vdash M : \tau \quad \tau \leq \sigma}{\Gamma \vdash M : \sigma}$$

the conversion function $\mathsf{coerce}_{\tau \leq \sigma}$ of type $\tau \to \sigma$ is inserted and we obtain the following term.

$$\mathsf{coerce}_{\tau \leq \sigma}(M)$$

Coercion $\mathsf{coerce}_{\tau \leq \sigma}$ is inductively defined on structure of types. If there are two base types bigint and int for integers where int is a subtype of bigint, we need to have a coercion primitive int2bigint of type int $\to$ bigint. A conversion function on function types is constructed as follows.

$$\lambda f.\lambda x.\text{coerce}_{\tau_2 \leq \sigma_2}(f(\text{coerce}_{\sigma_1 \leq \tau_1}(x)))$$

This is a coercion from $\tau_1 \rightarrow \tau_2$ to $\sigma_1 \rightarrow \sigma_2$.

We show that this interpretation of subtyping is safe with respect to execution time and stack space if the subtyping relation is a partial order. Intuitively, this holds because only a finite number of coercions can be applied to any value. If a subtyping relation is not a partial order, i.e., there exist two types τ and σ such that $\tau \leq \sigma$ and $\sigma \leq \tau$, we can easily construct counter examples for both execution time and stack space. A counter example for execution time is the following translation of term M of type τ,

$$\text{coerce}_{\sigma \leq \tau}(\text{coerce}_{\tau \leq \sigma}(\ldots(\text{coerce}_{\sigma \leq \tau}(\text{coerce}_{\tau \leq \sigma}(M)))))$$

where $\tau \leq \sigma$ and $\sigma \leq \tau$. The execution time to evaluate the coercions in the translation depends on the number of the coercions and cannot be bounded by a constant. It may be possible to avoid this silly translation, but it will be difficult to avoid this problem in general if we have equivalent types.

The conversion interpretation translates tail-call applications into non-tail-call applications. Let us consider the following translation of application $x\,y$.

$$\text{coerce}_{\tau \leq \sigma}(x\,y)$$

Even if $x\,y$ is originally at a tail-call position, after translation it is not at a tail-call position. Therefore, it is not straightforward to show the conversion interpretation preserves stack space asymptotically. In fact, if we have equivalent types, we can demonstrate a counter example. Let us consider the following program where types A and B are equivalent.

```
fun f (0, x : A) = x                    (* f: int * A -> A *)
  | f (n, x : A) = g (n-1, x)
and g (n, x : A) = f (n, x) : B         (* g: int * A -> B *)
```

We have a type annotation f (n, x) : B in the body of g and thus g has type A -> B. This program contains only tail-calls, and thus requires only constant stack space. By inserting conversion functions we obtain the following program:

```
fun f (0, x : A) = x
  | f (n, x : A) = B2A (g (n-1, x))
and g (n, x : A) = A2B (f (n, x))
```

where A2B and B2A are coercions between A and B. For this program, evaluation of f n requires stack space proportional to n since both the applications of f and g are not tail-calls.

In order to preserve time and stack space complexity, it is essential that the subtyping relation is a partial order. This ensures that there is no infinite subtyping chain of types if we consider only structural subtyping. Thus only a finite number of conversions can be applied to any value if the subtyping relation is a partial order.

3   Language and Conversion Interpretation

In this section we introduce a call-by-value functional language with subtyping and its conversion interpretation. We consider a call-by-value functional language with the following syntax.

$$V ::= x \mid \bar{i} \mid \underline{i} \mid \lambda x.M \mid \mathtt{fix}^n\, x.\lambda y.M$$
$$M ::= V \mid M\,M \mid \mathtt{let}\ x = M\ \mathtt{in}\ M$$

There are two families of integers: $\bar{i}$ and $\underline{i}$ are integer values of types bigint and int respectively. The language includes bounded recursive functions where $\mathtt{fix}^n\, x.\lambda y.M$ is expanded at most n times [4]. Any closed program with usual recursive functions can be simulated by bounded recursive functions.

For this language we consider a simple type system extended with subtyping. The types of the language are defined as follows.

$$\tau ::= \mathsf{bigint} \mid \mathsf{int} \mid \tau \to \tau$$

We consider two base types bigint and int where int is a subtype of bigint. A metavariable σ is also used to denote a type. The subtyping relation $\tau_1 \leq \tau_2$ is given by the following three rules.

$$\tau \leq \tau \qquad \mathsf{int} \leq \mathsf{bigint} \qquad \frac{\sigma_1 \leq \tau_1 \quad \tau_2 \leq \sigma_2}{\tau_1 \to \tau_2 \leq \sigma_1 \to \sigma_2}$$

The rule for transitivity is not included here because it can be derived from the other rules for this subtyping relation. We write $\tau < \sigma$ if $\tau \leq \sigma$ and $\tau \not\equiv \sigma$. It is clear that the subtyping relation is a partial order. The typing judgment has the following form:

$$\Gamma \vdash M{:}\tau$$

where Γ is a type assignment of the form $x_1{:}\tau_1, \ldots, x_n{:}\tau_n$. The rules of the type system are defined as follows.

$$\Gamma \vdash \bar{i}{:}\mathsf{bigint} \qquad\qquad \Gamma \vdash \underline{i}{:}\mathsf{int}$$

$$\frac{x{:}\tau \in \Gamma}{\Gamma \vdash x{:}\tau} \qquad\qquad \frac{\Gamma \vdash M_1{:}\tau_1 \to \tau_2 \quad \Gamma \vdash M_2{:}\tau_1}{\Gamma \vdash M_1 M_2{:}\tau_2}$$

$$\frac{\Gamma, x{:}\tau_1 \vdash M{:}\tau_2}{\Gamma \vdash \lambda x.M{:}\tau_1 \to \tau_2} \qquad\qquad \frac{\Gamma \vdash M{:}\sigma \quad \sigma \leq \tau}{\Gamma \vdash M{:}\tau}$$

$$\frac{\Gamma, y{:}\tau_1 \to \tau_2, x{:}\tau_1 \vdash M{:}\tau_2}{\Gamma \vdash \mathtt{fix}^n\, y.\lambda x.M{:}\tau_1 \to \tau_2} \qquad \frac{\Gamma \vdash M_1{:}\tau_1 \quad \Gamma, x{:}\tau_1 \vdash M_2{:}\tau}{\Gamma \vdash \mathtt{let}\ x = M_1\ \mathtt{in}\ M_2{:}\tau}$$

Note that let-expressions do not introduce polymorphic types. They are used to simplify definition of coercions.

We consider a standard natural semantics for this language. A judgment has the following form: $M \Downarrow V$. The rules are given as follows.

$$V \Downarrow V \qquad \frac{M_1 \Downarrow V_1 \quad M_2[V_1/x] \Downarrow V}{\mathtt{let}\ x = M_1\ \mathtt{in}\ M_2 \Downarrow V}$$

$$\frac{M_1 \Downarrow \lambda x.M \quad M_2 \Downarrow V_2 \quad M[V_2/x] \Downarrow V}{M_1 M_2 \Downarrow V}$$

$$\frac{M_1 \Downarrow \mathtt{fix}^{k+1}\ y.\lambda x.M \quad M_2 \Downarrow V_2 \quad M[\mathtt{fix}^k\ y.\lambda x.M/y][V_2/x] \Downarrow V}{M_1 M_2 \Downarrow V}$$

When the recursive function $\mathtt{fix}^{k+1} y.\lambda x.M$ is applied, the bound of the recursive function is decremented.

To formalize the conversion interpretation we need to introduce a target language without subtyping that includes a coercion primitive. We consider the following target language. The only extension is the coercion primitive int2bigint from int into bigint.

$$W ::= x \mid \underline{i} \mid \overline{i} \mid \lambda x.N \mid \mathtt{fix}^n\ x.\lambda y.N$$

$$N ::= W \mid N\ N \mid \mathtt{let}\ x = N\ \mathtt{in}\ N \mid \mathsf{int2bigint}(N)$$

The operational semantics and type system of the language are almost the same as those of the source language. The rule of subsumption is excluded from the type system. The typing rule and evaluation of coercion are defined as follows.

$$\frac{N \Downarrow \underline{i}}{\mathsf{int2bigint}(N) \Downarrow \overline{i}} \qquad \frac{\Gamma \vdash N{:}\mathsf{int}}{\Gamma \vdash \mathsf{int2bigint}(N){:}\mathsf{bigint}}$$

The conversion interpretation is defined inductively on structure of the typing derivation of a program: the translation $\mathcal{C}[\![\Gamma \vdash M{:}\tau]\!]$ below gives a term of the target language.

$$\mathcal{C}[\![\Gamma \vdash x{:}\tau]\!] = x$$

$$\mathcal{C}[\![\Gamma \vdash \lambda x.M{:}\tau_1 \to \tau_2]\!] = \lambda x.\mathcal{C}[\![\Gamma, x{:}\tau_1 \vdash M{:}\tau_2]\!]$$

$$\mathcal{C}[\![\Gamma \vdash \mathtt{fix}^n\ y.\lambda x.M{:}\tau_1 \to \tau_2]\!] = \mathtt{fix}^n\ y.\lambda x.\mathcal{C}[\![\Gamma, y{:}\tau_1 \to \tau_2, x{:}\tau_1 \vdash M{:}\tau_2]\!]$$

$$\mathcal{C}[\![\Gamma \vdash M_1 M_2{:}\tau_2]\!] = \mathcal{C}[\![\Gamma \vdash M_1{:}\tau_1 \to \tau_2]\!]\mathcal{C}[\![\Gamma \vdash M_2{:}\tau_1]\!]$$

$$\mathcal{C}[\![\Gamma \vdash M{:}\tau]\!] = \mathsf{coerce}_{\sigma \leq \tau}(\mathcal{C}[\![\Gamma \vdash M{:}\sigma]\!])$$

$$\mathcal{C}[\![\Gamma \vdash \mathtt{let}\ x = M_1\ \mathtt{in}\ M_2{:}\tau_2]\!] = \mathtt{let}\ x = \mathcal{C}[\![\Gamma \vdash M_1{:}\tau_1]\!]\ \mathtt{in}\ \mathcal{C}[\![\Gamma \vdash M_2{:}\tau_2]\!]$$

The coercion used in the translation is defined inductively on structure of derivation of subtyping as follows [1].

$$\mathsf{coerce}_{\tau \leq \tau}(M) = M$$

$$\mathsf{coerce}_{\mathsf{int} \leq \mathsf{bigint}}(M) = \mathsf{int2bigint}(M)$$

$$\mathsf{coerce}_{\tau_1 \to \tau_2 \leq \sigma_1 \to \sigma_2}(M) = \mathtt{let}\ x = M\ \mathtt{in}\ \lambda y.\mathsf{coerce}_{\tau_2 \leq \sigma_2}(x(\mathsf{coerce}_{\sigma_1 \leq \tau_1}(y)))$$

Note that $\mathsf{coerce}_{\tau \leq \tau}(M)$ must be not only extensionally equivalent to M, but also intensionally equivalent to M. If we adopt $(\lambda x.x)\,M$ for $\mathsf{coerce}_{\tau \leq \tau}(M)$, we have the same problem when we have equivalent types, and thus execution time and stack space are not preserved.

We define two measures, $\lfloor \tau \rfloor$ and $\lceil \tau \rceil$, of types as follows.

$$\begin{array}{ll}
\lfloor \mathsf{int} \rfloor = 0 & \lceil \mathsf{int} \rceil = 1 \\
\lfloor \mathsf{bigint} \rfloor = 1 & \lceil \mathsf{bigint} \rceil = 0 \\
\lfloor \tau_1 \to \tau_2 \rfloor = \lceil \tau_1 \rceil + \lfloor \tau_2 \rfloor & \lceil \tau_1 \to \tau_2 \rceil = \lfloor \tau_1 \rfloor + \lceil \tau_2 \rceil
\end{array}$$

It is clear that $\sigma < \tau$ implies $\lfloor \sigma \rfloor < \lfloor \tau \rfloor$ and $\lceil \sigma \rceil > \lceil \tau \rceil$. Since $\lfloor \tau \rfloor$ and $\lceil \tau \rceil$ are non-negative integers, we also obtain the following properties.

$$\tau_n < \ldots < \tau_1 < \tau_0 \quad \Rightarrow \quad \lfloor \tau_n \rfloor < \ldots < \lfloor \tau_1 \rfloor < \lfloor \tau_0 \rfloor \quad \Rightarrow \quad n \leq \lfloor \tau_0 \rfloor$$

$$\tau_0 < \tau_1 < \ldots < \tau_n \quad \Rightarrow \quad \lceil \tau_0 \rceil > \lceil \tau_1 \rceil > \ldots > \lceil \tau_n \rceil \quad \Rightarrow \quad n \leq \lceil \tau_0 \rceil$$

From the property we can estimate the maximum number of conversions applied a value of τ_0. In the following program, we know that $n \leq \lceil \tau_0 \rceil$ by the property.

$$\mathsf{coerce}_{\tau_{n-1} \leq \tau_n}(\ldots (\mathsf{coerce}_{\tau_0 \leq \tau_1}(V)))$$

Intuitively, this is the property that ensures that conversion interpretation preserves execution time and stack within a factor determined by types in a program.

4   Preservation of Stack Space

We show that coercion interpretation of subtyping preserves stack space within a factor determined by types occurring in a program. Strictly speaking, the factor is determined by the types occurring in the typing derivation used in translation of a program. We prove this property by the method of logical relations.

First we extend the operational semantics to profile stack space usage. The extended judgment has the form $M \Downarrow^n V$ where n models the size of stack space required to evaluate M to V. The following are the extended rules.

$$\frac{}{V \Downarrow^1 V} \qquad \frac{M_1 \Downarrow^m V_1 \quad M_2[V_1/x] \Downarrow^n V}{\mathtt{let}\ x = M_1\ \mathtt{in}\ M_2 \Downarrow^{\max(m+1,n)} V}$$

---

[1] We assume that $\tau_1 \to \tau_2 \leq \tau_1 \to \tau_2$ is not derived from $\tau_1 \leq \tau_1$ and $\tau_2 \leq \tau_2$, but from the axiom.

$$\frac{M_1 \Downarrow^l \lambda x.M \quad M_2 \Downarrow^m V_2 \quad M[V_2/x] \Downarrow^n V}{M_1 M_2 \Downarrow^{\max(l+1,m+1,n)} V}$$

$$\frac{M_1 \Downarrow^l \mathtt{fix}^{k+1} y.\lambda x.M \quad M_2 \Downarrow^m V_2 \quad M[\mathtt{fix}^k y.\lambda x.M/y][V_2/x] \Downarrow^n V}{M_1 M_2 \Downarrow^{\max(l+1,m+1,n)} V}$$

This semantics is considered to model evaluation by an interpreter: $M \Downarrow^n V$ means that a standard interpreter requires n stack frames to evaluate M to V. In the rule of application, evaluation of M_1 and M_2 are considered as non-tail-calls and evaluation of the body of the function is considered as a tail-call. This is the reason that the number of stack frames used to evaluate the application is $\max(l + 1, m + 1, n)$.

This semantics and the correspondence to a semantics modeling evaluation after compilation is discussed in [10]: the ratio to the stack space used by compiled executable code is bounded by the size of a program.

By the rule for values, a value V is evaluated to itself with 1 stack frame. Instead, you can choose $V \Downarrow^0 V$ as the rule for values. This choice does not matter much because the difference caused by the choice is always only 1 stack frame. We have chosen our rule to simplify our proofs.

We write $e \Downarrow^n$ if $e \Downarrow^n v$ for some v and $e \Downarrow^{\leq n}$ if $e \Downarrow^m$ for some $m \leq n$.

The main result of this section is that the conversion interpretation preserves stack space within a factor determined by the sizes of types appearing in a program.

Theorem 1. *Let $C[\![\emptyset \vdash M{:}\tau]\!] = N$ and let C be an integer such that $C > \lfloor \sigma \rfloor + 3$ for all σ appearing in the derivation of $\emptyset \vdash M{:}\tau$. If $M \Downarrow^n V$ then $N \Downarrow^{\leq Cn} W$ for some W.*

Let us consider the following translation where the type of $\lambda x.\underline{1}$ is obtained by subsumption for int $\to$ int $\leq$ int $\to$ bigint.

$$C[\![(\lambda x.\underline{1})\underline{2}]\!] = (\mathtt{let}\ y = \lambda x.\underline{1}\ \mathtt{in}\ \lambda z.\mathsf{int2bigint}(y\ z))\underline{2}$$

The source program is evaluated with 2 stack frames.

$$(\lambda x.\underline{1})\underline{2} \Downarrow^2 \underline{1}$$

On the other hand, the translation is evaluated with 4 stack frames.

$$\frac{\lambda x.\underline{1} \Downarrow^1 \lambda x.\underline{1} \quad \dfrac{V \Downarrow^1 V \quad \underline{2} \Downarrow^1 \underline{2} \quad \dfrac{(\lambda x.\underline{1})\ \underline{2} \Downarrow^2 \underline{1}}{\mathsf{int2bigint}((\lambda x.\underline{1})\ \underline{2}) \Downarrow^3 \overline{1}}}{(\lambda z.\mathsf{int2bigint}((\lambda x.\underline{1})\ z))\ \underline{2} \Downarrow^3 \overline{1}}}{(\mathtt{let}\ y = \lambda x.\underline{1}\ \mathtt{in}\ \lambda z.\mathsf{int2bigint}(y\ z))\underline{2} \Downarrow^3 \overline{1}}$$

where $V \equiv \lambda z.\mathsf{int2bigint}((\lambda x.\underline{1})\ z)$. In this case, the factor of increase is $3/2$.

We prove the main theorem by the method of logical relations. Before defining the logical relations we define the auxiliary relation $V_1 V_2 \downarrow^n V$ defined as follows.

$$\frac{M[V_2/x] \Downarrow^n V}{(\lambda x.M)V_2 \downarrow^n V} \qquad \frac{M[V_2/x][\mathtt{fix}^k y.\lambda x.M/y] \Downarrow^n V}{(\mathtt{fix}^{k+1} y.\lambda x.M)V_2 \downarrow^n V}$$

By using this relation we can combine the two rules for the evaluation of the application into the following rule.

$$\frac{M_1 \Downarrow^l V_1 \quad M_2 \Downarrow^m V_2 \quad V_1 V_2 \Downarrow^n V}{M_1 M_2 \Downarrow^{\max(l+1,m+1,n)} V}$$

This reformulation simplifies the definition of the logical relations and our proof. We define logical relations $V \approx^C_\tau W$ indexed by a type τ and a positive integer C as follows.

$$\underline{i} \approx^C_{\mathsf{int}} \underline{i}$$
$$V \approx^C_{\mathsf{bigint}} \overline{i} \qquad V = \underline{i} \text{ or } V = \overline{i}$$
$$V \approx^C_{\tau_1 \to \tau_2} W \qquad \begin{cases} \text{for all } V_1 \approx^C_{\tau_1} W_1, \text{ if } VV_1 \Downarrow^{n+1} V_2 \\ \text{then } WW_1 \Downarrow^{\leq Cn + \lfloor \tau_2 \rfloor + 3} W_2 \text{ and } V_2 \approx^C_{\tau_2} W_2 \end{cases}$$

We implicitly assume that V and W have type τ for $V \approx^C_\tau W$. The parameter C corresponds to the factor of increase of stack space usage. Note that the increase of stack space usage depends on only the range type τ_2 of a function type $\tau_1 \to \tau_2$. This is explained by checking the following translation of a function f of type $\tau_1 \to \tau_2$ [2].

$$\mathsf{coerce}_{\tau_1 \to \tau_2 \leq \sigma_1 \to \sigma_2}(f) \equiv \lambda y.\mathsf{coerce}_{\tau_2 \leq \sigma_2}(f \; \mathsf{coerce}_{\sigma_1 \leq \tau_1}(y))$$

In this translation, only the coercion $\mathsf{coerce}_{\tau_2 \leq \sigma_2}$ causes increase of stack space usage.

We first show that a conversion from τ to σ behaves well with respect to the logical relations.

Lemma 1. *If $\tau < \sigma$ and $V \approx^C_\tau W$ then $\mathsf{coerce}_{\tau \leq \sigma}(W) \Downarrow^2 W'$ and $V \approx^C_\sigma W'$ for some W'.*

Proof. By induction on derivation of $\tau < \sigma$.

Case: $\mathsf{int} \leq \mathsf{bigint}$. By the definition of $V \approx^C_{\mathsf{int}} W$, both V and W must be $\underline{i}$ for some i. Since $\mathsf{coerce}_{\mathsf{int} \leq \mathsf{bigint}}(\underline{i}) = \mathsf{int2bigint}(\underline{i})$, we have $\mathsf{int2bigint}(\underline{i}) \Downarrow^2 \overline{i}$ and $\underline{i} \approx^C_{\mathsf{bigint}} \overline{i}$.

Case: $\tau \equiv \tau_1 \to \tau_2$ and $\sigma \equiv \sigma_1 \to \sigma_2$ where $\sigma_1 \leq \tau_1$ and $\tau_2 \leq \sigma_2$. There are two subcases: $\tau_2 < \sigma_2$ and $\tau_2 \equiv \sigma_2$. We show the former case here. The proof the latter case is similar.

$$\mathsf{coerce}_{\tau \leq \sigma}(W) \Downarrow^2 \lambda y.\mathsf{coerce}_{\tau_2 \leq \sigma_2}(W(\mathsf{coerce}_{\sigma_1 \leq \tau_1}(y)))$$

Let $V_0 \approx^C_{\sigma_1} W_0$ and $VV_0 \Downarrow^{m+1} V_2$. By induction hypothesis,

$$\mathsf{coerce}_{\sigma_1 \leq \tau_1}(W_0) \Downarrow^{\leq 2} W_1$$

and $V_0 \approx^C_{\tau_1} W_1$ for some W_1. By definition of the logical relations

$$WW_1 \Downarrow^{\leq Cm + \lfloor \tau_2 \rfloor + 3} W_3$$

---

[2] Strictly speaking, it is $\mathsf{let}\ x = f\ \mathsf{in}\ \lambda y.\mathsf{coerce}_{\tau_2 \leq \sigma_2}(x\ \mathsf{coerce}_{\sigma_1 \leq \tau_1}(y))$.

and $V_2 \approx_{\tau_2}^C W_3$ for some W_3. Then we obtain the following evaluation.

$$\frac{W \Downarrow^1 W \quad \mathsf{coerce}_{\sigma_1 \leq \tau_1}(W_0) \Downarrow^{\leq 2} W_1 \quad W W_1 \Downarrow^{\leq Cm + \lfloor \tau_2 \rfloor + 3} W_3}{W(\mathsf{coerce}_{\sigma_1 \leq \tau_1}(W_0)) \Downarrow^{\leq \max(2,3,Cm + \lfloor \tau_2 \rfloor + 3)} W_3}$$

where $\max(2, 3, Cm + \lfloor \tau_2 \rfloor + 3) = Cm + \lfloor \tau_2 \rfloor + 3$.
By induction hypothesis,

$$\mathsf{coerce}_{\tau_2 \leq \sigma_2}(W_3) \Downarrow^2 W_2$$

and $V_2 \approx_{\sigma_2}^C W_2$ for some W_2. Then

$$\mathsf{coerce}_{\tau_2 \leq \sigma_2}(W(\mathsf{coerce}_{\sigma_1 \leq \tau_1}(W_0))) \Downarrow^{\leq Cm + \lfloor \tau_2 \rfloor + 4} W_2$$

where $Cm + \lfloor \tau_2 \rfloor + 4 \leq Cm + \lfloor \sigma_2 \rfloor + 3$

$\square$

The next lemma indicates that we can choose a constant C such that the evaluation of a source program and its translation are related by C. For ρ and ρ' two environments with the same domain, $\rho \approx_\Gamma^C \rho'$ means that they are pointwise related. The main theorem is obtained by restricting this lemma to $\Gamma = \emptyset$ and taking C such that $C > \lfloor \sigma \rfloor + 3$ for all σ appearing in the typing derivation.

Lemma 2. *Let C be an integer such that $C > \lfloor \sigma \rfloor$ for all σ appearing in the derivation of $\Gamma \vdash M{:}\tau$. Let $C[\![\Gamma \vdash M{:}\tau]\!] = N$ and $\rho \approx_\Gamma^C \rho'$. If $\rho(M) \Downarrow^{n+1} V$ then $\rho'(N) \Downarrow^{\leq Cn + \lfloor \tau \rfloor + 3} W$ and $V \approx_\tau^C W$ for some W.*

Proof. By lexicographic induction on derivation of $\Gamma \vdash M{:}\tau$ and the sum of bounds of recursive functions in M.

Case: $\Gamma \vdash M{:}\sigma$ is derived from $\Gamma \vdash M{:}\tau$ and $\tau \leq \sigma$. We assume $\tau < \sigma$. The case of $\tau \equiv \sigma$ is trivial. By definition, N must be $\mathsf{coerce}_{\tau \leq \sigma}(N_0)$ for some N_0 and $C[\![\Gamma \vdash M : \tau]\!] = N_0$. By induction hypothesis,

$$\rho'(N_0) \Downarrow^{\leq Cn + \lfloor \tau \rfloor + 3} W_0$$

and $V \approx_\tau^C W_0$ for some W_0. By Lemma 1,

$$\rho'(\mathsf{coerce}_{\tau \leq \sigma}(N_0)) \Downarrow^{\leq Cn + \lfloor \tau \rfloor + 3 + 1} W$$

and $V \approx_\sigma^C W$ for some W. The proof of this case completes since $Cn + \lfloor \tau \rfloor + 3 + 1 \leq Cn + \lfloor \sigma \rfloor + 3$.

Case: $\Gamma \vdash M_1 M_2{:}\tau_2$ is derived from $\Gamma \vdash M_1{:}\tau_1 \to \tau_2$ and $\Gamma \vdash M_2{:}\tau_1$. By the definition of the translation $N \equiv N_1 N_2$ for some N_1 and N_2.
$\rho(M_1 M_2) \Downarrow^{k+1} V$ is derived from $\rho(M_1) \Downarrow^l V_1$ and $\rho(M_2) \Downarrow^m V_2$ and $V_1 V_2 \Downarrow^n V$ where $l \leq k$, $m \leq k$ and $n \leq k + 1$. By induction hypothesis for M_1,

$$\rho'(N_1) \Downarrow^{C(l-1) + \lfloor \tau_1 \to \tau_2 \rfloor + 3} W_1$$

and $V_1 \approx^C_{\tau_1 \to \tau_2} W_1$ for some W_1. Then we have $\rho'(N_1) \Downarrow^{\leq Cl+2} W_1$ because $\lfloor \tau_1 \to \tau_2 \rfloor + 1 \leq C$. By induction hypothesis for M_2,

$$\rho'(N_2) \Downarrow^{C(m-1)+\lfloor \tau_1 \rfloor + 3} W_2$$

and $V_2 \approx^C_{\tau_1} W_2$ for some W_2. Then we also have $\rho'(N_2) \Downarrow^{\leq Cm+2} W_2$ because $\lfloor \tau_1 \rfloor + 1 \leq C$. By definition of the logical relations

$$W_1 W_2 \downarrow^{\leq C(n-1)+\lfloor \tau_2 \rfloor + 3} W$$

and $V \approx^C_{\tau_2} W$ for some W. We have the following inequality.

$$\max(Cl + 2 + 1, Cm + 2 + 1, C(n-1) + \lfloor \tau_2 \rfloor + 3) \leq Ck + \lfloor \tau_2 \rfloor + 3$$

Hence,

$$\rho'(N_1 N_2) \Downarrow^{\leq Ck+\lfloor \tau_2 \rfloor + 3} W$$

Case: $\Gamma \vdash \mathtt{fix}^{a+1} y.\lambda x.M{:}\tau_1 \to \tau_2$ is derived from $\Gamma, y{:}\tau_1 \to \tau_2, x{:}\tau_1 \vdash M{:}\tau_2$. By definition, $\mathcal{C}[\![\Gamma, y{:}\tau_1 \to \tau_2, x{:}\tau_1 \vdash M{:}\tau_1]\!] = N$ for some N. We have the following evaluation.

$$\rho(\mathtt{fix}^{a+1} y.\lambda x.M) \Downarrow^1 \rho(\mathtt{fix}^{a+1} y.\lambda x.M)$$

$$\rho'(\mathtt{fix}^{a+1} y.\lambda x.N) \Downarrow^1 \rho'(\mathtt{fix}^{a+1} y.\lambda x.N)$$

Let $V \approx^C_{\tau_1} W$ and $\rho(M)[V/x][\rho(\mathtt{fix}^a y.\lambda x.M)/y] \Downarrow^{n+1} V'$. By induction hypothesis,

$$\rho(\mathtt{fix}^a y.\lambda x.M) \approx^C_{\tau_1 \to \tau_2} \rho'(\mathtt{fix}^a y.\lambda x.N)$$

Let $\rho_0 = \rho[V/x][\rho(\mathtt{fix}^a y.\lambda x.M)/y]$ and $\rho'_0 = \rho'[W/x][\rho'(\mathtt{fix}^a y.\lambda x.N)/y]$. We have $\rho_0 \approx^C_{\Gamma, y:\tau_1 \to \tau_2, x:\tau_1} \rho'_0$. By induction hypothesis,

$$\rho'_0(N) \Downarrow^{Cn+\lfloor \tau_2 \rfloor + 3} W'$$

and $V' \approx^C_{\tau_2} W'$. Hence, $\rho(\mathtt{fix}^{a+1} y.\lambda x.M) \approx^C_{\tau_1 \to \tau_2} \rho'(\mathtt{fix}^{a+1} y.\lambda x.N)$.

$\square$

5   Preservation of Execution Time

We introduce the operational semantics profiling execution time and outline the proof that the coercion interpretation of subtyping is also safe with respect to execution time. The operational semantics for execution time is a simple extension of the standard semantics as that for stack space. As the previous section, we first extend judgment of operational semantics to the following form:

$$M \Downarrow^n V$$

where n represents execution time to evaluate M to V. For the rule of application we use an auxiliary relation: $V_1 V_2 \Downarrow^n V$ as before. The rules are given as follows.

$$V \Downarrow^1 V \qquad \frac{M_1 \Downarrow^m V_1 \quad M_2[V_1/x] \Downarrow^n V}{\texttt{let } x = M_1 \texttt{ in } M_2 \Downarrow^{m+n+1} V}$$

$$\frac{M_1 \Downarrow^l V_1 \quad M_2 \Downarrow^m V_2 \quad V_1 V_2 \Downarrow^n V}{M_1 M_2 \Downarrow^{l+m+n+1} V}$$

$$\frac{M[V_2/x] \Downarrow^n V}{(\lambda x.M)V_2 \Downarrow^n V} \qquad \frac{M[V_2/x][\texttt{fix}^k y.\lambda x.M/y] \Downarrow^n V}{(\texttt{fix}^{k+1} y.\lambda x.M)V_2 \Downarrow^n V}$$

All the rules are a straightforward extension of the standard rules.

Then it is shown that the conversion interpretation preserves execution time within a factor determined by the types appearing in a program.

Theorem 2. *Let $\mathcal{C}[\![\emptyset \vdash M : \tau]\!] = N$ and let C be an integer such that $C > 7\lfloor\sigma\rfloor$ for all σ appearing in the derivation of $\emptyset \vdash M : \tau$. If $M \Downarrow^n V$ then $N \Downarrow^{\leq Cn} W$ for some W.*

The factor of slowdown $7\lfloor\sigma\rfloor$ is bigger than the factor of increase of stack space $\lfloor\sigma\rfloor$. To prove this theorem, w use the method of logical relations which are indexed by a slowdown factor as well as a type. The relations $V \approx_\tau^C W$ are defined as follows.

$$\underline{i} \approx_{\text{int}}^C \underline{i}$$
$$V \approx_{\text{bigint}}^C \overline{i} \qquad V = \underline{i} \text{ or } V = \overline{i}$$
$$V \approx_{\tau_1 \to \tau_2}^C W \qquad \begin{cases} \text{for all } V_1 \approx_{\tau_1}^C W_1, \text{ if } V V_1 \Downarrow^{n+1} V_2 \\ \text{then } W W_1 \Downarrow^{Cn+7\lfloor\tau_1 \to \tau_2\rfloor+1} W_2 \text{ and } V_2 \approx_{\tau_2}^C W_2 \end{cases}$$

The important difference from the relations for stack space is that slowdown of the applications depends on the domain type τ_1 as well as the range type τ_2 of a function type $\tau_1 \to \tau_2$.

With this definition, the main theorem is proved in the same manner as the proof for stack space. It is shown that a conversion function behaves well with respect to the logical relations as before. Then the generalization of the main theorem is proved by induction on the derivation of the conversion interpretation of a program.

6   Conclusions and Related Work

We have shown that conversion interpretation of subtyping preserves execution time and stack space within a factor determined by the types in a program if the subtyping relation is a partial order. Type-directed unboxing of Leroy is a translation similar to conversion interpretation of subtyping, but it does not preserve execution time and stack space. This is because conversions of equivalent types appear in type-directed unboxing.

We have considered only a very simple type system which does not include product types and recursive types. We believe the results in this paper can be easily extended for product types. However, our results cannot be extended for recursive types. If we consider recursive types, cost of one application of coercion cannot be bounded by a constant as Leroy discussed in his work on type-directed unboxing for polymorphic languages [8]. Thus the conversion interpretation does not preserve execution time nor stack space usage in the presence of subtyping on recursive types.

We have shown that the conversion interpretation is safe with respect to time and stack space by the method of logical relations. We believe the conversion interpretation is also safe with respect to heap space, but it will be difficult to adopt the same method for heap space. We have no idea how to formalize logical relations for heap space because the semantics profiling heap space is much more complicated than those for time and stack space.

In the rest of this section I review other proof methods to show safety of program transformations with respect to performance.

David Sands studied time safety of transformations for call-by-name languages [16,15]. In his study he extended applicative bisimulation and its context lemma to account execution time. Applicative bisimulation with the context lemma greatly simplifies safety proofs of many program transformations. As with the method of logical relations, it will be difficult to extend this method if we consider heap space or various extensions of languages.

Another approach is to analyze states of evaluation more directly, where proofs are often based on induction on length of evaluation. Blelloch and Greiner showed that an implementation of NESL based on an abstract machine preserves execution time and space within a constant factor based on this approach [2]. Minamide showed that the CPS transformation preserves space within a constant factor [9]. Gustavsson and Sands developed a theory of a space improvement relation for a call-by-need programming language [5,6]. They clarified their proofs by considering evaluation of programs with holes based on a context calculus [17]. Bakewell and Runciman proposed an operational model for lazy functional programming languages based on graph rewriting [1]. As a proof method for the model they considered an extension of bisimulation.

Acknowledgments

This work is partially supported by Japan Society for the Promotion of Science, Grant-in-Aid for Encouragement of Young Scientists of Japan, No. 13780193, 2001.

References

1. A. Bakewell and C. Runciman. A model for comparing the space usage of lazy evaluators. In *Proceedings of the 2nd International ACM SIGPLAN Conference on Principles and Practice of Declarative Programming*, pages 151–162, 2000.

2. G. E. Blelloch and J. Greiner. A provably time and space efficient implementation of NESL. In *Proceedings of the ACM SIGPLAN International Conference on Functional Programming*, pages 213–225, 1996.
3. V. Breazu-Tannen, C. A. Gunter, and A. Scedrov. Computing with coercions. In *Proceedings of the 1990 ACM Conference on LISP and Functional programming*, pages 44–60, 1990.
4. C. A. Gunter. *Semantics of Programming Languages*, chapter 4. The MIT Press, 1992.
5. J. Gustavsson and D. Sands. A foundation for space-safe transformations of call-by-need programs. In *Proceedings of the Third International Workshop on Higher Order Operational Techniques in Semantics (HOOTS99)*, volume 26 of *ENTCS*, 1999.
6. J. Gustavsson and D. Sands. Possibilities and limitations of call-by-need space improvement. In *Proceedings of the Sixth ACM SIGPLAN International Conference on Functional Programming*, pages 265–276, 2001.
7. N. Heintze. Control-flow analysis and type systems. In *Proceedings of the 1995 International Static Analysis Symposium*, volume 983 of *LNCS*, pages 189–206, 1995.
8. X. Leroy. Unboxed objects and polymorphic typing. In *the 19th ACM SIGPLAN-SIGACT Symposium on Principles of Programming Languages*, pages 177–188, 1992.
9. Y. Minamide. A space-profiling semantics of call-by-value lambda calculus and the CPS transformation. In *Proceedings of the Third International Workshop on Higher Order Operational Techniques in Semantics (HOOTS99)*, volume 26 of *ENTCS*, 1999.
10. Y. Minamide. A new criterion for safe program transformations. In *Proceedings of the Forth International Workshop on Higher Order Operational Techniques in Semantics (HOOTS)*, volume 41(3) of *ENTCS*, Montreal, 2000.
11. Y. Minamide and J. Garrigue. On the runtime complexity of type-directed unboxing. In *Proceedings of the Third ACM SIGPLAN International Conference on Functional programming*, pages 1–12, 1998.
12. Y. Minamide, G. Morrisett, and R. Harper. Typed closure conversion. In *Proceeding of the ACM Symposium on Principles of Programming Languages*, pages 271–283, 1996.
13. J. C. Mitchell. *Foundations for Programming Languages*, chapter 10. The MIT Press, 1996.
14. A. Ohori. A polymorphic record calculus and its compilation. *ACM Transaction on Programming Languages and Systems*, 17(6):844–895, 1995.
15. D. Sands. A naive time analysis and its theory of cost equivalence. *Journal of Logic and Computation*, 5(4):495–541, 1995.
16. D. Sands. Proving the correctness of recursion-based automatic program transformations. *Theoretical Computer Science*, 167(1&2):193–233, 1996.
17. D. Sands. Computing with contexts: A simple approach. In *Proceedings of the Second Workshop on Higher-Order Operational Techniques in Semantics (HOOTS II)*, volume 10 of *ENTCS*, 1998.

A Generic Programming Extension for Clean

Artem Alimarine and Rinus Plasmeijer

Nijmegen Institute for Information and Computing Sciences,
1 Toernooiveld, 6525ED, Nijmegen, The Netherlands,
{alimarin,rinus}@cs.kun.nl

Abstract. Generic programming enables the programmer to define functions by induction on the structure of types. Defined once, such a generic function can be used to generate a specialized function for any user defined data type. Several ways to support generic programming in functional languages have been proposed, each with its own pros and cons. In this paper we describe a combination of two existing approaches, which has the advantages of both of them. In our approach overloaded functions with class variables of an arbitrary kind can be defined generically. A single generic definition defines a kind-indexed family of overloaded functions, one for each kind. For instance, the generic mapping function generates an overloaded mapping function for each kind.
Additionally, we propose a separate extension that allows to specify a customized instance of a generic function for a type in terms of the generated instance for that type.

1 Introduction

The standard library of a programming language normally defines functions like equality, pretty printers and parsers for standard data types. For each new user defined data type the programmer often has to provide similar functions for that data type. This is a monotone, error-prone and boring work that can take lots of time. Moreover, when such a data type is changed, the functions for that data type have to be changed as well. Generic programming enables the user to define a function once and specialize it to the data types he or she needs. The idea of generic programming is to define the functions by induction on the structure of types. This idea is based on the fact that a data type in many functional programming languages, including Clean, can be represented as a sum of products of types.

In this paper we present a design and implementation of a generic extension for Clean. Our work is mainly based on two other designs. The first is the generic extension for Glasgow Haskell, described by Hinze and Peyton Jones in [1]. The main idea is to automatically generate methods of a type class, e.g. equality. Thus, the user can define overloaded functions generically. The main limitation of this design is that it only supports type classes, whose class variables range over types of kind $\star$.

The second design described by Hinze in [2] is the one used in the Generic Haskell Prototype. In this approach generic functions have so-called kind-indexed

T. Arts and M. Mohnen (Eds.): IFL 2001, LNCS 2312, pp. 168–185, 2002.

types. The approach works for any kind but the design does not provide a way to define overloaded functions generically.

The design presented here combines the benefits of the kind-indexed approach with those of overloading. Our contributions are:

- We propose a generic programming extension for Clean that allows for kind-indexed families of overloaded functions defined generically. A generic definition produces overloaded functions with class variables of any kind (though current implementation is limited to the second-order kind).
- We propose an additional extension, customized instances, that allows to specify a customized instance of a generic function for a type in terms of the generated instance for that type.

The paper is organized as follows. Section 2 gives an introduction to generic programming by means of examples. In Section 3 our approach is described. We show examples in Generic Clean and their translation to non-generic Clean. In section 4 we discuss the implementation in more detail. In section 5 we describe customized instances. Finally, we discuss related work and conclude.

2   Generic Programming

In this section we give a short and informal introduction to generic programming by example. First we define a couple of functions using type constructor classes. Then we discuss how these examples can be defined generically.

2.1   Type Constructor Classes

This subsection demonstrates how the equality function and the mapping function can be defined using overloading. These examples are the base for the rest of the paper. We will define the functions for the following data types:

```
:: List a      = Nil | Cons a (List a)
:: Tree a b    = Tip a | Bin b (Tree a b) (Tree a b)
```

The overloaded equality function for these data types can be defined in Clean as follows:

```
class eq t :: t t → Bool
instance eq (List a) | eq a where
    eq Nil Nil                      = True
    eq (Cons x xs) (Cons y ys)      = eq x y && eq xs ys
    eq x y                          = False
instance eq (Tree a b) | eq a & eq b where
    eq (Tip x) (Tip y)              = eq x y
    eq (Bin x lxs rxs) (Bin y lys rys) = eq x y && eq lxs lys && eq rxs rys
    eq x y                          = False
```

All these instances have one thing in common: they check that the data constructors of both compared objects are the same and that all the arguments of these constructors are equal. Note also that the context restrictions are needed for all the type arguments, because we call the equality functions for these types.

Another example of a type constructor class is the mapping function:

class *fmap t* :: $(a \rightarrow b)$ $(t\ a) \rightarrow (t\ b)$
instance *fmap List* **where**
    fmap f Nil   = *Nil*
    fmap f (Cons x xs)   = *Cons (f x) (fmap f xs)*

The class variable of this class ranges over types of kind $\star \rightarrow \star$. In contrast, the class variable of equality ranges over types of kind $\star$. The tree type has kind $\star \rightarrow \star \rightarrow \star$. The mapping for a type of this kind takes two functions: one for each type argument.

class *bimap t* :: $(a \rightarrow b)$ $(c \rightarrow d)$ $(t\ a\ c) \rightarrow (t\ b\ d)$
instance *bimap Tree* **where**
    bimap fx fy (Tip x)   = *Tip (fx x)*
    bimap fx fy (Bin y ls rs) = *Bin (fy y) (bimap fx fy ls) (bimap fx fy rs)*

In general the mapping function for a type of arity n, takes n functions: one for each type argument. In particular, the mapping function for types of kind $\star$ is the identity function. This remark is important for section 3 where we define a mapping function for types of all kinds.

2.2   Generic Classes

In this subsection we show how to define the equality function generically, i.e. by induction on the structure of types. The user provides the generic definition of equality once. This definition can be used to produce the equality function for any specific data type. The approach described in this subsection assumes only generic definitions for classes, whose class variables range over types of kind $\star$. This is the approach described by Peyton Jones and Hinze in [1]. We present it here for didactic reasons. In the next section we will present our approach, based on Hinze's kind-indexed types [2], which does not have the limitation of kind $\star$.

The structure of a data type can be represented as a sum of products of types. For instance, a Clean data type

$$:: T\ a_1\ ...\ a_n = K_1\ t_{11}\ ...\ t_{1l_1}|\ ...\ |K_m\ t_{m1}\ ...\ t_{ml_m}$$

can be regarded as

$$T^\circ\ a_1\ ...\ a_n = (t_{11} \times ... \times t_{1l_1}) + ... + (t_{m1} \times ... \times t_{ml_m})$$

List and *Tree* from the previous section can be represented as

$List^\circ\ a$ = $1 + a \times (List\ a)$
$Tree^\circ\ a\ b$ = $a + b \times (Tree\ a\ b) \times (Tree\ a\ b)$

To encode such a representation in Clean we use the following types for binary sums and products.

```
:: UNIT       = UNIT
:: PAIR a b   = PAIR a b
:: EITHER l r = LEFT l | RIGHT r
```

N-ary sums and products can be represented as nested binary sums and products. The *UNIT* type is used to represent the product of zero elements, the *EITHER* type is a binary sum and the *PAIR* type is a binary product. With these types *List°* and *Tree°* can be represented as (in Clean a synonym type is introduced with :==)

```
:: List° a      :== EITHER UNIT (PAIR a (List a))
:: Tree° a b    :== EITHER a (PAIR b (PAIR (Tree a b) (Tree a b)))
```

Note that these types are not recursive. For instance, the right hand side of *List°* refers to the plain *List* rather than to *List°*. So, the encoding affects only the "top-level" of a type definition. The recursive occurrences of *List* type are converted to List° "lazily". In this way it is easy to handle mutually recursive types (see [1]).

We need conversion functions to convert between a data type T and its generic representation $T°$. For example, the conversion functions for lists are

```
fromList                     :: (List a) → List° a
fromList Nil                 = LEFT UNIT
fromList (Cons x xs)         = RIGHT (PAIR x xs)
toList                       :: (List° a) → List a
toList (LEFT UNIT)           = Nil
toList (RIGHT (PAIR x xs))   = Cons x xs
```

Now we are ready to define the equality generically. All the programmer has to do is to specify the instances for unit, sum, product and primitive types.

```
class eq t :: t t → Bool
instance eq Int where
    eq x y                      = eqInt x y
instance eq UNIT where
    eq UNIT UNIT                = True
instance eq (PAIR a b) | eq a & eq b where
    eq (PAIR x1 x2) (PAIR y1 y2) = eq x1 y1 && eq x2 y2
instance eq (EITHER a b) | eq a & eq b where
    eq (LEFT x) (LEFT y)        = eq x y
    eq (RIGHT x) (RIGHT y)      = eq x y
    eq x y                      = False
```

This definition is enough to produce the equality functions for almost all data types: an object of a data type can be (automatically) converted to the generic representation using the conversion functions and the generic representations can be compared using the instances above. The integers are compared with the predefined function *eqInt*. We use integers as the only representative of primitive types. Other primitive types can be handled analogously. The *UNIT* type has only one inhabitant; the equality always return *True*. Pairs are compared component-wise. Binary sums are equal only when the constructors are equal and their arguments are equal. In general a data types may involve arrows. To handle such data types the user has to provide an instance on the arrow type ($\rightarrow$). Since equality cannot be sensibly defined for arrows, we have omitted the instance: comparing types containing arrows will result in a compile time overloading error.

These definitions can be used to produce instances for almost all data types. For instance, when the programmer wants the equality functions to be generated for lists and trees, (s)he specifies the following

instance *eq (List a)* **generic**
instance *eq (Tree a b)* **generic**

These definitions can be used to generate the following instances:

instance *eq (List a)* | *eq a* **where**
    eq x y = eq (fromList x) (fromList y)
instance *eq (Tree a b)* | *eq a* & *eq b* **where**
    eq x y = eq (fromTree x) (fromTree y)

So, we can implement the equality on arbitrary types using the equality on their generic representations. It is important to note that the way we convert the arguments and the results to and from the generic representation depends on the type of the generic function. The compiler generates these conversions automatically as described in section 4.4.

When we try to use the same approach to define *fmap* generically, we have a problem. The type language has to be extended for lambda abstractions on the type level. See [3] for details. Another problem is that we need to provide different mapping functions for different kinds: like *fmap* for kind $\star \rightarrow \star$, *bimap* for kind $\star \rightarrow \star \rightarrow \star$ and so on. Both of these problems are solved by the approach with kind-indexed types [2]. In our design, described in the following section, we use this approach in combination with type constructor classes.

3   Generics in Clean

In this section we show how generic functions can be defined and used in Clean. We use the mapping function as an example. To define the generic mapping function we write

generic *map* a_1 a_2 :: $a_1 \rightarrow a_2$
instance *map Int* **where**
    map x   = x
instance *map UNIT* **where**
    map x   = x

instance *map PAIR* **where**
    map mapx mapy (PAIR x y) = PAIR (mapx x) (mapy y)
instance *map EITHER* **where**
    map mapl mapr (LEFT x)   = LEFT (mapl x)
    map mapl mapr (RIGHT x) = RIGHT (mapr x)

The **generic** definition introduces the type of the generic function. The **instance** definitions provide the mapping for the primitive types, *UNIT*, *PAIR* and *EITHER*.

The reader has probably noticed that the instances do not seem to "fit" together: they take a different number arguments. The function for integers takes no additional arguments, only the integer itself. Similarly, the function for *UNIT* takes only the *UNIT* argument; mapping for types of kind $\star$ is the identity function. The functions for *EITHER* and *PAIR* take two additional arguments; mapping for types of kind $\star \to \star \to \star$ needs two additional arguments: one for each type argument. The generic definition is actually a template that generates an infinite set of mapping classes, one class per kind. So, using the definition above we have defined

class $map_\star$ t $::$ $t \to t$
class $map_{\star \to \star}$ t $::$ $(a_1 \to a_2)\, (t\ a_1) \to (t\ a_2)$
class $map_{\star \to \star \to \star}$ t $::$ $(a_1 \to a_2)\, (b_1 \to b_2)\, (t\ a_1\ b_1) \to (t\ a_2\ b_2)$
...

The class for kind $\star$ has the type of the identity function. The other two classes are renamings of *fmap* and *bimap* class from the previous section. The instances are bound to the classes according to the kind of the instance type.

instance $map_\star$ *Int* **where**
    $map_\star$ *x*   = *x*
instance $map_\star$ *UNIT* **where**
    $map_\star$ *x*   = *x*
instance $map_{\star \to \star \to \star}$ *PAIR* **where**
    $map_{\star \to \star \to \star}$ *mapx mapy (PAIR x y) = PAIR (mapx x) (mapy y)*
instance $map_{\star \to \star \to \star}$ *EITHER* **where**
    $map_{\star \to \star \to \star}$ *mapl mapr (LEFT x) = LEFT (mapl x)*
    $map_{\star \to \star \to \star}$ *mapl mapr (RIGHT x) = RIGHT (mapr x)*

The programmer does not have to write the kind indexes, they are assigned automatically by the compiler.

For convenience we introduce a type synonym for the type specified in the **generic** definition of mapping:

$:: Map\ a_1\ a_2 :== a_1 \to a_2$

The type of the generic mapping for a type of any kind can be computed using the following algorithm [2]:

$:: Map_\star\ t_1\ t_2 \quad :== Map\ t_1\ t_2$
$:: Map_{k \to l}\ t_1\ t_2 :== \forall a_1\ a_2.\ (Map_k\ a_1\ a_2) \to Map_l\ (t_1\ a_1)\ (t_2\ a_1)$

The mapping function for a type t of a kind k has type:

class map_k t $::$ Map_k t t

The type specified in a generic declaration, like Map, is called the polykinded type [2] of the generic function. We have to note that, though the type of map has two type arguments, the generated classes have only one class argument. It holds for all generic functions: the corresponding classes always have one class argument. It remains to be researched how to extend the approach for classes with more than one argument. In this example, we use type Map_k t t with both arguments filled with the same variable t. It means that the consumed argument has the same top level structure as the produced result. We need two type variables to indicate that the structure does not have to be the same at the lower level. In the example of the reduce function at the end of this section we will give an idea about how to find the generic type of a function.

The programmer specifies which instances must be generated by the compiler. For $List$ we write:

instance map $List$ **generic**

The mapping for types of kind $\star \rightarrow \star$, like lists, can be used as usually, but the user now has to explicitly specify which map of the generated family of maps to apply. This is done by giving the kind between $\{|$ and $|\}$ as in

$map\{|\star \rightarrow \star|\}$ inc $(Cons\ 1\ (Cons\ 2\ (Cons\ 3\ Nil)))$

Similarly, we can also get the mapping for type $Tree$, which is of kind $\star \rightarrow \star \rightarrow \star$.

instance map $Tree$ **generic**

It can be used as in

$map\{|\star \rightarrow \star \rightarrow \star|\}$ inc dec $(Bin\ 1\ (Tip\ 2)\ (Tip\ 3))$

In this example the values in the tips of the tree are incremented, the values in the branches of the tree are decremented. From now on for readability reasons we will write kind indexes as subscripts.

Let's go back to the equality example and see how to define generic equality in Clean:

```
generic eq t                                    :: t t → Bool
instance eq Int where
    eq x y                                      = eqInt x y
instance eq UNIT where
    eq x y                                      = True
instance eq PAIR where
    eq eqx eqy (PAIR x1 y1) (PAIR x2 y2) = eqx x1 x2 && eqy y1 y2
instance eq EITHER where
    eq eql eqr (LEFT x) (LEFT y)            = eql x y
    eq eql eqr (RIGHT x) (RIGHT y)          = eqr x y
    eq eql eqr x y                          = False
```

In this definition, like in the definition of map, the instances have additional arguments depending on the kind of the instance type. Again, the programmer specifies the instances to be generated, say:

instance *eq List* **generic**
instance *eq Tree* **generic**

This will result in two instances: $eq_{\star\to\star}$ *List* and $eq_{\star\to\star\to\star}$ *Tree*. The equality can be used as in

$eq_{\star\to\star}\ eq_\star\ [1,2,3]\ [1,2,3] \Rightarrow True$
$eq_{\star\to\star\to\star}\ eq_\star\ eq_\star\ (Bin\ 1\ (Tip\ 2)\ (Tip\ 3))\ (Bin\ 1\ (Tip\ 2)\ (Tip\ 3)) \Rightarrow True$
$eq_{\star\to\star}\ (\lambda x\ y\to eq_\star\ (length\ x)\ (length\ y))\ [[1,2],[3,4]]\ [[1,1],\ [2,2]] \Rightarrow True$

In the last line the two lists are equal if they are of the same length and the lengths of the element lists are equal.

One can see that this equality is more general than one defined in Section 2: the user can specify how to compare the elements of the structure. However, it is inconvenient to pass the "dictionaries" (such as $eq_\star$) manually every time. For this reason we generate additional instances that turn explicit dictionaries into implicit ones:

instance $eq_\star$ *(List a)* | *eq a* **where**
$\quad eq_\star\ x\ y = eq_{\star\to\star\to\star}\ eq_\star\ x\ y$
instance $eq_\star$ *(Tree a b)* | *eq a* & *eq b* **where**
$\quad eq_\star\ x\ y = eq_{\star\to\star\to\star}\ eq_\star\ eq_\star\ x\ y$

Such instances make it possible to call

$eq_\star\ [1,2,3]\ [1,2,3]$
$eq_\star\ (Bin\ 1\ (Tip\ 2)\ (Tip\ 3))\ (Bin\ 1\ (Tip\ 2)\ (Tip\ 3))$

with the same effect as above.

The equality operator defined as a type class in the standard library of Clean can now be defined using the generic equality:

(==) **infixr** *5 :: t t $\to$ Bool* | $eq_\star$ *t*
(==) x y = $eq_\star$ x y

Consider an application of *map*

$map_{\star\to\star}\ (\lambda x \to 0)\ [[1,2],\ [3,4]]$

What would it return: [0,0] or [[0,0], [0,0]]? The overloading will always choose the first. If the second is needed, the user has to write

$map_{\star\to\star}\ (map_{\star\to\star}\ (\lambda x \to 0))\ [[1,2],\ [3,4]]$

As one more example we show the right reduce function, which is a generalization of *foldr* on lists. It takes a structure of type a and an "empty" value of type b and collapses the structure into another value of type b. Thus, the type is $a \to b \to b$, where a is the structure, i.e. a is a generic variable, and b is a parametrically polymorphic variable.

generic *rreduce a :: a b → b*
instance *rreduce Int* **where**
    rreduce x e = e
instance *rreduce UNIT* **where**
    rreduce x e = e
instance *rreduce PAIR* **where**
    rreduce redx redy (PAIR x y) e = redx x (redy y e)
instance *rreduce EITHER* **where**
    rreduce redl redr (LEFT x) e = redl x e
    rreduce redl redr (RIGHT x) e = redr x e

Reducing types of kind $\star$ just returns the "empty" value. The instance for pairs uses the result of reduction for the second element of the pair as the "empty" argument for reduction of the first element. To reduce the sum we just reduce the arguments.

The function is an example of a parametrically polymorphic function: here b is a non-generic type variable. We can define the standard *foldr* function that is defined on types of kind $\star \to \star$ using *rreduce*.

foldr :: (a b → b) b (t a) → b | rreduce$_{\star \to \star}$ t
foldr op e x = rreduce$_{\star \to \star}$ op x e

How do we come up with the type for generic reduce knowing the type of reduce for lists (*foldr*)? The type of a standard definition for *foldr* is:

foldr :: (a → b → b) b [a] → b

If it is generalized to any type of kind $\star \to \star$, it becomes

foldr :: (a → b → b) b (t a) → b

The type *(t a)* is the structure that we are collapsing. The first argument is the function that we apply to the elements of the structure, i.e. it is folding for type a of kind $\star$. So, we can choose the type $(a \to b \to b)$ as the generic type. With this generic type we get

class *rreduce$_\star$ a*   :: *a b → b*
class *rreduce$_{\star \to \star}$ a*   :: $(a_1 \to b \to b)$ $(a\ a_1)$ $b \to b$
class *rreduce$_{\star \to \star \to \star}$ a* :: $(a_1 \to b \to b)$ $(a_2 \to b \to b)$ $(a\ a_1\ a_2)$ $b \to b$

The type for kind $\star \to \star$ is the same as the type of *foldr*, except that the last two arguments are flipped. This idea of finding out the generic type can be used for other functions that normally make sense for types of kind $\star \to \star$.

4   Implementation

In this section we describe how the generic definitions are translated to classes and instances of non-generic Clean. Suppose we need to specialize a generic function g to a data type T, i. e. generate an instance of g for T. A generic definition in general looks like

generic $g\ a_1\ ...\ a_r$ :: $G\ a_1\ ...\ a_r\ p_1\ ...\ p_s$

Here G is the polykinded type of the generic function g, a_i are polykinded type variables and p_i are polymorphic type variables (i.e. the function is parametrically polymorphic with respect to them). We will denote $p_1 \ldots p_s$ as $\boldsymbol{p}$.

To generate the instance for a data type T the following has to be specified by the user

instance g T **generic**

A data type T has the following form

$$:: T\ a_1\ \ldots\ a_n\ =\ K_1\ t_{11}\ \ldots\ t_{1l_1}\ |\ \ldots\ |K_m\ t_{m1}\ \ldots\ t_{ml_m}$$

As an example in this section we will use the generic equality function defined in the previous section and its specialization to lists

$$:: Eq\ a\ :==\ a \to a \to Bool$$
generic $eq :: Eq\ a$
$$:: List\ a\ =\ Nil\ |\ Cons\ a\ (List\ a)$$
instance $eq\ List$ **generic**

Here is a short summary of what is done to specialize a generic function g to a data type T. The following subsections give more details.

- Create the class g_k for the kind k of the data type T, if not already created. The instance on T becomes an instance of that class (Section 4.1).
- Build the generic representation T° for the type T. Also build the conversion functions between T and T° (Section 4.2)
- Build the specialization of g to the generic representation T°. We have all the ingredients needed to build the specialization because the type T° is defined using sums and products. The instances for sums and products are provided by the user as part of the generic definition. (Section 4.3).
- The generic function is now specialized to the generic representation T°, but we need to specialize it to the type T. We generate an adaptor that converts the function for T° into the function for T (Section 4.4).
- Build the specialization to the type T. It uses the specialization to T° and the adaptor. The instance g_k on T is the specialization of the generic function g to the type T. (Section 4.3).
- For convenience we additionally create shorthand instances for kind $\star$ (Section 4.5).

4.1   Kind-Indexed Classes

The polykinded type of a generic function is used to compute the type of the function for a kind using the following algorithm [2]:

$$G_\star \qquad t_1\ \ldots\ t_r\ \boldsymbol{p}\ :==\ G\ t_1\ \ldots\ t_r\ \boldsymbol{p}$$
$$G_{k_1 \to k_2}\ t_1\ \ldots\ t_r\ \boldsymbol{p}\ :==\ \forall a_1 \ldots a_r.(G_{k_1}\ a_1\ \ldots\ a_r\ \boldsymbol{p}) \to G_{k_2}\ (t_1\ a_1)\ \ldots\ (t_r\ a_r)\ \boldsymbol{p}$$

From now on we will use the following shorthands:

$$G' \ t \ \boldsymbol{p} \ := = G \ t \ ... \ t \ \boldsymbol{p}$$
$$G'_k \ t \ \boldsymbol{p} \ := = G_k \ t \ ... \ t \ \boldsymbol{p}$$

where t in each right hand side occurs r times.

The generic extension translates a generic definition into a family of class definitions, one class per kind. The class has one class argument of kind k and one member. The type of the member is the polykinded type of the generic function specialized to kind k:

class $g_k \ t \ :: \ G'_k \ t \ \boldsymbol{p}$

Unlike [2], we use the polykinded types to type the class members rather than functions.

Each instance of a generic function is bound to one of the classes according to the kind of the instance type. For our example we have so far

class $eq_{*\to*} \ t \ :: \ (Eq \ a) \ \to \ Eq \ (t \ a)$
instance $eq_{*\to*} \ List$ **where** $eq_{*\to*} \ eqa = ...$

where the body of the instance is still to be generated.

4.2   Generic Type Representation

To specialize a generic function to a concrete data type one needs to build the generic representation of that type. This is rather straightforward. The algorithms of building the generic representation types and the conversion functions are described by Hinze in [4]. The conversion functions are packed into a record defined in the generic prelude:

$$:: \ Iso \ a \ a^\circ = \{iso \ :: \ a \ \to \ a^\circ, \ osi \ :: \ a^\circ \ \to \ a\}$$

Here we just give an example of the generic type representation and the isomorphism for the list type:

$$List^\circ \ a \ := = EITHER \ UNIT \ (PAIR \ a \ (List \ a))$$
$$iso_{List} \ :: \ Iso \ (List \ a) \ (List^\circ \ a)$$
$$iso_{List} \ = \ \{iso = isoList, osi = osiList\}$$

where	$isoList \ Nil$	$= \ LEFT \ UNIT$
	$isoList \ (Cons \ x \ xs)$	$= \ RIGHT \ (PAIR \ x \ xs)$
	$osiList \ (LEFT \ UNIT)$	$= \ Nil$
	$osiList \ (RIGHT \ (PAIR \ x \ xs))$	$= \ Cons \ x \ xs$

4.3   Specialization

In this subsection we show how to specialize a generic function g to a data type T. It is done by first specializing it to the generic type representation T°. This specialization g_{T° is then used to build the specialization g_T to the data type T. The specialization to the generic T° is:

$$g_{T^\circ} :: G'_k \ T^\circ \ \boldsymbol{p}$$
$$g_{T^\circ} \ v_1 \ ... \ v_n = \mathcal{S}(g, \{a_1 := v_1, ..., a_n := v_n\}, T^\circ)$$

The following algorithm is used to generate the right hand side by induction on the structure of the generic representation:

$$\begin{array}{lll}
\mathcal{S}(g, \mathcal{E}, a) & = \mathcal{E}[a] & \textit{type variables} \\
\mathcal{S}(g, \mathcal{E}, T) & = g_T & \textit{type constructors} \\
\mathcal{S}(g, \mathcal{E}, t \ s) & = \mathcal{S}(g, \mathcal{E}, t) \ \mathcal{S}(g, \mathcal{E}, s) & \textit{type application} \\
\mathcal{S}(g, \mathcal{E}, t \to s) & = g_\to \ \mathcal{S}(g, \mathcal{E}, t) \ \mathcal{S}(g, \mathcal{E}, s) & \textit{arrow type}
\end{array}$$

Type variables are interpreted as value variables bound in the environment $\mathcal{E}$, type constructors T as instances g_T of the generic function g on the data type T, type application as value application and arrow type as application of the instance of g for the arrow type. In [2] Hinze proves that the functions specialized in this way are well-typed. For the equality on $List^\circ$ the specialization is:

$$eq_{List^\circ} :: (Eq \ a) \to Eq \ (List^\circ \ a)$$
$$eq_{List^\circ} \ eqa = eq_{EITHER} \ eq_{UNIT} \ (eq_{PAIR} \ eqa \ (eq_{List} \ eqa))$$

The functions eq_{EITHER}, eq_{PAIR} and eq_{UNIT} are instances of the generic equality for the corresponding types. The function eq_{List} is the specialization to lists that we are generating.

The specialization to T is generated using the specialization to T°:

$$g_T :: G'_k \ T \ \boldsymbol{p}$$
$$g_T \ v_1 \ ... \ v_n = adaptor \ (g_{T^\circ} \ v_1 \ ... \ v_n)$$
$$\textbf{where} \ \ adaptor \ \ :: (G' \ (T^\circ \ a_1 \ ... \ a_n) \ \boldsymbol{p}) \to G' \ (T \ a_1 \ ... \ a_n) \ \boldsymbol{p}$$
$$adaptor \ \ = ...$$

The adaptor converts the function for T° into the function for T. The adaptors are generated using bidirectional mappings [1], described in the next subsection. The equality specialized to lists is

$$eq_{List} :: (Eq \ a) \to Eq \ (List \ a)$$
$$eq_{List} \ eqa = adaptor \ (eq_{List^\circ} \ eqa)$$
$$\textbf{where} \ \ adaptor :: (Eq \ (List^\circ \ a)) \to Eq \ (List \ a)$$
$$adaptor = ...$$

The mutually recursive definitions of eq_{List} and eq_{List° show why we do not need type recursion in the generic type representation: the function converts lists to the generic representations as needed.

Now it is easy to fill in the instance for the type T. It is just the specialization to the type T.

instance $g_k \ T$ **where** $g_k = g_T$

The instance of the equality for lists is:

instance $eq_{\star \to \star} \ List$ **where** $eq_{\star \to \star} = eq_{List}$

4.4   Adaptors

Adaptors are more complicated than one would expect. The reason is that generic function types and data types may contain arrows. Since the arrow type is contravariant in the argument position, we need bidirectional mapping functions to map it [1]. We define bidirectional mapping by induction on the structure of types as a special generic function predefined in the compiler:

generic $bmap\ a\ b :: Iso\ a\ b$

It is automatically specialized to all data types in the following way

instance $bmap\ T$ **where**
$$bmap\ v_1\ ...\ v_n\ =\ \{iso{=}isoT,\ osi{=}osiT\}$$
     where $isoT\ (K_1\ x_{11}\ ...\ x_{1m_1})\ =\ K_1\ x'_{11}\ ...\ x'_{1m_1}$

            ...

            $isoT\ (K_m\ x_{m1}\ ...\ x_{ml_m})\ =\ K_m\ x'_{m1}\ ...\ x'_{ml_m}$
            $osiT\ (K_1\ x_{11}\ ...\ x_{1m_1})\ =\ K_1\ x''_{11}\ ...\ x''_{1m_1}$

            ...

            $osiT\ (K_m\ x_{m1}\ ...\ x_{ml_m})\ =\ K_m\ x''_{m1}\ ...\ x''_{ml_m}$

Here $x_{ij} :: t_{ij}$ is the jth argument of the data constructor K_i. New constructor arguments x'_{ij} and x''_{ij} are given by

$$x'_{ij}\ =\ (\mathcal{S}(bmap, \{a_1 := v_1, \ldots, a_n := v_n\}, t_{ij})).iso\ x_{ij}$$
$$x''_{ij}\ =\ (\mathcal{S}(bmap, \{a_1 := v_1, \ldots, a_n := v_n\}, t_{ij})).osi\ x_{ij}$$

The environment passed to $\mathcal{S}$ binds the type arguments of the data type T to the corresponding function arguments. For example, the instance for lists is

instance $bmap\ List$ **where**
$$bmap\ v\ =\ \{iso{=}isoList,\ osi{=}osiList\}$$
     where $isoList\ Nil$ $=\ Nil$
            $isoList\ (Cons\ x\ xs)$ $=\ Cons\ (v.iso\ x)\ ((bmap_{List}\ v).iso\ xs)$
            $osiList\ Nil$ $=\ Nil$
            $osiList\ (Cons\ x\ xs)$ $=\ Cons\ (v.osi\ x)\ ((bmap_{List}\ v).osi\ xs)$

The instance for the arrow is predefined as

instance $bmap\ (\rightarrow)$ **where**
$$bmap\ bmaparg\ bmapres\ =\ \{iso{=}isoArrow,\ osi{=}osiArrow\}$$
     where $isoArrow\ f\ =\ bmapres.iso \cdot f \cdot bmaparg.osi$
            $osiArrow\ f\ =\ bmapres.osi \cdot f \cdot bmaparg.iso$

This instance demonstrates the need for pairing the conversion functions together.

   This generic function is used to build bidirectional mapping for a generic function type:

$$bmap_g\ ::\ Iso_{kind(G)}\ G\ ...\ G$$
$$bmap_g\ v_1\ ...\ v_r\ u_1\ ...\ u_s$$
$$=\ \mathcal{S}(bmap, \{a_1 := v_1, \ldots, a_r := v_r, p_1 := u_1, \ldots, p_s := u_s\}, G\ \boldsymbol{a}\ \boldsymbol{p})$$

The function lifts the isomorphisms for the arguments to the isomorphism for the function type. In the function type the data type *Iso* is used as a polykinded type. It is instantiated to the type of the generic function G. The right hand side is defined by induction on the structure of type G. For the generic equality we have

$$bmap_{eq} :: (Iso\ a\ a^\circ) \to (Iso\ (Eq\ a)\ (Eq\ a^\circ))$$
$$bmap_{eq}\ v = bmap_{\to}\ v\ (bmap_{\to}\ v\ bmap_{Bool})$$

Bidirectional mapping for the primitive type *Bool* is the identity mapping, because it has kind $\star$.

Now we can generate the body of the adaptor:

$$adaptor = (bmap_g\ iso_T\ ...\ iso_T\ isoId\ ...\ isoId).osi$$

The a-arguments are filled in with the isomorphism for the data type T and the p-arguments with the identity isomorphism. In the current implementation ps are limited to kind $\star$, so we use the identity to map them. In our example of the equality on lists the adaptor is

$$adaptor = (bmap_{eq}\ iso_{List}).osi$$

4.5   Shorthand Instances for Kind $\star$

For each instance on a type of a kind other than $\star$ a shorthand instance for kind $\star$ is created. Consider the instance of a generic function g for a type $T\ a_1\ ...\ a_n$, $n \geq 1$. The kind k of the type T is $k = k_1 \to ... \to k_n \to \star$.

instance $g_\star\ (T\ a_1\ ...\ a_n)\ |\ g_{k_1}\ a_1\ \&\ ...\ \&\ g_{k_n}\ a_n$ **where**
   $g_\star = g_k\ g_{k_1}\ \cdots\ g_{k_n}$

For instance, for the equality on lists and trees we have

instance $eq_\star\ [a]\ |\ eq_\star\ a$ **where**
   $eq_\star\ x\ y = eq_{\star \to \star}\ eq_\star\ x\ y$
instance $eq_\star\ Tree\ a\ b\ |\ eq_\star\ a\ \&\ eq_\star\ b$ **where**
   $eq_\star\ x\ y = eq_{\star \to \star \to \star}\ eq_\star\ eq_\star\ x\ y$

These instances make it is possible to call $eq_\star\ [1,2,3]\ [1,2,3]$ instead of $eq_{\star \to \star}\ eq_\star$ $[1,2,3]\ [1,2,3]$: they turn explicit arguments into dictionaries of the overloading system.

5   Customized Instances

Generic functions can be defined to perform a specific task on objects of a specific data type contained in any data structure. Such generic functions have the big advantage that they are invariant with respect to changes in the data structure.

Let's for example consider terms in a compiler.

```
:: Expr   = ELambda Var Expr
          |  EVar Var
          |  EApp Expr Expr
:: Var    = Var String
```

We can define a generic function to collect free variables in any data structure (e.g. parse tree):

```
generic fvs t                    :: t → [Var]
instance fvs UNIT where fvs x = []
instance fvs Int where fvs x    = []
instance fvs PAIR where
    fvs fvsx fvsy (PAIR x y)    = removeDup(fvsx x ++ fvsy y)
instance fvs EITHER where
    fvs fvsl fvsr (LEFT l)      = fvsl l
    fvs fvsl fvsr (RIGHT r)     = fvsr r
instance fvs Var where fvs x   = [x]
instance fvs Expr where
    fvs (ELambda var expr)      = removeMember var (fvs⋆ expr)
    fvs (EVar var)              = fvs⋆ var
    fvs (EApp fun arg)          = removeDup(fvs⋆ fun ++ fvs⋆ arg)
```

$UNIT$s and Ints do not contain variables, so the instances return empty lists. For pairs the variables are collected in both components; the concatenated list is returned after removing duplicates. For sums the variables are collected in the arguments. The instance on Var returns the variable as a singleton list. For lambda expressions we collect variables in the lambda body and filter out the lambda variable. For variables we call the instance on variables. For applications we collect the variables in the function and in the argument and return the concatenated list.

Now, if the structure containing expressions (e.g. a parse tree) changes, the same generic function can still be used to collect free variables in it. But if the expression type itself changes we have to modify the last instance of the function accordingly. Let's have a closer look at the last instance. Only the first alternative does something special - it filters out the bound variables. The other two alternatives just collect free variables in the arguments of the data constructors. Thus, except for lambda abstractions, the instance behaves as if it was generated by the generic extension. The generic extension provides a way to deal with this problem. The user can refer to the generic implementation of an instance that (s)he provides. In the example the instance on $Expr$ can be written more compactly:

```
instance fvs Expr where
    fvs (ELambda var expr) = removeMember var (fvs⋆ expr)
    fvs x                  = fvs{|generic|} x
```

The name $fvs\{|\textbf{generic}|\}$ is bound to the generic implementation of the instance in which it occurs. The code generated for the instance on *Expr* is:

$$
\begin{aligned}
fvs^{g}_{\mathrm{Expr}}\ x &= (bmap_{fvs}\ iso_{\mathrm{Expr}}).osi\ (fvs_{\mathrm{Expr}^{\circ}}\ x) \\
fvs_{\mathrm{Expr}}\ (ELambda\ var\ expr) &= removeMember\ var\ (fvs_{\mathrm{Expr}}\ expr) \\
fvs_{\mathrm{Expr}}\ x &= fvs^{g}_{\mathrm{Expr}}\ x
\end{aligned}
$$

Here fvs^{g}_{Expr} denotes the function generated for $fvs\{|\textbf{generic}|\}$. The function for the generic representation $fvs_{Expr^{\circ}}$ is generated as usually.

6   Related Work

Generic Haskell is an extension for Haskell based on the approach of kind-indexed types, described in [2]. Despite pretty different notation, generic definitions in Generic Haskell and Clean are similar. The user provides the polykinded type and cases for sums, products, unit, arrow and primitive types. In Generic Haskell an overloaded function cannot be defined generically. It means that, for instance, equality operator ($==$) has to be defined manually. In Clean overloaded functions are supported. For instance, the equality operator in Clean can be defined in terms of the generic function eq:

$$
\begin{aligned}
(==)\ \textbf{infixr}\ 5 &:: t\ t \to Bool\ |\ eq_{\star}\ t \\
(==)\ x\ y &= eq_{\star}\ x\ y
\end{aligned}
$$

Currently Generic Haskell does not support the module system. Clean supports the module system for generics in the same way as it does it for overloaded functions.

Glasgow Haskell supports generic programming as described in [1]. In GHC generic definitions are used to define default implementation of class members, giving systematic meaning to the **deriving** construct. Default methods can be derived for type classes whose class argument is of kind $\star$. That means that functions like mapping cannot be defined generically. In Clean a **generic** definition provides default implementation for methods of a kind-indexed family of classes. For instance, it possible in Clean to customize how elements of lists are compared:

$$
eq_{\star \to \star}\ (\lambda x\ y \to eq_{\star}\ (length\ x)\ (length\ y))\ [[1,2],[3,4]]\ [[1,1],\ [2,2]] \Rightarrow True
$$

This cannot be done in GHC, since the equality class is defined for types of kind $\star$. In Clean one generic definition is enough to generate functions for all (currently up to second-order) kinds. This is especially important for functions like mapping.

In [5] Chen and W. Appel describe an approach to implement specialization of generic functions using dictionary passing. Their work is a the intermediate language level; our generic extension is a user level facility. Our implementation is based on type classes that are implemented using dictionaries. In SML/NJ the kind system of the language is extended, which we do not require.

PolyP [6] is a language extension for Haskell. It is a predecessor of Generic Haskell. PolyP supports a special **polytypic** construct, which is similar to our **generic** construct. In PolyP, to specify a generic function one needs to provide two additional cases: for type application and for type recursion. PolyP generic functions are restricted to work on regular types. A significant advantage of PolyP is that recursion schemes like catamorphisms (folds) can be defined. It remains to be seen how to support such recursion schemes in Clean.

In [8] Lämmel, Visser and Kort propose a way to deal with generalized folds on large systems of mutually recursive data types. The idea is that a fold algebra is separated in a basic fold algebra and updates to the basic algebra. The basic algebras model generic behavior, whereas updates to the basic algebras model specific behavior. Existing generic programming extensions, including ours, allow for type indexed functions, whereas their approach needs type-indexed algebras. Our customized instances (see section 5) provide a simple solution for dealing with type-preserving (map-like) algebras (see [8]). To support type-unifying (fold-like) algebras we need more flexible encoding of the generic type representation.

7   Conclusions and Future Work

In this paper we have presented a generic extension for Clean that allows to define overloaded functions with class variables of any kind generically. A generic definition generates a family of kind-indexed type (constructor) classes, where the class variable of each class ranges over types of the corresponding kind. For instance, a generic definition of map defines overloaded mapping functions for functors, bifunctors etc. Our contribution is in extending the approach of kind-indexed types [2] with overloading.

Additionally, we have presented an extension that allows for customization of generated instances. A custom instance on a type may refer to the generated function for that type. With this feature a combination of generic and specific behavior can be expressed.

Currently our prototype lacks optimization of the generated code. The overhead introduced by the generic representation, the conversion functions and the adaptors is in most cases unacceptable. But we are convinced that a partial evaluator can optimize out this overhead and yield code comparable with handwritten one. Our group is working on such an optimizer.

Generic Clean currently cannot generate instances on array types and types of a kind higher then order 2. Class contexts in polykinded types are not yet supported. To support pretty printers and parsers the data constructor information has to be stored in the generic type representation. The current prototype has a rudimentary support for uniqueness typing. Uniqueness typing in polykinded types must be formalized and implemented in the compiler. As noted in section 6 our design does not support recursion schemes like catamorphisms. We plan to add the support in the future.

Acknowledgements

We are grateful to Sjaak Smetsers for fruitful discussions and comments on this paper. For helpful comments we are also grateful to Peter Achten, Marko van Eekelen and three anonymous referees. We would like to thank Ralf Hinze for the discussion of customized instances.

References

1. Ralf Hinze and Simon Peyton Jones. *Derivable Type Classes.* In Graham Hutton, editor, Proceedings of the Fourth Haskell Workshop, Montreal, Canada, September 17, 2000
2. Ralf Hinze. *Polytypic values possess polykinded types.* In Roland Backhouse, J.N. Oliveira, editors, Proceedings of the Fifth International Conference on Mathematics of Program Construction (MPC 2000), Ponte de Lima, Portugal, July 3-5, 2000.
3. Ralf Hinze. *A New Approach to Generic Functional Programming.* In Proceedings of the 27th Annual ACM SIGPLAN-SIGACT Symposium on Principles of Programming Languages, Boston, Massachusetts, January 19-21, 2000.
4. Ralf Hinze. *A Generic Programming Extension for Haskell* In Erik Meijer, editor, Proceedings of the Third Haskell Workshop, Paris, France, September 1999. The proceedings appear as a technical report of Universiteit Utrecht, UU-CS-1999-28.
5. Juan Chen and Andrew W. Appel. *Dictionary Passing for Polytypic Polymorphism* Princeton University Computer Science TR-635-01, March 2001.
6. P. Jansson and J. Jeuring, *PolyP - a polytypic programming language extension,* POPL '97: The 24th ACM SIGPLAN-SIGACT Symposium on Principles of Programming Languages, ACM Press 470–482, 1997.
7. M. J. Plasmeijer, M.C.J.D. van Eekelen *Language Report Concurrent Clean. Version 1.3.* Technical Report CSI R9816, Faculty of mathematics and Informatics, Catholic University of Nijmegen, June 1998. Also available at www.cs.kun.nl/~clean/Manuals/manuals.html
8. Ralf Lämmel, Joost Visser, and Jan Kort. *Dealing with large bananas.* In Johan Jeuring, editor, Workshop on Generic Programming, Ponte de Lima, July 2000. Technical Report UU-CS-2000-19, Universiteit Utrecht.

Author Index

Lecture Notes in Computer Science

For information about Vols. 1–2238
please contact your bookseller or Springer-Verlag